Adam Chapnick

The Middle Power Project: Canada and the Founding of the United Nations

UBCPress · Vancouver · Toronto

15 14 13 12 11 10 09 08 07 06 05   5 4 3 2 1

Printed in Canada on acid-free paper

Library and Archives Canada Cataloguing in Publication

Chapnick, Adam, 1976-
   The middle power project : Canada and the founding of the
United Nations / Adam Chapnick.

Includes bibliographical references and index.
ISBN 13: 978-0-7748-1247-4 (bound); 978-0-7748-1248-1 (pbk.)
ISBN 10: 0-7748-1247-8 (bound); 0-7748-1248-6 (pbk.)

   1. United Nations – Canada – History – 20th century. I. Title.

FC242.C48 2005   341.23'71'09044   C2005-904338-5

Canadä

UBC Press gratefully acknowledges the financial support for our publishing
program of the Government of Canada through the Book Publishing Industry
Development Program (BPIDP), and of the Canada Council for the Arts, and
the British Columbia Arts Council.

This book has been published with the help of a grant from the Canadian
Federation for the Humanities and Social Sciences, through the Aid to Scholarly
Publications Programme, using funds provided by the Social Sciences and
Humanities Research Council of Canada.

Printed and bound in Canada by Friesens
Set in Stone by Artegraphica Design Co. Ltd.
Copy editor: Robert Lewis
Proofreader: Dianne Tiefensee

UBC Press
The University of British Columbia
2029 West Mall
Vancouver, BC V6T 1Z2
604-822-5959 / Fax: 604-822-6083
www.ubcpress.ca

Contents

Acknowledgments

Erica Berman's love and support are the driving force behind any successes that I have had over the past five years.

The Chapnick and Berman families were also there whenever I needed them, and the Rossman family provided the most wonderful home away from home while I was in Ottawa. Robert Bothwell's detailed and thorough comments and suggestions on an earlier version of the manuscript made it much better than it ever could have been otherwise. Few will ever know as much about Canadian history as he does. Bob Accinelli was utterly reliable when I had questions on American foreign policy, and Bill Young provided access to his own personal papers, which helped to shed light on some of the personalities of the day. William Walker and John English also provided particularly helpful comments on an earlier version of the manuscript. Marilyn Laville answered more phone calls and e-mails than I care to remember and remained positive and accommodating no matter what I asked. Kathy Rasmussen was a wonderful office companion in the early years of this project and set an example of how senior PhDs should treat their juniors. Mike Carroll was the most helpful person with whom I spoke about travel and accommodations for research trips. Urs Obrist went above and beyond the call of duty in translating the Stipernitz thesis. Judith Robertson not only granted me an interview and access to her own papers, but also connected me with others who were able to help with my research. She and June Rogers provided me with a sense of their fathers that I could not have found anywhere else and have remained helpful supporters ever since I first met them. Brian Horgan was a better host than anyone could have asked for while I was in London. Norman Hillmer came through as he always has, and I cannot imagine ever having finished this book without his reassuring words and e-mails. Finally, Emily Andrew has been an exceptional editor. She and the rest of the staff at UBC Press are models of efficiency and professionalism. Working with them has been a privilege.

The research for this book was made possible by an unbelievably helpful group of support staff and archivists, including: Louise Nugent, Jennifer Francisco, and the rest of the staff in the History Department, University of Toronto; Heather Home and the Queen's University Archives staff; Karen Rohan at the Library of the American Foreign Policy Association; Gayle Fraser and Jennifer McNenly formerly of the Library of the Canadian Institute of International Affairs; Apollonia Steele and Marlys Chevrefils at the University of Calgary Library, Special Collections; Richard Virr at McGill University Library, Special Collections; the staff at Library and Archives Canada (particularly the circulation crew, who are polite, professional, and amazingly patient); the staff at the University of Toronto Archives; Henry Pilon at Trinity College Archives (Toronto); the staff at Robarts Library, University of Toronto, in Resource Sharing, Data, Maps, and Government Documents and in the Microform Reading Room; Pat Molesky and the staff at the Glenbow Museum Archives in Calgary; National Archives of England, Wales, and the United Kingdom; Christine Penney and the staff at the University of Birmingham Library, Special Collections; Corinne Miller, Helen Lafleur, Jane Boyko, and the staff at the Bank of Canada Archives in Ottawa; the staff at the National Archives and Records Administration, College Park, Maryland; the staff at the Library of Congress, Washington, DC; Michele Dale and the staff at the Archives of Ontario; Jude Brimmer and the staff at the Churchill Archives Centre, Cambridge; Oliver House and the staff at the Bodleian Library, Oxford; the staff at the Durham University Library, Archives and Special Collections; Robert Clark and the staff at the Franklin Delano Roosevelt Library, Hyde Park; Ramona Kohrs at the Dag Hammarskjöld (United Nations) Library, New York; and the staff at the Seeley G. Mudd Library, Princeton.

I would also like to thank the master and fellows of Massey College for permission to consult the Vincent Massey Papers; Robert Bothwell for permission to consult the Robert Selkirk Bothwell Papers; Lady Avon for permission to consult the Avon Papers; Graham Fraser for permission to consult the Blair Fraser Papers; William Young for access to his personal papers; the Bank of Canada for access to the Louis Rasminsky Papers; James S. Hutchison for access to the Bruce Hutchison Fonds; Lord Hilfax for permission to cite from the Halifax Papers; and Judith Robertson for access to her personal papers; and Julia Matthews for permission to cite from the James Gibson interview.

Money for the research for this book was provided by: the Social Sciences and Humanities Research Council; Massey College through the Jack and Rita Catherall and Evelyn Catherall Travel Scholarships (two awards); the University of Toronto Centre for International Studies through the Sir Val

Duncan Travel Grant (two awards); the University of Toronto School of Graduate Studies through the Associates of the University of Toronto Travel Award/SGS Travel Grant; the Department of History, University of Toronto; and the Franklin and Eleanor Roosevelt Institute Grants Program.

Acronyms

AIPO	American Institute of Public Opinion
AO	Archives of Ontario, Toronto, Ontario, Canada
APOP	Australian Public Opinion Poll
BCA	Bank of Canada Archives, Ottawa, Ontario, Canada
BL	Bodleian Library, Oxford University, Oxford, UK
CAAE	Canadian Association for Adult Education
CAB	Cabinet Office Papers
CAC	Churchill Archives Centre, Churchill College, Cambridge University, Cambridge, UK
CBC	Canadian Broadcasting Corporation
CCEC	Canadian Council for Education in Citizenship
CCF	Co-operative Commonwealth Federation
CFR	Council on Foreign Relations
CIIA	Canadian Institute of International Affairs
CIPO	Canadian Institute of Public Opinion
DCER	*Documents on Canadian External Relations*
DEA	Department of External Affairs
DHL	Dag Hammarskjöld Library, United Nations, New York, USA
DO	Dominions Office (Papers)
DUL	Durham University Library, Archives and Special Collections, Durham, UK
ECOSOC	(United Nations) Economic and Social Council
EPA	Empire Parliamentary Association
FDRL	Franklin Delano Roosevelt Library, Hyde Park, New York, USA
FO	Foreign Office (Papers)
FRUS	*Foreign Relations of the United States*
G&M	*Globe and Mail*
IPR	Institute of Pacific Relations
ISO	(US) Division of International Security and Organization
LAC	Library and Archives Canada, Ottawa, Ontario, Canada

LC	Library of Congress, Manuscript Division, Washington, DC, USA
MHF	Records of the Office of European Affairs (Matthews-Hickerson File) 1934-47
MP	member of Parliament
NARA	National Archives and Records Administration at College Park, Maryland, USA
NAUK	National Archives of England, Wales, and the United Kingdom, Kew, UK
NFB	National Film Board
PCO	Privy Council Office
PHP	post-hostilities problems
POQ	*Public Opinion Quarterly*
PSF	President's Secretary's Files
QUA	Queen's University Archives, Kingston, Ontario, Canada
RIIA	Royal Institute of International Affairs
SML	Seeley G. Mudd Manuscript Library, Princeton, New Jersey, USA
SS	Secretary of State
SSDA	Secretary of State for Dominion Affairs
SSEA	Secretary of State for External Affairs
UBSC	University of Birmingham Library, Special Collections, Birmingham, UK
UN	United Nations (Organization)
UNCIO	*Documents of the United Nations Conference on International Organization, San Francisco, 1945*
UNRRA	United Nations Relief and Rehabilitation Administration
UNSC	United Nations Security Council
UT	University of Toronto Archives, Toronto, Ontario, Canada
UTTC	University of Toronto, Trinity College Archives, Toronto, Ontario, Canada
WCA	World Citizens Association
WFP	*Winnipeg Free Press*
WIB	Wartime Information Board

1
Introduction

We are a conservative and steady people, hardly daring to
believe in our own capacity in the more complex affairs of
statecraft, afraid to test that capacity too far with new systems
and experiments ...

We are among the few peoples still in the first throes of collective
growth ... We have, every one of us, the feeling that we are
involved in a process of perpetual expansion, development and
revision, whose end we cannot see.

We have the feeling, not of an old and settled resident in his
father's house, but of a young man building a new house for
himself, without any clear plan in his head and wondering how
large his future family will be ...

If this is not yet a rounded and settled national character, it is,
assuredly, the soil out of which a character is growing as surely
as a boy grows into a man. It has grown these last few years
faster than we have stopped to realize.[1]

– Bruce Hutchison

With these words, the Canadian journalist Bruce Hutchison captured the
spirit of a country entering one of the most profound periods of change in
its history. When the Second World War began, Canada was governed by a
prime minister who was afraid of international commitments and an
undersecretary of state for external affairs with neutralist, if not isolationist,
tendencies. While technically independent, Canada was considered by the
international community to be a British dominion lacking a foreign policy

of its own. Over the next five years, Canada became a self-proclaimed middle power and an active, enthusiastic participant in the creation of the most recognized symbol of internationalism of its time: the United Nations Organization (UN). Forced by a brutal war to abandon their ambivalence toward the world outside of North America, Canadians reinvented themselves as concerned and responsible global citizens. They learned that security meant more than just military strength yet were still able to acknowledge the importance of harmony between the great powers to a stable international system.

There has yet to be a thorough, published account of Canada's contribution to the founding of the UN, but a number of writers have considered the national postwar planning process more generally.[2] Some, like the former diplomat turned commentator John Holmes, have been relatively guarded in their enthusiasm for their country's achievements: "We did our homework in post-hostilities planning," he wrote, "and consequently we had about as much influence on the nature of the UN Charter as a country of our size could approximately expect even though we had, of course, to accept a scheme designed to a large extent by the great powers."[3] Others have been less reserved, attributing to Canada "considerable influence"[4] and noting how it had become "richer, immeasurably more powerful, confident and armed to the teeth both with righteousness and the weapons of war."[5] On the whole, regardless of their initial hesitancies, most analysts agree that the establishment of the United Nations changed, and indeed improved, the character of the modern world – and Canadians along with it.

But in their haste to celebrate what was new, many of these writers have neglected to recognize how much of the old remained. The charter that emerged from the San Francisco Conference in June 1945 was neither perfect nor radically different from the old Covenant of the League of Nations. One international commentator later explained: "The founding fathers of the United Nations were realistic enough to accept the necessity of operating within the confines of the existing power structure and to recognize the grave dangers of future conflict among the superpowers."[6] The charter, wrote another, was "a political document compounded by practical politicians who compromised on many contentious issues and produced a paper which, while satisfactory to nobody on all points, had obtained the approval of at least two-thirds of all delegations for every paragraph."[7]

The changes that took place within Canada have also been romanticized. The Canadian general public, which had previously shown virtually no interest in international relations, did indeed begin to advocate a greater role for its government in the new world order. And Canada certainly was an active and founding member of the United Nations. It was not, however, the leading middle power that so many have made it out to be. Because national histories have fixated so intently on "the Canadian preoccupation with Canada's place in the world, a preoccupation with status, position, influence and power,"[8] they have consistently overestimated the country's international standing when the Second World War came to a close. In the case of the United Nations, they have focused almost exclusively on the period from 1943 through 1945, overlooking the lack of Canadian involvement, and by extension influence, in the earlier years.[9]

Between 1939 and 1941, while officials in Great Britain and the United States quietly cooperated with interested nongovernmental organizations to create the bureaucratic infrastructure necessary to design a new world order, their colleagues in Ottawa showed virtually no interest in postwar planning. There were individuals in groups such as the Canadian Institute of International Affairs (CIIA) who did take reconstruction questions seriously, but until 1942, or even 1943, they had no legitimate political outlet for their concerns.

In 1942 the Canadian government was unaware that its great-power allies had begun to formalize their visions of the general structure of the next world organization. It was therefore difficult for proponents of greater internationalism to convince their prime minister, William Lyon Mackenzie King, to move ahead aggressively with a national planning exercise. A leading civil servant stationed outside of Ottawa, Hume Wrong, was more forward-thinking. In January 1942 he conceived what has since become known as the functional principle. This theory of international representation was originally developed to ensure that during the war, states with the capacity and willingness to contribute positively would receive influence commensurate with their contribution. From the principle's inception, however, Wrong and his closest colleagues knew that Canada's brand of functionalism – one that had been developed by diplomats rather than by soldiers – would be more applicable to discussions of the future peace.

The functional principle was tested in this future context in 1942 and 1943 during negotiations to establish the first global postwar organization, the United Nations Relief and Rehabilitation Administration (UNRRA). The original composition of the UNRRA executive set a precedent for the structure of the United Nations, and the results of the UNRRA meetings therefore mark Canada's first direct involvement in the shaping of the postwar world. Throughout the negotiations, poor coordination and miscommunication among the country's top officials and political leaders resulted in a decision to compromise the functional principle and put its future usefulness as a foreign-policy tool into question. The outcome of the UNRRA planning meetings should therefore be seen as a failure, indicative of the country's lack of worldly experience.

Already suffering in the polls after a divisive national debate over conscription and seeking to respond to accusations at home and in the United States that Canada had not been contributing its fair share to the war,

Mackenzie King's Liberal government had no choice but to become more comfortable with international engagement as the UNRRA talks progressed. In 1943 when the newly instituted Wartime Information Board informed the prime minister that the Canadian people were now seriously interested in postwar reconstruction, he grudgingly allowed his staff in the Department of External Affairs to contribute to the formal planning exercises then taking place in the United Kingdom. Thanks to its British ties, its close relationship with the United States, and its political, economic, and military investment in the war, Canada was invited to join these postwar discussions well before any other nongreat power. Consequently, the six month period that followed the end of the UNRRA negotiations saw the extent of Canada's relative influence in shaping the new world order reach its peak. King was privy to confidential Anglo-American planning ideas before the rest of the small-power leaders, and Canada's impact on the Moscow Conference of October 1943 justified proclamations both in the media and on Parliament Hill that the country had begun to function as the foremost representative of the intermediate and small states.

After Moscow, as it became more obvious that the United States had replaced Great Britain as the dominant power in the West and that London would need the support of the dominions to maintain its international legitimacy as a world leader, an increasingly confident national public questioned Canada's proper role within the British Commonwealth of Nations. This was an important issue that would enshrine the concept of helpful fixer in the Canadian national mentality and allow the King government to assume a more independent position on the world stage, but it was also an all-consuming issue in late 1943 and early 1944. Discussions about the old empire overwhelmed the public, the press, the academic community, and Parliament, while officials in the United Kingdom and the United States were finalizing their first drafts of the UN Charter. Their results, arrived at with only minimal input from Canada, were not that different from the document that eventually emerged from San Francisco.

In the summer of 1944, while the great powers formally discussed their visions of the future at the Dumbarton Oaks Conference, Canadian officials did a particularly poor job of making certain that their government's opinions were heard and taken seriously. This disappointing performance was the result primarily of the inability of the country's most important planners to reconcile their conflicting approaches to conceiving a new world order. When officials Lester Pearson and Escott Reid refused to heed their superiors' warnings to negotiate cautiously, Norman Robertson and Hume Wrong denied them access to information that they needed to perform effectively at the Canadian Embassy in the United States. This conflict between the aggressive internationalists in Washington and the cautious pragmatists in Ottawa has generally been underemphasized by Canadian historians, just as it was never acknowledged or managed by Mackenzie King, who was also the minister of external affairs.

Instead, most of the importance traditionally assigned by Canadian analysts to the period leading up to the San Francisco Conference is associated with the development of the amorphous middle power concept. Canada, among others, vaguely demanded that a distinction be made on the world organization's executive committee – the United Nations Security Council – between the moderately powerful states, like itself, and the utterly powerless. Once again, the Canadian negotiators were unsuccessful. It was simply too difficult to devise reasonable and widely acceptable criteria by which to differentiate among the nongreat. Moreover, as a country that was still relatively new to world affairs, Canada lacked the bureaucratic infrastructure and the resources necessary to develop a network of like-minded medium-sized states that might have worked together to achieve this end.

The more optimistic civil servants, like Pearson and Reid, were hardly deterred, and the national press certainly continued to promote Canada as the leader of the secondary countries, but the most significant Canadian contribution to the new world organization eventually came from those who had all but abandoned the middle power project. In early 1945, led once again by Hume Wrong, officials in the East Block[10] involved in the UN negotiations turned their thoughts to an issue of international order closer to Mackenzie King's heart: the impact of social and economic stability on world peace and global security. Accompanying this new focus was the belief that, for the United Nations to be successful, the great powers – then the United States, the United Kingdom, the Soviet Union, China, and France – would have to be allowed to dominate the more traditional security field.

Thus, while most Canadians anticipated that their country would make its greatest impact at the San Francisco Conference by defining a role for the middle powers and establishing the functional principle as a basis for determining representation on international bodies, Canada's best opportunity for real influence lay in the socio-economic arena. Thanks to its effective preparation and genuine commitment, the Canadian delegation was successful in rewriting and expanding the articles in the Dumbarton Oaks proposals that defined and characterized the new organization's Economic and Social Council. Other initiatives ended less positively. The concept of functionalism was only partly included in the new charter. And the middle power campaign ended before it began. At San Francisco it was not a Canadian but rather Australia's foreign minister, Herbert Evatt, who led the smaller states in a drive to reduce the influence of the great powers. During the negotiations, the representatives from Ottawa were in fact complicit in ensuring that the veto power granted to the United Kingdom, the United States, the Soviet Union, China, and France was further-reaching than many of their colleagues from the medium- and smaller-sized countries would have preferred. Caution clearly ruled under Mackenzie King: international prestige was not worth the risk of another great-power conflict.

Their initial optimism now tempered by increasing tensions between the Western allies and the Soviet Union, most Canadian participants acknowledged the results of the United Nations Conference on International Organization to be a wake-up call. It was time to accept that their country was a small, albeit independent and active, nation on the world stage. It could have an impact on international issues that did not require a substantial military commitment, but in a Cold War environment, when it came to security, the will of the great powers reigned supreme. For the great majority of the Canadian delegation, the process that would lead to what one historian has called "the destruction of the idealist impulse in Canadian life"[11] was all but over.

It was not over for those who had followed the conference through the press. Politicians, academics, journalists, and those few officials who managed to maintain some of their idealism viewed the San Francisco experience as evidence of Canada's new, elevated place in world affairs. They spoke and wrote wistfully of their country's position as a middle power leader and trumpeted Canada's half-triumphs at the negotiations as complete victories. For them, as the late historian C.P. Stacey has explained, Canada was "the centre of the world."[12] They interpreted changes that had taken place internally as international achievements.

This was an understandable response, one that is common historically among peoples who have committed themselves to a new national identity and have then proceeded to try to "bring reality into alignment with their vision."[13] Nevertheless, it has resulted in a consistent overstatement of Canada's importance to the planning of the United Nations during the Second World War. As a small state undergoing "a profound period of apprenticeship in the trade of international relations,"[14] Canada was on the periphery during what were primarily great-power negotiations. In well over its head and coming to grips with an expanded role in the international community for which it had not asked, Canada's successes on the world stage were relatively minor. None of this diminishes the importance to Canadian history of the process of founding the United Nations. Rather, instead of assessing the significance of this period in terms of how Canada changed the world, it is time to consider more carefully how planning a new world order changed Canada.

2
Two Steps Behind
(Beginnings through January 1942)

When it came to peacemaking, William Lyon Mackenzie King was a natural. His upbringing, his religion, and his education had made him a strong believer in faith, hope, and human reason. He applied these values to his academic training and eventually received a PhD from Harvard recognizing the quality of his research on labour negotiation and social reform. From 1914 to 1917 he consulted for the Rockefeller Foundation, quickly becoming one of the world's foremost experts on mediation and conflict resolution.

In 1918, writing in the shadows of the First World War, he published his only significant scholarly work, *Industry and Humanity*. It was meant to be a discourse on the future of industrial relations, but its promotion of negotiation and conciliation as means of conflict resolution was equally relevant to the management of global affairs. International conflict, King reasoned, was just like industrial strife, and "the acceptance of nations of the principle of investigation before resort to hostilities would mark the dawn of a new era in the history of the world."[1] These thoughts were hardly original – at this precise moment, the American president, Woodrow Wilson, was trying to embody them in the League of Nations Covenant – but they were sincere, and King carried them with him throughout his tenure as Canada's prime minister and minister of external affairs.

Where King and Wilson differed was on the value of formal international organizations. To the Canadian, problems were best solved by people, not structures, and conciliation "was always the best of methods to employ in adjusting differences."[2] King was also not a deep student of international events; maintaining domestic harmony concerned him far more than his country's involvement abroad. Nevertheless, he was Canada's leading political figure and could not always avoid thinking about his global responsibilities. A confidential contemporary biographical sketch of the prime minister, likely from the late 1930s or the early 1940s, listed his interpretation of these duties as threefold: "to gain and maintain Canada's recognition as an independent unified nation bound to the Commonwealth only by ties of loyalty to the Crown; to support Great Britain and the Empire in bad days as well as in good, but to do so because it is in Canada's best interest; and finally to promote close friendship between Canada and the United States and thus a closer understanding between the United States and Great Britain."[3]

This tempered approach to foreign policy reflected the generally ambivalent attitude toward international affairs and world order shared by much of the Canadian public into the early 1940s. When the war began, the electorate was still recovering from the strains of the conscription controversy of 1917 and from the economic and social impact of the Great Depression. Canadians sought comfort in the so-called fireproof house of North America and did not pay attention to talk of a new international organization to replace the old and ineffective League of Nations. It is therefore not surprising that King saw little need to contemplate the potentially controversial postwar peace during the first years of the Second World War.

His great-power allies in the United Kingdom and the United States were thinking differently. The failure of the League of Nations had demonstrated to them the need for a new, workable framework for international organization, and they started to devise strategies for postwar reconstruction before the formal conflict with Hitler had even begun. It was not until 1941, under new administrative leadership and with the national war effort expanding, that Canada's Department of External Affairs was given King's grudging permission to begin to catch up. By then Canadian officials were clearly starting from behind.

While Mackenzie King might not have cared for the idea of a new world organization, a number of other educated Canadians, who formed part of what the historian Douglas Owram has called the national "brain trust," felt differently.[4] Most of them were members of the Canadian Institute of International Affairs (CIIA). Founded in 1928 as a sister organization to Britain's Royal Institute of International Affairs (RIIA), it aimed to promote a greater general awareness of international problems, particularly with reference to Canada and the British Empire. Since, as one scholar has explained, in the 1920s and the 1930s, "the CIIA's membership comprised virtually everyone in Canada interested in foreign policy in a serious way,"[5] CIIA activists were often affiliated with other bodies committed to internationalism and collective security. Members could be found, for example, at meetings of both the League of Nations Society and the Canadian Association for Adult Education (CAAE).

On 20 November 1940 a number of CIIA leaders, including Brooke Claxton, who was an affiliate of the League of Nations Society and a Liberal backbencher, E.A. Corbett of the CAAE, the Canadian film commissioner,

John Grierson, and the University of New Brunswick president, Norman Mackenzie, attended an informal conference of educational authorities. The next day, the foursome helped found the Canadian Council for Education in Citizenship (CCEC). The CCEC had two main objectives: "To stimulate in the minds of all Canadians a greater appreciation of the meaning and implications of democracy as a way of life" and to promote a greater understanding of the challenges of postwar reconstruction both at home and abroad.[6]

Throughout the war, the council collaborated with a variety of governmental and nongovernmental agencies to help shape public opinion and to promote a more internationalist approach to Canadian external relations. In 1940, however, most of its work was restricted to the voluntary sector; access to the official body responsible for foreign-policy development, the Department of External Affairs, was either limited or nonexistent. Part of the problem was the undersecretary of state for external affairs, O.D. Skelton. He was, like King, a Presbyterian, a first-rate academic with a PhD in political economy, and a liberal at heart. He shared his prime minister's suspicions of Britain's political leadership and had never forgotten that following the British blindly into battle in 1914 had nearly destroyed his country. In the late 1930s, while Hitler moved on Austria and Czechoslovakia, Skelton became the leader of "the isolationist intelligentsia" in the East Block. He argued incessantly that Canada would not survive entrance into another European conflict. By implication, there was no reason to seriously contemplate the peace that might follow.[7]

Not all of Skelton's staff shared his views. Most of the young, well-educated, forthright nationalist intellectuals whom he hired to serve beneath him between 1925 and 1940 envisioned Canada as an active player in world affairs and, over time, as a significant contributor to the Allied cause in the Second World War. Nevertheless, under their leader's shadow, they generally kept their desires for a more dynamic policy to themselves.

For the most part, this system worked effectively. One recruit, Charles Ritchie, recalled his first impressions of the office in 1934: "The Department of External Affairs at that time was as small as Canada's place on the map of international politics. Its future was being shaped by a handful of unusually gifted men ... They worked together without feeling for respective rank, without pomposity, with humour, desisting pretence, intolerant of silliness and scathing in their contempt for self-advertisement."[8] Thanks in large part to Skelton's leadership, this atmosphere of youthful enthusiasm and general cohesiveness remained intact through the first sixteen months of the Second World War.

On 28 January 1941, however, the sixty-two-year-old undersecretary, who had been coping with relatively serious heart trouble for years, suffered a fatal heart attack in his car on his way back to the East Block from lunch.

His passing was a tremendous blow to Mackenzie King, who trusted him more than he did any other civil servant, and to the Canadian policy establishment as a whole. The Department of External Affairs was particularly hard hit. One officer later recalled: "He was the firm foundation of our department, at home and abroad. He was more. He was the centre of all its decisions and of many of those of the government. He appeared to be irreplaceable." And he had never had the time to develop or mentor a successor.[9]

The selection of the next undersecretary marked a turning point in the history of Canadian external relations and, more specifically, in Canada's approach to shaping the future world order; with Skelton gone, so too was the most significant long term impediment in Ottawa to constructive postwar planning. According to the historian John Hilliker, the process of choosing a replacement was basically one of elimination. Assistant Undersecretary Laurent Beaudry did not want the position; the legal adviser John Read lacked the required background in politics and economics; Hugh Keenleyside, who had worked in the legation in Japan and had also recently served as King's personal emissary in discussions with the United States, was a difficult political choice because of his unpopular defence of the interests of Canada's Japanese. That left three of Skelton's best recruits from the 1920s: Oxford graduates Hume Wrong, Lester (Mike) Pearson, and Norman Robertson.[10]

A professor of history at the University of Toronto and the son of its founding historian, Hume Wrong was best known for his superior intellect. After his death in 1954, one colleague recalled fondly: "It was his capacity for bold, dispassionate and objective thinking and of following through to whatever his trained rational processes of thought and experience would lead him, despite the pressures and distractions of the day, that made Hume Wrong such a tower of strength in those days of diplomatic pioneering for Canada."[11] Among himself, Pearson, and Robertson, Wrong was senior and therefore an obvious choice for Skelton's job.

But, along with being "the most substantial of all these people," he was also, according to King's former assistant James Gibson, "the most pointed and the least tolerant."[12] He had a quick temper, and as his colleague Lester Pearson once explained: "Hume didn't try to get people to like him particularly. He didn't make many concessions. He wouldn't go out of his way to placate people because of their political position if he thought they were wrong ... And he wouldn't mind calling a spade a spade, [or] calling it a bloody shovel if he had to." This attitude did not find favour with Canada's prime minister. In fact, Wrong's contemporary John Deutsch once said: "[Mackenzie] King was death on him." Without King's support, he never stood a chance for the promotion.[13]

Lester Pearson's situation was different. According to Wrong's daughter, June Rogers: "Mike liked everybody, and everybody liked Mike."[14] Pearson's charm was extraordinary. A former colleague, the well-respected and usually critical Maurice Pope, wrote of him: "It was always not only a pleasure but an inspiration to find oneself associated in anything with the one and only Mike."[15] Others found that he delivered less than he appeared to promise, especially intellectually. The president of the National Research Council, for example, conceded his impeccable charm but called the former semiprofessional athlete "just an educated ballplayer."[16] Another suggested that he had "a massive ego."[17]

Pearson had been doing excellent work in London under Canada's high commissioner, Vincent Massey. With Wrong out of consideration for the undersecretary's position, he seemed to be the next logical choice. Not in the same intellectual class as his former academic colleague in the History Department at the University of Toronto, he still held an Oxford degree, worked extremely hard, and was the best public-relations spokesperson in the diplomatic civil service. Yet his friend and associate Walter Gordon remembered, "there may have been some question as to whether Mike, with his breezy cheerful manner, would be the best man to establish an intimate relationship with the lugubrious Prime Minister."[18] Hilliker has speculated that Pearson might not have been chosen because, being in London, he was simply out of King's mind, but Gordon's explanation merits consideration as well: Mackenzie King demanded full and unquestioning obedience, and Lester Pearson was outspoken and ambitious.[19]

That left Norman Robertson. Although the youngest and most junior of the qualified candidates, he was also the best person for the job. Robertson, wrote one colleague, "had great intellectual gifts and extraordinary mental capacity. He could read and assimilate a dispatch of a cabinet paper in half the time of anyone else. He remembered everything he had read and was able to bring to bear on the consideration of any subject not only a vast amount of knowledge but also good judgment and a ready resourcefulness."[20] Trained as an economist, he had also already caught the attention of the prime minister through his performance as a trade negotiator at a series of international meetings in the late 1930s.

Admittedly, Robertson's daughter Judith has conceded modestly, he "didn't have that easy affability that Mr. Pearson had." He was, however, far better suited to work with Mackenzie King. He was humble, he took great pride in serving his country, and he had no political ambitions.[21] To his biographer, Jack Granatstein, Robertson was "the model civil servant ... His role was to advise, and he performed that task superbly, offering his political masters the benefit of his well-stocked brain and his deep learning."[22] On 28 January, only hours after King had learned of Skelton's death, he offered Robertson the position.

The new undersecretary shared many of his predecessor's personal qualities: exceptional intelligence, a preference for settling internal conflicts quietly, and somewhat lacklustre organizational skills. At the same time, the much more youthful Robertson had been influenced by profoundly different worldly experiences. Too young to have fought in the First World War, he had developed a more tolerant attitude toward Great Britain and was more comfortable than Skelton seeing Canada actively involved in international affairs.

Robertson's views coincided nicely with those of the officials around him; however, his age (he was not yet thirty-seven) made it difficult for some of them to accept him initially as their superior. One might therefore suggest that the loss of Skelton robbed the department of its direction, but it would be more accurate to say that under their new leader, the young, nationalistic officers gained the freedom to become more flexible and adventurous in their approaches to world affairs.

Hume Wrong seems to have taken the news of Robertson's appointment quite well. Wrong had first met him only in 1939, but from the very beginning, Rogers remembers, "he was just tremendously impressed." When Wrong's wife, Joyce, became bitter that her husband had been passed over for the promotion, he "quickly told her that she was making a big mistake and would not think this if she met Norman."[23] During the war years, Robertson and Wrong established a mutually beneficial and trusting working relationship. The new undersecretary was unprepared, and in some ways ill-suited, for his additional responsibilities, and he came to rely on the colleague whom he called "the ablest man in the service" to handle the organizational duties of the office, which seemed to baffle him. Robertson showed the utmost respect for Wrong's abilities and his intellect, and Wrong, in turn, never questioned Robertson's judgment or his senior status.[24]

The same cannot be said for Lester Pearson. Shortly after King's disappointing announcement, in a speech – given with reluctance – at the Canadian Club, he declared: "I think Norman was the right choice for the job. I shall be pleased and honoured to work under him."[25] But the public statement and his private diary writings tell different stories. Upon his more permanent recall to Ottawa to assume the post of joint assistant undersecretary of state for external affairs (along with Keenleyside) in late March, Pearson wrote revealingly: "Of course I don't like the idea really of going back to the Department, except as Under-Secretary, and I am not quite sure what this post of Joint Assistant Under-Secretary means. My own view is that it means that Mr. King wants Norman Robertson as a sort of super personal assistant and is going to give him the rank of Under-Secretary for that reason, while I am to be brought back to do the work that the Under-Secretary would normally be doing, without being given the rank."[26] Two months later, in a personal letter to Vincent Massey, he left the impression that he had not yet completely overcome his disappointment.[27]

Pearson was jealous, and colleagues admitted later that his frustration was noticeable. Robertson's former assistant once said of him and Pearson: "There was a state of suppressed tension between the two that prevented fruitful relations throughout their entire association ... I am sure, in my own mind, that Mike Pearson was never at ease with Norman."[28] Another associate concurred, noting that Pearson's attitude in the early 1940s caused the relationship to become "ambiguous and difficult."[29] As for Robertson, it was not coincidental that it was Wrong to whom he would turn in planning the new world order and Pearson who would soon be isolated in Washington.[30] After January 1941, therefore, the department's old cohesiveness – which Charles Ritchie had so fondly recalled in 1934 – was no longer in evidence.

The increasingly difficult relationship among some of Canada's top civil servants did not immediately affect the country's official plans for the postwar period. This was not because the diplomats were able to put their rivalries aside; rather, at the official level in 1941, such planning was simply not yet taking place. The situation was different in the nongovernmental sector. In April 1941 members of the World Citizens Association (WCA), a group made up of specialists in international relations from Canada, the United States, and Europe, met in Lake Forest, Illinois, to discuss their visions of a postwar world. Among their conclusions was the statement: "A firm and lasting partnership among the democracies, founded not only upon the recognition of their common interests, but upon acceptance of their responsibilities toward other nations, constitutes the first of the peace aims – the indispensable foundation for all future plans." There was a need for a more elaborate version of the League of Nations, one that would invoke the concepts of regionalism and universalism. Planning for this new organization, they maintained, should begin immediately.[31]

In May the executive committee of Canada's 4,000-person League of Nations Society, which included at least one member of the WCA, passed a resolution urging the Canadian government to form a committee on postwar organization.[32] Less than two weeks later, Brooke Claxton – who had links to both the society and the CIIA and who was well-acquainted with representatives of the WCA – sent a letter to Robertson urging immediate action. He waited three weeks for a response and then wrote again, this time attaching a detailed memorandum recommending that his government sponsor a thorough study of international reconstruction.[33]

However interested Robertson might have been personally, it appears that the combination of the immediate stresses brought on by his new position – learning the job, earning the respect of his peers, attempting to establish a sense of structure within one of the most disorganized departments in Ottawa – and the hiring restrictions that had been imposed throughout the civil service in the early years of the war precluded any consideration of the distant future. Himself a partisan Liberal, Claxton might have tried to approach Robertson's superior, Mackenzie King, but during the war, King was (justifiably) inaccessible to anyone but his closest advisers.

The Canadian government's inability, or unwillingness, to contemplate the postwar era between 1939 and 1941 left it a full two years behind its Anglo-American great-power allies in the planning process. In the United Kingdom the RIIA initiated its dialogue on postwar political reconstruction in May 1939, three months prior to Hitler's attack on Poland.[34] While Mackenzie King was bracing his country for the possibility of war, the RIIA's world-order preparatory group held its first meeting at Chatham House on 17 July 1939. The discussion emphasized the importance of maintaining the rule of law in international relations.[35]

Unlike the CIIA, which struggled to be heard in Ottawa through much of 1941, the RIIA had already established close links to the government in London. Its impact was evident in October 1939 when Lord Lothian, the British ambassador in Washington, alluded publicly to a future global federation. His comments foresaw an international order in which regional organizations would police the world under the umbrella of a unifying executive body. Lothian was acting boldly in expressing this idea to a people who had, in his own words, "been taught to justify their own abandonment of international co-operation in 1920 by discrediting [President Woodrow] Wilson and all his works and their own action in 1917-1919 and by crediting all other governments and peoples with the basest motives," but his experience in the United States made him confident that America was "gradually becoming reconciled to the necessity of playing a hand in some form of world organization not for war but to prevent world war."[36]

His instincts were correct. On 16 September 1939 the US secretary of state, Cordell Hull, saw fit to appoint Leo Pasvolsky his special assistant responsible primarily for postwar settlement issues. In December the secretary and his new assistant gathered the department's senior officers, and together they created what eventually became an advisory committee on problems of foreign relations. Working within the Division for the Study of Problems of Peace and Reconstruction, the committee discussed "possibilities of political arrangements for the maintenance of peace ... methods of limitation of national sovereignty [and] problems of general machinery of international co-operation."[37] Again, unlike the government in Ottawa, the government in Washington immediately accepted support from its RIIA equivalent, the Council on Foreign Relations.

All of the American preparation took place in relative secrecy. During the so-called phoney war of 1939 and early 1940, President Roosevelt feared that the still isolationist general public would not accept US political involvement in what it felt was a European conflict.[38] When Hitler marched through France, however, things began to change. Almost immediately, Roosevelt pursued closer military and economic ties with both Canada and Great Britain. In August 1940 Canada and the United States signed the Ogdensburg Agreement, creating a permanent joint board on defence for North America. The United States then agreed to exchange some of its old destroyers with the United Kingdom for long-term leases on a series of naval bases in and around Newfoundland. When the American Lend-Lease Act – designed to provide financial aid in the form of munitions to Britain and its European allies – threatened Canada's economic security and caused Mackenzie King to complain that his country was being "overlooked" by both the US and the UK, Cordell Hull promised to "endeavor to guard against this omission in the future."[39] Canada and the United States then quickly signed an agreement at Hyde Park that restored continental economic stability.

When it came to North Atlantic political cooperation, perhaps because they did not find Canada sufficiently important, but also at least in part because the Canadians had not undertaken any formal planning themselves, the American and British officials collaborated more exclusively. As a first step, Winston Churchill made Lord Halifax – a senior minister who kept in regular touch with representatives of the RIIA – his new ambassador to Washington.

Halifax arrived in the United States just as President Roosevelt announced to Congress that he anticipated a postwar system founded upon what became known worldwide as the four freedoms.[40] The new ambassador made inquiries into the implications of the speech but initially discovered very little. It did not take him long to realize why. In a letter to Britain's foreign secretary a few weeks later, he expressed amazement at the sensitivity of American political officials "to the ripples of public opinion."[41] Indeed, in 1941, according to the American Institute of Public Opinion (AIPO), only one-third of voting Americans were thinking about how world peace might be maintained after the end of what most felt was a European war.[42] Critics of Roosevelt who would later accuse him of lacking "long range vision"[43] misunderstood his intentions. In January 1941 the US president admitted to one long-time adviser that the isolationist impulse still prevalent among the American people obligated him to continue the postwar strategizing, to which he was utterly committed, in relative secrecy.[44]

America's public silence inadvertently held back the progress of the Canadian internationalists. Without evidence of what their US colleagues had been doing, they could not convince their government that it was being left behind. Specifically, Mackenzie King was unaware that on 3 February 1941 the United States had formalized its planning process by establishing a division of special research. It was tasked with foreign-policy analysis related specifically to changes in international relations. Leo Pasvolsky, fast becoming the State Department's foremost expert on international organization, was made chief of the new unit.[45]

At about the same time, President Roosevelt sent his personal assistant, Harry Hopkins, to London to propose what would have to be, given the German naval threat in the Atlantic, a secret encounter between himself and Prime Minister Churchill to discuss wartime collaboration. Originally planned for the early spring, scheduling problems postponed the conference until the late summer. Roosevelt had considered Ottawa as a meeting place but decided against it to avoid having to explain to Mackenzie King that he could not be invited. Later asked why, he answered simply, "I really couldn't take him."[46] In America's view, Canada had no place at a summit of two major leaders.

The government in London did not entirely agree. After the fall of France, and with the threat of a German invasion imminent, Canada and the rest of the dominions had become crucial to Britain's national defence. At the end of March 1941, when the committee on reconstruction considered the implications of sharing Britain's postwar plans with the United States, one civil servant reminded his colleagues that any discussions that excluded the increasingly important dominion governments would have to be treated as preliminary.[47] Unfortunately for Canada, Australia, New Zealand, and South Africa, the British Foreign Office (FO) did not share his concerns. Still convinced that Britain could remain a great power on its own, the FO ignored instructions to improve communication between London and the Commonwealth governments.

In June, with just over eight weeks left until the Anglo-American meeting, Canada had yet to learn anything about Britain's postwar thinking. When Canadian High Commissioner Vincent Massey finally received the opportunity to press Britain for more information, he argued forcefully that since Canada would have a significant role to play in the peace process, it was important that it be kept informed. The vagueness of the response from the Foreign Office suggests that it did not agree.[48]

Mackenzie King, therefore, did not know about the meeting between Roosevelt and Churchill that began on 9 August 1941. Nor was he aware that it took place in Canada's backyard, on a pair of battleships in Argentia Harbour on the coast of Newfoundland. The meeting demonstrated that Canada was not needed to mediate between its greatest allies. After just two days of talks, having gotten along effortlessly, the parties exchanged drafts of a joint public statement.[49]

Of the eight points in what was called the Atlantic Charter, it was the last one that would have the greatest political impact on the future world order. The British had proposed that both countries pledge to create an "effective international organization" after the war. Roosevelt, however, was reluctant to risk the response of the still isolationist American public to such a bold statement.[50] He preferred to speak of a joint US-UK police force to safeguard Europe during the inevitable postwar transition period. Churchill, who was more concerned personally with military strategy and who, indeed, had already privately declared himself "too old to have anything to do with postwar planning,"[51] brought the problem to his much more forward-thinking Cabinet by telegraph and found a compromise. Rather than explicitly referring to an international organization, he proposed to include the words "pending the establishment of a wider and more permanent system of general security." The internationalists in Great Britain would be disappointed, but they could be convinced to regard the result "as an interim and partial settlement of war aims" and as an assurance that their government's vision of the future was developing responsibly. Roosevelt too would not be entirely pleased, but he would accept the new wording so that he could emerge from the talks with what he needed: a joint public statement of principles.[52]

In the end, the eighth article read:

> They believe that all of the nations of the world, for realistic as well as spiritual reasons must come to the abandonment of the use of force. Since no future peace can be maintained if land, sea or air armaments continue to be employed by nations which threaten, or may threaten, aggression outside of their frontiers, they believe, pending the establishment of a wider and permanent system of general security, that the disarmament of such nations is essential. They will likewise aid and encourage all other practicable measures which will lighten for peace-loving peoples the crushing burden of armaments.[53]

When Mackenzie King learned of the Argentia meeting, he was hurt, if not upset. He did not mind that Roosevelt and Churchill had excluded him per se, but holding the talks so close to Canada without his knowing had made both him and his country look unimportant. Clearly, this would not sit well with the Canadian public, particularly during a period when it was being asked to make sacrifices for the sake of the war.[54] Sensing trouble, Norman Robertson attempted to downplay the importance of the Atlantic Charter to his prime minister. It did not really contain any new ideas, he explained. It served merely to publicize a set of principles that would underlie future discussions of international relations.[55]

While perhaps true of some of the articles, this was not at all the case in terms of world organization. To the British Foreign Research and Press Service, Churchill had now committed Great Britain, at least in principle, to "some form of continuing security system."[56] American officials also believed that the declaration was important, although they could not quite determine what the final article meant. It might have been referring to a great-power police force, but alternatively it could have been promoting a new, structured international organization. In either case, one officer noted confidently: "To be compatible with American desires and acceptable to our electorate the international body [would] have to be built to our specifications."[57]

He had good reason to feel secure. By drafting the charter in such vague terms, the United Kingdom had made a significant concession to the United States. On behalf of the rest of the international community, including its own dominions, it had assured the government in Washington, at least implicitly, that America would have the final word on the composition of any new world organization. Indeed, as the historian David Reynolds has argued: "1941 marked the U.S.A.'s self-conscious assertion of her potential as a great power, even though she was not at war – a situation that often reduced the British Government to diplomatic impotence."[58] Since the fall of France, Britain had been the single most dominant power in wartime planning. Quickly, however, this was beginning to change.

At the time, Mackenzie King could not have been aware of the power shift; he was too focused on his constituents to pay close attention. The Conservatives were effectively criticizing his government for failing to have been represented at Argentia. In August, setting aside Norman Robertson's attempts to calm him, King told Britain's new high commissioner to Canada, Malcolm MacDonald, that he would have to visit London to reaffirm his country's worldly importance.[59]

During his three-week stay in the fall of 1941, the Canadian prime minister made certain that both he and his electorate got the reassurance that they needed. On 4 September, King delivered a particularly well-received speech at Mansion House that earned public praise from Churchill. The momentum from the talk carried through the rest of the trip. According to two historians of Canadian external affairs, King's visit to London "proved a source of inspiration to the whole Canadian people and strengthened the conviction of many that Canada had a distinct and significant role to play in the existing world crisis."[60]

Perhaps they were right, but King had not converted Brooke Claxton. Canada's exclusion from Argentia had convinced him that the government could not be counted on to take a leadership role in postwar planning. In October he moved successfully that the CIIA create its own research group to study the implications of the Atlantic Charter.[61] In November, at the annual meeting of its national council, the CIIA dedicated all of its available resources to the postwar period. Records of the minutes noted this new focus: "During the course of the discussion, emphasis was placed by the speakers on the very great responsibility which the Institute must accept for considering the pressing problems of postwar reconstruction in Canada, and in the world, with special attention to the relations between Great Britain, the United States and Canada. There was a general feeling that, at a time when Governments are heavily engaged in the business of carrying on the war, a unique organization like the C.I.I.A. must accept responsibility for considering how the peace can be won."[62]

Ironically, just as the CIIA abandoned its faith in the Canadian government, Norman Robertson finally began to mobilize the Department of External Affairs. Since wartime restrictions prevented him from hiring the additional staff necessary to pursue an internationalist agenda in the traditional way, he sought temporary help from his former academic colleagues. Himself a University of British Columbia graduate, Robertson first asked the professor of political science and economics Henry Angus to move to Ottawa and assume the position of departmental "special assistant." Angus was a member of the CIIA and had studied the Versailles settlement in depth. He was expected to contribute constructively to postwar discussions. George Glazebrook, known to Pearson from the History Department of the University of Toronto, soon joined him. Glazebrook had sat on the CIIA research committee that had been tasked with looking into the shape of the postwar world. In all, approximately twenty university professors eventually worked for External Affairs during the war, nearly all of whom had direct or at least indirect ties to the CIIA. The recruitment of these academics created a planning infrastructure within the Canadian civil service that was similar to those already established in Great Britain and the United States. Two years after the Anglo-American process of planning the postwar order had started, Canada was finally taking its first small step forward.[63]

Beyond the East Block, however, this step was hardly noticeable. Domestically, Canada's most significant wartime concern in late 1941 remained the possibility of conscription. The former prime minister, Arthur Meighen, had revived Conservative support for compulsory service in November, and after the Japanese attack on the United States at Pearl Harbor on 7 December, even Mackenzie King had begun to contemplate ways of releasing his government from its commitment to a purely volunteer overseas military force.

The Canadian public expressed relief that America had finally joined the conflict and responded willingly to the never-ending orders coming from the office of the new minister of munitions and supply, C.D. Howe. Most of the country hardly noticed that the great powers were once again acting alone. Shortly after Pearl Harbor, Churchill and Roosevelt met privately in Washington to coordinate their military efforts through what they described as a supreme war council. To maintain the support of the smaller contributing forces, they discussed a possible joint declaration of what Roosevelt called the United Nations – a pledge by the UK, the US, and all of their allies to abide by the principles of the Atlantic Charter and to pursue victory until the enemy had surrendered.[64] After they learned of these decisions, some of the more activist members of Canada's Department of External Affairs expressed a legitimate concern that the new command structure would set a precedent for great-power control during the postwar period as well. Thinking back to 1919, they began to formulate strategies to ensure that Canada's influence after the war would be commensurate with its current and projected military and economic contributions.[65]

Because they had become dependent on Canadian economic support, the British were initially sympathetic. Lord Halifax implored Cordell Hull to grant the dominions a degree of status on the Anglo-American supreme war council. The results of his efforts, however, were disappointing and reflective of Great Britain's diminishing influence in the alliance. The State Department claimed that additional members would render the body "unwieldy and ineffective." Instead, US officials suggested possible provisions for relevant governments to be represented on an ad hoc basis.[66]

America's inflexibility prevented Norman Robertson from viewing the United Nations Declaration until just three days before its scheduled release. When he finally saw it, the undersecretary was disappointed; first, Canada had been denied input into the draft; now, in the list of adherents, the great powers – in this case the United States, the United Kingdom, the Soviet Union, and China – had segregated themselves. "In terms of war potential or immediately effective contribution to the struggle," Robertson reported to Prime Minister King, "it is difficult to put what is left of Free China in a separate and higher category than that which will contain Canada, the Netherlands and India."[67]

Working at the Canadian Embassy in Washington at the time, Hume Wrong was instructed to deliver a memorandum expressing this and other concerns to America's assistant secretary of state, Adolf Berle. The cynical former Harvard Law School professor and noted Anglophobe did little more than shrug, citing the complications that could arise from reopening the declaration so close to its planned publication. Presumably following orders, Wrong responded sympathetically, stressing only that in the future the United States had best avoid sending messages to Ottawa through London; Canada expected direct communication. The two parted with the Canadian government seemingly committed to the declaration without reservations.[68]

It is difficult to determine how Mackenzie King felt about Berle's dismissive treatment of Wrong. On the day of their meeting, Winston Churchill was in Ottawa speaking to a joint session of the House of Commons and the Senate. The British prime minister gave what one member called "the speech of a great warrior, whose words of defiance inspired free men to fight irrevocably."[69] With his usual flare for the dramatic, Churchill called Canada "a potent magnet drawing together those in the new world and in the old world whose fortunes are now united in a deadly struggle for life and honour against the common foe."[70] An American witness to the event wrote of the unprecedented impact that the prime minister's presence had had on the country, noting that it had spurred the nation to a more determined war effort.[71] Any problems with the joint statement were therefore quickly forgotten.

The Declaration of the United Nations was released on 1 January 1942, with Canada among its twenty-six original signatories. To follow up, Britain and the United States established a series of combined boards to coordinate their military and economic war effort. The boards were managed by a combined chiefs-of-staff committee with offices in Washington and London. As a British dominion, Canada was not represented.

While, to some, the result might suggest that little had changed in Ottawa between 1939 and 1942, in reality, when it came to the postwar planning process, this was far from true. Canada had entered the war firmly committed to limiting its international liabilities. It had been led by a prime minister who preferred to ignore external relations and an undersecretary of state for external affairs who encouraged his isolationist tendencies. Just over two years later, it was fully engaged in what had become a truly global conflict. Unlike his predecessor in the East Block, Norman Robertson was comfortable with the internationalist views of organizations such as the CIIA and expected Canada to have a role in the future peace at least commensurate to its military and economic contribution to winning the war. Still, however, the new undersecretary's team was not as cohesive as it had been under O.D. Skelton. Also, because of its late start and Mackenzie King's continued aversion to global commitments, Canada remained far behind its allies in postwar planning. These factors, along with the Canadian public's still limited interest in reconstruction, would play a significant role the following year in the creation and composition of the first, precedent-setting postwar body: the United Nations Relief and Rehabilitation Administration.

3
Private Failure: Canada and the UNRRA (January 1942–November 1943)

At the diplomatic level, the fallout from the United Nations Declaration of 1 January 1942 was disheartening. Officially, the King government committed itself to the establishment of a new world organization after the war. Practically, it had little time for world affairs. Opposition to the Liberals was reaching a wartime high thanks to a divisive debate over conscription, and the prime minister was therefore virtually oblivious to reconstruction issues.

Perhaps because he was far away from the political crisis in Ottawa, Hume Wrong viewed the global situation differently. With memories of the First World War still fresh in his mind, he had already become seriously concerned about the impact of America's response to Pearl Harbor on Canada's ability to maintain its deserved place in the future international order. In a letter to Norman Robertson, he soon translated this concern into what has become known to many as "the single most important Canadian contribution to the theory and practice of international organization": the functional principle.[1]

This principle was tested when Canada faced its first real opportunity to affect the composition of the future world order during the meetings to create the United Nations Relief and Rehabilitation Administration (UNRRA). The result was a failure, albeit a private one. The Canadian diplomatic team lacked cohesiveness, and thanks to its preoccupation with the situation at home, the political leadership was unable to recognize the significance of the discussions until they were too far along. At the same time, the general public was hardly aware of the negotiations and never realized the opportunity that had been lost. As a result, although Canada's ability to influence the shape of the peace suffered, the public momentum that was slowly building in favour of proactive engagement in global affairs did not.

It was clear to Hume Wrong almost immediately that his message to Adolf Berle just prior to the publication of the United Nations Declaration had not convinced the Americans of Canada's independent status. In mid-January 1942 he learned that, with the joint chiefs of staff now in place, his country would be expected to communicate its wartime concerns to the United States through Great Britain. To the most pragmatic and logical of Canada's diplomats, this decision was both puzzling and troublesome. Clearly, he thought, in view of his country's geographical location and the importance of North American economic cooperation, it would be more efficient, and indeed more reasonable, to create a joint Anglo-Canadian mission to Washington. Otherwise, Ottawa would risk being robbed of the voice that it had earned as a significant contributor to the war thus far. Furthermore, without influence over wartime policy, it might lose its opportunity to affect the postwar talks.[2]

As he pondered the most effective way to promote Canadian interests at the policy level, Wrong inadvertently articulated what would become known as Canada's functional principle: "Each member of the grand alliance should have a voice in the conduct of war proportionate to its contribution to the general war effort. A subsidiary principle is that the influence of the various countries should be greatest in connection with those matters with which they are most directly concerned."[3] This argument – that a state's influence in international affairs should be commensurate with its interests and capacity to contribute to the issue in question – was ironically much less authentically Canadian than it was Anglo-American. Functionalism was a theory borrowed from a former junior officer at Britain's Foreign Research and Press Service, David Mitrany, and Wrong's interpretation drew from the old American adage "no taxation without representation."[4] Nonetheless, Wrong based his subsequent evaluation of five prospective means of increasing Canadian influence on this functional idea.

The first two policy options, which anticipated Canada as an equal to the US and the UK on all of the wartime boards, he dismissed out of hand as impractical and unrealistic. The third, to demand representation only on bodies where vital Canadian interests were at stake – true "functional representation" – he rejected as "very difficult." As a fourth option, his government might pursue a position either in partnership with the United Kingdom or in collaboration with the entire Commonwealth, replicating the situation of 1919. Lastly, Canada could refrain from seeking a place on any of the boards and focus instead on lobbying Washington and London individually. Wrong rejected this final idea as "quite impossible."

In the end, despite the difficulties that an agreement with the British would likely entail, and regardless of the impact on Canada's so-called independence, Wrong endorsed the fourth option. The functional principle, which was so easy to state, was "remarkably difficult to apply." He felt that Canada could have a more significant impact internationally as part of a greater Commonwealth unit.[5]

The following week, Wrong presented this idea to Britain's representative to the combined chiefs of staff in Washington, Sir John Dill. Quite quickly, it became clear that London would agree to a joint British-Commonwealth mission only if it alone had ultimate control. This would never have been acceptable to the government in Ottawa, so Dill and Wrong discussed ways that Canada might access the authorities in Washington more directly.[6]

With option four no longer available, Wrong reconsidered his third alternative. He used the functional principle to justify his request for an independent, executive-level Canadian mission. Despite the obvious difficulties that this could raise, he recognized that the results of these negotiations would set a precedent for discussions of the postwar order and refused to see Canada deprived of its due influence.

Wrong then looked for support from his political superiors in Ottawa, but his government initially seemed hesitant to interfere with the Anglo-American war (and postwar) plans.[7] The lack of leadership on foreign policy issues coming from the prime minister's office made him furious. "Mainly for reasons of internal political balance," he wrote to a colleague,

> the Government has hitherto adopted in these matters what may unkindly be called a semi-colonial position ... If we had sought earlier to undertake more extensive political responsibilities, it would be easier now to maintain our status. We have tended, however, to be satisfied with the form rather than the substance. Are we still looking mainly for the formal preservation of our status, or are we actually seeking to exert greater influence on the conduct of the alliance? I cannot answer this last question. I do not yet know what the real desires of the Canadian Government are in this respect ... because we have had no sure guidance from Ottawa.[8]

A statement from the Cabinet war committee arrived the next day, but it was not helpful. While the King government expressed its dissatisfaction with the situation, it concluded that there was nothing, at this point, that could be done.[9]

It was in this context – with Wrong having had little success in focusing attention on the postwar period – that talks to create the first international postwar structure opened in London and Washington. The results of the debate over what was originally described as the executive council of the United Nations Relief and Rehabilitation Administration served as what James Eayrs has called a "prototype" for the great powers in their design of the subsequent postwar international institutions.[10] Thanks to its physical distance from the wartime destruction, its booming economy, and its abundance of natural resources, Canada was positioned to be a significant international contributor to relief and rehabilitation efforts for the foreseeable future. As such, it should have been entitled to substantial input into any institution that would coordinate the global response to these issues. The talks therefore provided one of the first serious tests of the usefulness of the functional principle.

Although the Big Three – the US, the UK, and the Soviet Union – had met in London to discuss international relief in September 1941, the UNRRA negotiations began in earnest in response to a January 1942 Soviet memorandum. When asked by the British to collaborate on postwar planning, Moscow's ambassador to the UK, Ivan Maisky, replied: "In view of the fact [that] a number of important problems concerning the economic life of saving post-war Europe will have an international character, it is considered desirable at the present time to create an international organization ... in the form of an Inter-Allied Committee on Post-War Requirements."[11] By late February the Soviet Union had clarified that, in view of its own financial and military concerns, any form of successful international cooperation would have to start with postwar relief.

From the beginning, the great powers assumed that they would take the lead. As Roosevelt explained to his undersecretary, Sumner Welles: "This [was] not the time to talk about the post-war position of small nations."[12] Preliminary discussions in anticipation of a meeting with the Soviets were therefore limited to Great Britain and the United States. Representing the British was Sir Frederick Leith-Ross of the Treasury. According to Norman Robertson, he was one of the few opponents of great-power exclusivity. Leith-Ross was not afraid to challenge the Americans and was generally sympathetic to the interests of the smaller states.[13] He negotiated with the US assistant secretary of state, Dean Acheson, a man recalled by one Canadian as "a person of brilliant intellect ... honest and straightforward to the point of it hurting."[14] Acheson's rather sharp personality made it difficult to interpret his opinion of the lesser powers. One might have thought that he summarily dismissed them, but it is equally as likely that he listened carefully and then rejected their ideas as impractical.

In March 1942 Leo Pasvolsky briefed Acheson on the proposed design of the new organization. It included an executive, or steering, committee composed of between five and seven states, including the US, the UK, the Soviet Union, and China.[15] Acheson developed the proposal and soon invited Leith-Ross to Washington for a more detailed conversation. True to Robertson's analysis, the British Treasury representative strove to open up the negotiations to the smaller powers, but his suggestion does not seem to have been taken seriously in the United States. Washington was already sufficiently concerned about the rather large size of the proposed executive.

These worries were shared by Leith-Ross's own Foreign Office (FO), which itself preferred a more restricted body. The FO felt so strongly about its position that it contracted the great-power body to four before sending a revised proposal to Canada for preliminary approval. When it received the memorandum, Mackenzie King's Cabinet war committee noted immediately that, in view of the global expectations of a significant Canadian contribution to the UNRRA, Canada's exclusion from the executive seemed inappropriate. Nevertheless, the ministers approved the idea in principle and pledged to raise their concerns at a later date. The next week, after their country was denied executive standing on two other combined boards, some members of the Cabinet began to question their decision to stay silent on the UNRRA. For most of them, however, this concern was hardly more than a query.[16]

Norman Robertson was more seriously alarmed. National prestige, he admitted to Leith-Ross, was a factor in his thinking, but international recognition of Canada's contribution to the war and the peace to follow was also important to maintaining morale at home, particularly during a time when the Canadian military was inactive in Europe.[17] Leith-Ross himself was sympathetic, but he could not be of much help in view of the position of his powerful Foreign Office. Excluding select members of the British Treasury, any real sympathy for Canada's position lay not in London but in Washington.[18]

Leith-Ross did convey Robertson's comments to his government, but the preliminary response that he received was negative. Reiterating the need for efficiency, an internal British memorandum made the same argument that Cordell Hull had put forward in discussions on the composition of the supreme war council the previous December: the smaller powers could perhaps sit on the executive body on an ad hoc basis when their interests were affected directly. Full membership would be permitted only on the lower-level committees. When the Canadian concerns were forwarded to Washington, the response of the US officers was initially more amenable. They recognized how important Canada would be to international relief plans and how its support would be crucial to the success of the organization. But the British were adamant. In July 1942 the Americans gave in.[19]

It was around this time that a significant change took place at External Affairs. Hume Wrong was suddenly called back to Ottawa to work as Robertson's primary assistant, and Lester Pearson was transferred to Washington. In the United States, Jack Hickerson noted the abruptness of the switch. When he later asked about it, Robertson replied vaguely that, "in a move of that sort nothing was gained by delay and it was simpler to confront both individuals with a fait accompli rather than enter into long preliminary discussions and negotiations."[20] There is no question that there were legitimate reasons for Robertson to send Pearson to Washington, but it is also worth noting that, along with his disappointment in not getting the undersecretary's position himself, Pearson had already spoken out against his new superior on the UNRRA issue. He personally did not see the need for Canada to have a permanent position on the executive. Hume Wrong, on the other hand, agreed with Robertson completely.

Pearson arrived in Washington with an incomplete understanding of the state of the negotiations. Because he was unaware of America's prior willingness to consider the Canadian position, he concluded that the United States and Great Britain had always been equally intransigent on the size of the council. That being the case, he wrote: "I do not think we will ever alter it merely by complaining about the way we are being treated. It might indeed be better frankly to accept the inevitability of 'two-power' war control in theory and see how we can protect our own interests in practice within this limitation."

Pearson's solution was based on a watered-down interpretation of the same functional principle that Wrong had espoused six months earlier: Canada should abandon the campaign for membership on the UNRRA executive in exchange for greater rights of representation when its interests were being considered. "The one thing to be avoided in these cases," he wrote in a memorandum, "is ill-feeling and controversy. Even when we are in the right, we won't win our case very often, if ever, by insisting on our full rights. It is, in a sense, humiliating to admit this, but, nevertheless, I think it is a fact."[21] Perhaps if Pearson had been made aware of the initial American proposal for a council of between five and seven, he would have concluded differently. But it seems that any opportunity for Canada to learn of the changes was lost in the diplomatic transition.

From this point onward, a combination of inexperience and a lack of policy direction caused the Canadian representatives in Ottawa and Washington to work at cross-purposes. Less than a day after a meeting with Leith-Ross, during which his own Canadian colleagues argued strongly for executive-level representation, Pearson told J. Pierrepont Moffat, the US minister in Ottawa, that he personally sympathized with the great-power position and hoped that together they could soothe Canada's "wounded feelings."[22] The Cabinet war committee contradicted him the next day. Its minutes show that "the proposals submitted did not provide for adequate Canadian representation in organization of post-war relief and rehabilitation measures."[23]

The Department of External Affairs considered the situation in mid-August. Under Robertson's guidance, it produced three options: Canada could demand that all of the United Nations be consulted on every issue; it could campaign for the creation of "a group of medium belligerents" that might receive treatment different from that afforded the rest of the smaller states; or, based on the functional principle, it could "press for recognition of Canada as having a unique position approaching that of the four major powers." The undersecretary's former mentor, Professor Angus, concluded that in the cases of postwar relief and reconstruction, as well as in negotiations for the peace settlement, the government should pursue the final option.[24] The deputy minister of finance, the powerful and influential

Clifford Clark, agreed. Nevertheless, he reflected regretfully, "I think we are probably guilty of not having thought through this problem long before this and of having clear-cut proposals to make. It is high time that we should formulate specific proposals which would represent the application of Canada's case ... We should then take a strong line, and if we fail in our representations, we fail – but the responsibility is on other shoulders."[25] His comments came at an ideal time. The conscription issue was temporarily under control and the Liberal Party had gained confidence from victories in three crucial federal by-elections. Clark's sentiments found the ear of the Cabinet war committee, and it voted in early September to inform the United Kingdom, in writing, that Canada would not accept the proposed composition of the UNRRA's executive council.[26]

Coincidentally, the British were reconsidering their own position. The war was destroying their economy, and Canadian support was needed to maintain their international standing alongside the United States. A warning from Malcolm MacDonald that the Canadians now believed that the United States was viewing the UNRRA debate more sympathetically seems to have prompted a policy change.[27]

Just weeks after receiving the Cabinet war committee's stern memorandum, Leith-Ross and the rest of the Treasury developed a proposal to increase membership to seven on what was now being called the policy committee. This would allow them to include Canada as well as representatives from Europe and Latin America. They sent the proposal to the British war Cabinet, and it was considered at the committee level on 12 October. In what could only have been an awkward briefing, the ministers around the table were reminded that their own Foreign Office had originally rejected an American recommendation to create a larger executive. Now, after the increasingly confident King government warned them that further wartime economic assistance might become contingent upon a satisfactory solution to the UNRRA situation, the entire Cabinet, save the representatives from the Foreign Office, recommended that the Treasury's proposal be accepted. As for Foreign Secretary Anthony Eden's staff, they continued to fear the Soviet reaction to the inclusion of nongreat powers on significant postwar bodies and therefore refused to make the decision unanimous.[28]

The Cabinet debate in London clarified a dispute within British policy circles over the optimal shape of the postwar world. The Dominions Office, along with MacDonald and Leith-Ross, felt that the former colonies were crucial to the long-term prospects of the Commonwealth as a world power. The Foreign Office, along with Prime Minister Churchill, was more confident in Great Britain's ability to negotiate with the United States and the Soviet Union independently. Evidently, in this case Churchill did not care to press the point. The former view prevailed, and the United Kingdom reversed its position on the composition of the council.[29]

To avoid sending the impression that any negotiations had taken place behind the back of the Soviet Union, the British sought Moscow's approval before informing Washington of its new position. On 17 November, Maisky received an aide-memoire proposing that the policy committee be expanded to seven. His preliminary reaction was positive (and misleading), so the British copied the suggestion to the United States.[30] Three weeks later, Maisky made a formal reply, this time citing serious concerns with an enlarged committee. Still, Leith-Ross and his staff remained optimistic, hoping that additional face-to-face negotiations with the Soviets might clear up the problem.[31]

The Treasury, however, could not control the Foreign Office. On 22 December, Eden's team notified the United States directly that Maisky was entirely opposed to nongreat power representation. The next day, an uninformed (or simply stubborn) Dominions Office representative advised the government in Ottawa that Great Britain still planned to propose expanding the committee to seven.[32] The Canadians, some of whom were growing increasingly concerned about the postwar implications of these negotiations, were now aware of two contradictory policy proposals. They chose to ignore the first and responded positively to the second.

Their decision was naive and unrealistic. Dean Acheson emerged from a meeting with two Soviet representatives on 30 December convinced that their position was final. A week later, he recommended to Cordell Hull that, while remaining flexible, the United States should support Maisky over Leith-Ross.[33] On behalf of the British war Cabinet, the Foreign Office continued to press the Americans, but it did so with little passion.[34]

When the British met with the Soviets on 11 January 1943, Ambassador Litvinov argued convincingly that the composition of the UNRRA executive would set a precedent for all future postwar negotiations. Consequently, the USSR – already the firmest believer in the need for great-power exclusivity – could not diverge from the four-power set-up.[35] Still, the representatives from the United Kingdom were not deterred. In conversations with the Americans, they continued to maintain that it might be possible to convince the Soviets that, since postwar economic planning was sufficiently different from political negotiations, greater flexibility was permissible.[36]

When the results of these disappointing discussions were reported to the Cabinet war committee in Ottawa, war production was expanding, unemployment was negligible, and a new nationalist spirit was building across the country. Therefore, for perhaps the first time since the war began, King and his colleagues were in a position to recognize and effectively respond to what was clearly an attempt by the great powers to assume total control of the shape of the postwar order. The minutes of the 21 January Cabinet meeting reflect a determination that had rarely been evident to this point. The ministers agreed that "the United Nations could not be divided into one group of great powers exercising responsibility for political and military settlements, and another group excluded from responsibility regardless of size and importance." Through Robertson, King ordered Lester Pearson to convey the Canadian position assertively in Washington.[37]

Pearson and Acheson's reports of their meeting on 26 January are substantially different. In a short diary entry, the Canadian recounts that he found Acheson "friendly enough" but also intransigent.[38] The American's recollection is more revealing. He notes, for example, that Pearson "agreed that in the political and military fields Canada would not expect a position equal to the four great powers," a stance that clearly contradicts the Cabinet conclusions of less than a week earlier. Moreover, Pearson seems to have suggested that, although he did not expect his government to agree, he personally would have been interested in a compromise through which Canada would receive a leading position on the supply committee of the organization.[39] It was this last point – that the King government might be willing to put aside its concerns in exchange for greater standing on a committee of suppliers – that was communicated from Washington to London. That day, the Americans determined that if the Soviets still insisted on a four-power policy committee, it was time to go forward.[40]

The British remained divided. Leith-Ross's group at the Treasury, along with staff from the Dominions Office, thought that adequate Canadian representation was "an issue of principle" and urged the Cabinet to remain firm. The Foreign Office, on the other hand, was prepared to give way completely.[41]

Before they could make a decision, Canada's Cabinet war committee elected to plead its case directly to the United States. Pearson, who would be delivering the message, disagreed with this strategy, arguing that it would be easier to oppose a concrete proposal that excluded Canada than to continue to object theoretically. When Robertson overruled him, he dutifully arranged to meet with both Welles and Acheson a few days later.[42] As per the undersecretary's orders, Pearson was to present the Americans with a strongly worded memorandum:

> The Canadian Government considers that the enlargement of the Policy Committee (if this Committee retains in the final scheme the importance given to it in the draft proposals) is necessary to insure the effectiveness of the Relief Administration. Unless this change is made or other alterations with equivalent effects are adopted, Canada, and no doubt other countries, will not be able to cooperate in the work of the administration as fully as they would be prepared to if they were responsible partners in a joint enterprise.

It concluded with an articulation of the functional principle that looked ahead to the future world order:

No lasting international system can be based on the concentration of influence and authority in bodies composed of a few large Powers to the exclusion of the rest. Such a system would be a denial of the democratic principle. It would also be unreal, for it is not always the largest Powers that have the greatest contribution to make to the work of these bodies, or the greatest stake in their success. In the opinion of the Canadian Government, representation of countries on international bodies should be determined on a functional basis whenever functional criteria can be applied; this principle can be given wide application, particularly in the case of international economic and technical organizations such as the Relief Administration.[43]

The meeting was entirely unsuccessful; President Roosevelt's attitude toward relations with the Soviet Union was clear, and the American decision had already been made before Pearson arrived.[44]

On 17 February representatives of the United States, the United Kingdom, the Soviet Union, and China met in Acheson's office in Washington to discuss the matter one last time. After Lord Halifax argued the Canadian case, the Chinese and Soviet representatives reaffirmed their opposition. Acheson then echoed their comments. With Great Britain now appearing to be the only state delaying the negotiations, Halifax relented, reserving the right to revisit the issue after a draft proposal had been circulated to the other United Nations.[45] Still, King and the rest of his Cabinet remained firm. "To agree to participate in an organization to which Canada would be expected to be a major contributor without an effective voice in its direction," the prime minister maintained at a war-committee meeting, "would be to sacrifice the essential support of the Canadian people for the whole undertaking."[46]

Two days later, before the government had made its position clear to the staff in Washington, Pearson learned of a possible compromise. If Canada withdrew its objection, the chair of the supply committee – a position that might be reserved specifically for a Canadian – could be invited to sit with the policy committee whenever supply issues were under consideration. An intrigued Pearson telegraphed Ottawa immediately but did not wait for an official response before beginning to negotiate independently.[47] Just as it had with Acheson in January, this willingness to discuss a compromise left the impression in the United States that the modification – along with a tactical, aesthetic change to the name of the executive body from the policy committee to the central committee – would eventually satisfy Canadian concerns.[48]

Such an interpretation could not have been more mistaken. Clifford Clark fumed. "Thank you, boys, but count us out," he proposed to say. "We are still trying to run a democracy and there is some historical evidence to support the thesis that democracies cannot be taxed without representation."

Clark advised Norman Robertson to refuse to even discuss a compromise. "What is done in this case will set the pattern for postwar economic organization as well as for postwar political organization," he warned. "If we have any trump cards, it is in connection with this matter." The undersecretary conveyed this view to the Cabinet, and it seems to have received unanimous support.[49]

Once again, however, the message was changed on its way to Washington. Pearson did tell Acheson that his government had rejected the compromise, but he admitted in his diary that he "did not use as strong and undiplomatic language as that of the telegram informing me of the rejection." More specifically, he neglected to read the paragraph that included Clark's comments verbatim.[50] Given Pearson's refusal to convey the true extent of Canada's disapproval, and the American desire for this problem to simply go away, it should not be surprising that Acheson reported the conversation as follows: "He [Pearson] was not prepared to say that the Canadian Government would push its position of actually refusing to join the proposed relief organization." Not long after, Adolf Berle informed Hume Wrong that as far as he was concerned, Canada had never made its position clear to the American negotiators.[51]

After two more strongly worded letters from Malcolm MacDonald to Lord Halifax pleading with the ambassador to remain firm, the more senior Anthony Eden crossed the Atlantic to join, and hopefully help complete, the discussions in Washington.[52] In his talks with the Americans, Eden floated his own compromise: to maintain the small size of the central committee while still responding to the Canadian concerns, Canada could take Britain's place among the four powers as the Commonwealth representative. Robertson conveyed the idea to King but recommended against it. Despite the position of prominence that the country would attain in relief matters, representing the entire Commonwealth would send the wrong message; Canada would appear to be speaking for Great Britain. If this were true, then the British might surely speak for the Canadian government in other situations. Moreover, the undersecretary added, the proposal "would not be of much value as a precedent in determining the composition of other postwar bodies."[53]

While Eden prepared to travel from Washington to Ottawa to negotiate with the Canadians one final time, Pearson interfered again. He spoke to a number of members of Eden's staff (along with the foreign secretary himself) and was, in his own words, "disloyal enough to my Government to give them some off-the-record advice as to the best way to approach Mackenzie King on the subject." "Personally," he wrote in his diary, "I think that we will have to accept the compromise, which makes us Chairman of the Suppliers Committee, and that there is no reason why we should not ...

With the right handling, we could make a big thing out of this chairman-ship and play a big part in the Organization."[54] The report to Hume Wrong made no mention of these thoughts.[55]

Pearson was called back to Ottawa on 26 March to help prepare for Eden's visit. At lunch with Robertson, Wrong, and Clifford Clark, he listened as Clark argued strenuously against any UNRRA compromise. Later that day, Pearson spoke personally with the prime minister in an attempt to persuade him against Clark's assertive stance.[56]

Upon his arrival in Ottawa, Eden was presented with two sets of contra-dictory advice, both of which emphasized the relevance of the UNRRA talks to the future world order. The first stressed the importance of great-power harmony and, therefore, urged him to find a way to make the Canadians compromise. The second stressed the significance of the dominions to Britain's place in the postwar international hierarchy. The stronger and more loyal they were, the better placed the United Kingdom would be to influ-ence, if not control, the other soon-to-be-created world organizations.[57]

At a meeting of King's Cabinet war committee, Eden stood by the posi-tion that his Foreign Office had taken from the beginning. He emphasized the importance of the supply committee and the influential role that Canada would have as chair, attempted to reassure the prime minister and his col-leagues that representation on the policy committee would not set a prece-dent for subsequent postwar organizations, and agreed that future global authority should derive from all nations, not just the great powers. The Canadians were not convinced. Mackenzie King closed the meeting by warn-ing Eden that his government would actively contest the proposed compo-sition not only of the UNRRA, but also of any similar organization.[58]

The foreign secretary was clearly shaken. He quickly drafted a personal letter to King, informing him that the American and Soviet demands left Britain with no choice but to give in.[59] That same day, he met with Robertson and the secretary of the war committee, Arnold Heeney, offering what Robertson described as "an exchange of letters between Canada and the United States (the latter speaking on behalf of the Big Four), confirming our understanding that any arrangements arrived at with regard to the position of the Central and Supplies Committees of the Relief Organization would not be a precedent fixing the Canadian relationship to other post war agen-cies which might be established." When Robertson openly doubted the value of the written assurance, Eden "argued quite vigorously."[60]

The final decision was made at a meeting of the Cabinet war committee on 7 April. At least two ministers, J.L. Ralston of National Defence and C.D. Howe of Munitions and Supply, spoke in favour of the compromise. Two more, J.L. Ilsley of Finance and Chubby Power of National Defence for Air, spoke against. By this point, however, the political atmosphere in Canada had changed once again. Thanks in large part to the success of the federal government's intervention in the economy, the Co-operative Commonwealth Federation (CCF) – recognized across the country as the leading advocate of state-sponsored economic initiatives – was quickly rising in the polls, and Mackenzie King worried that the Liberal Party's popularity would suffer if it were blamed for obstructing the future peace by refusing to give in. Moreover, the prime minister thought to himself, the national public had not been privy to the UNRRA talks, and a Canadian chair of a supply committee would be widely interpreted as an object of pride. With his prompting, the war committee accepted the great-power proposal with the caveat that it be made explicitly clear that the decision would not constitute a precedent for the future.[61]

Soon after, Pearson was asked to convey the decision to the British and the Americans. They were, in his words, "delighted." Taking at least partial credit for the change in government policy, he wrote in his diary: "I hope we play our cards right now and put a good man on the Supplies Committee. We have a chance to play a big part in this Organization."[62] In an outcome that, in retrospective, calls into question Pearson's overall motivations, he himself was appointed Canada's temporary representative. The draft UNRRA proposal was distributed to the rest of the United Nations, and although concerns were raised by some of the smaller powers, an agreement was eventually signed by forty-four states on 9 November 1943. Canada never received the written assurance that Eden had promised.

Most Canadian officials were disappointed. Vincent Massey, for example, wrote to Robertson and to Mackenzie King: "I can not help feeling sooner or later we shall have to be very 'tough' indeed in connection with our relation to these post-war international bodies. The 'big power' complex seems to be unfortunately far too present and we will suffer from it, I think, until we have scored a victory in some such issue as the recent one, and have secured full acknowledgement of the right of Canada to sit on international bodies which for functional reasons it is right and proper that she should."[63] A few weeks later, at dinner with a visiting Malcolm MacDonald, the two high commissioners commiserated over the inability, or unwillingness, of Canadian policy makers to assert themselves to their British counterparts. "They won't stand up to their opposite numbers here and state their views firmly and candidly," Massey lamented afterward in his diary. "I am convinced," he concluded, "that what we need more and more in Canada is a positive sense of our own position in the world and our responsibilities which can only lead to our being more respected provided good feeling and good manners are maintained."[64]

This was unquestionably part of the problem. In 1942 Canada was not yet prepared as a nation to assert itself the way that the functional principle demanded. And by the time that the government in Ottawa had achieved sufficient political stability at home to allow it to consider the potential ramifications of its lack of interest in world affairs, it was almost too late to affect the UNRRA discussions. Things might still have ended differently, but an obviously ambitious Lester Pearson took advantage of an opportunity to advance a personal agenda in the face of clear and firm instructions to the contrary. His success, combined with a decline in the Liberals' political fortunes in the spring of 1943, meant that Canada failed to achieve the standing on the UNRRA policy committee that, for all intents and purposes, it deserved.

The 1942-43 UNRRA discussions were probably the best opportunity the Canadian government had to assert itself in the shaping of the structure of the future United Nations. It did not have the same leverage over its allies on nonrelief issues; moreover, with the UNRRA decision serving as a precedent, neither Great Britain nor the United States would again feel the same obligation to worry about the willingness of the smaller powers to follow their lead.[65] That said, the negotiations were a failure for only some of those who had been intimately involved. For others, they provided an opportunity to shine on the world stage. And for everyone else, they were just a wake-up call to a slowly maturing country. Most Canadians did not know what might have been and could not have understood the significance of the precedent that had been set. For them, the allegedly positive outcome of the UNRRA talks was simply another step toward a new international identity.

4

Public Success: Canada and the New Internationalism (January 1942–November 1943)

Since most Canadians – the media, the nongovernmental sector, and the general public – were unaware of the Department of External Affairs' struggles in the early stages of the United Nations Relief and Rehabilitation Administration (UNRRA) negotiations, once the first conscription crisis ended, they began gradually to shift their focus to the world around them with great optimism. Canadians saw an opportunity to make a substantial contribution to postwar reconstruction and came to view their country as a leading intermediate power. Consequently, the Liberal government soon felt increasing pressure to take an active role in planning the new world order. A personal visit by Britain's charismatic foreign secretary, Anthony Eden, to Ottawa in late March 1943 added to the internationalist momentum. During his stay, he briefed the Cabinet war committee on plans for the future world organization even before he had spoken formally with the Soviet representatives. This action, along with his comments in a subsequent public speech, made Canadians believe that they were being taken seriously by their great-power allies.

The enthusiasm was both contagious and inspiring. After Eden left, the Cabinet war committee began to respond to the calls of its newly created Wartime Information Board (WIB) to become more proactive in world affairs; Mackenzie King officially endorsed the functional principle and enshrined it as the guiding philosophy behind Canada's approach to international relations; and Canadian diplomats made an important contribution to the words, if not to the meaning, of the period's most significant achievement in the field of postwar planning: the Moscow Declaration.

At the same time, it is easy to exaggerate the long-term impact of the events of this period on Canada's international standing. Certainly, the country was making unprecedented strides in its development as a global actor; however, by the end of the meetings in Moscow, even though the government in Ottawa had only just begun its national planning process, the general framework for the new world organization had already been set, derived from a process that minimized the significance of the nongreat states. The great-power summit of October 1943 also affirmed the increasing importance of the Soviet Union to the postwar order. Unlike the British, who encouraged dominion participation in world affairs to enhance their own declining position, the Soviets had less patience for countries that they generally regarded as colonies. The combination of this new powerful player and Mackenzie King's still relatively cautious approach to international diplomacy meant that after Moscow, despite public feelings to the contrary, the Canadian planners for the new world organization once again found themselves on the outside looking in.

Canada's journey from isolationism to internationalism began slowly. Public opinion polls in January 1942 showed that few Canadians recognized the importance of international organizations, and most only half-heartedly believed in their potential effectiveness.[1] Among the national media, only one significant paper, the Liberal-Independent *Winnipeg Free Press*, was actively promoting the establishment of a new system of collective security.

Leading the solitary campaign was the paper's editor, the well-respected and upright J.W. Dafoe. Dafoe had been heavily involved in the League of Nations negotiations that followed the First World War, and he was, by all accounts, a committed internationalist and a firm believer in the value of collective security.[2] His mouthpiece was a self-described "Liberal with a small 'L,'" Grant Dexter.[3] The well-connected journalist was, according to one colleague, "the ablest political reporter Canada ever produced."[4] The two were fully backed by the paper's owner, Victor Sifton, and its managing editor, George Ferguson. Together, these forward-thinking Canadian nationalists hoped to enhance their country's place in the world. In the wake of the pending changes to the world order, they believed that Canada had the opportunity to redefine itself as a capable and responsible member of the international community. They would do whatever they could to make this happen.

Since Dexter and Dafoe were both active in the Canadian Institute of International Affairs (CIIA), they took their case to its 1,400-person membership. Beginning in January 1942 the institute published three consecutive articles on Canada and the postwar world in its *Behind the Headlines* series. The University of Manitoba professor R.O. MacFarlane explained the advantages of a system of collective security to small nations, the value of the League of Nations to Canadian society more generally, and the benefits and drawbacks of universal and regional security organizations.[5] The CIIA also commissioned the University of Toronto historian George Glazebrook (before he was drafted into External Affairs) to write a brief history of the Canadian role at the Paris Peace Conference of 1919. Like their colleagues in the United States and Great Britain, members of the CIIA believed that understanding the policies of the past would help to create a better future.

Unfortunately, when Glazebrook asked his contacts in Ottawa to help him research the links between the old League of Nations and the plans for the new world organization, the officials at the Department of External Affairs – at this point overwhelmed by problems surrounding Canada's relationship with the United States – responded negatively. "We are not yet ready to contemplate [that] now," wrote one officer. Perhaps, he added, "it might be better for people's minds to lie fallow for two years."[6] Glazebrook need not have taken the rejection personally. When executives from the League of Nations Society met with representatives of the King government and urged them to create a formal committee on the postwar order, they too were unsuccessful.[7] The opposition Conservatives were hardly more helpful. In March, House Leader R.B. Hanson suggested to Parliament that contemplating the peace could wait until the war was over.[8]

The government's attitude began to change near the end of May when it finally saw fit to respond to a memorandum of five months earlier. Back in January, Escott Reid, a thirty-seven-year-old former secretary of the CIIA with, in his own words, a propensity "to intellectual and moral arrogance,"[9] had warned his government of a growing American tendency "to order Canada around." "In matters of high policy in the realm of foreign affairs," he claimed, "Canada does not make decisions; it has decisions forced on it." He recommended that Mackenzie King strengthen the legation in Washington, enhance the Department of External Affairs, separate the posts of prime minister and minister of external affairs, and "make the construction of an effective collective system" the country's most significant political priority.[10]

King had initially chosen to ignore the junior officer. His position paper arrived just ten days before the prime minister was to announce what was certain to be a divisive national plebiscite to release the government from its promise not to impose conscription, and Liberal support in the polls was already down. Five months later, with the American media now questioning Canada's military commitment to the war – and citing King's unwillingness to impose conscription as evidence – he decided that something had to be done. On 28 May the Prime Minister's Office asked the Montreal public-relations expert and former political lobbyist Charles Vining to evaluate the impact of Canadian publicity in the United States. Vining's seventy-two-page report concluded that Reid's assessment of the state of the Canadian-American relationship was absolutely correct. Canada's inability to promote its wartime contribution effectively in Washington was diminishing its credibility as a loyal ally. Consequently, Americans were growing less sympathetic to Canadian concerns.[11]

To ensure that this state of affairs did not spill over into the postwar period, when Canada would likely be even more dependent on American favour, Vining anticipated the creation of the Wartime Information Board, a governmental organization designed to promote Canadian international achievements within and outside of the country in place of the ineffective Bureau of Public Information. In September, King created the nonpartisan WIB. Vining was the first chair, and Phillippe Brais, the government leader in Quebec's Legislative Council, was appointed vice chair.[12]

Four months later, under the leadership of the Canadian Citizenship Council's cofounder, Norman Mackenzie, the WIB began to issue the prime minister confidential reports on the overall state of the country. They were based primarily on public opinion data and always ended with policy recommendations. King received the documents personally and distributed them to his Cabinet and other trusted advisers at his own discretion. Considering his subsequent decisions, he clearly took them seriously.

When it came to postwar planning, the WIB emphasized its international aspect. An early report forcefully argued that the Canadian people needed more information from their government, particularly in terms of its attitude toward the negotiation of the upcoming peace. It was less important that the plans be specific or even acceptable; public morale would improve so long as it was clear that the leadership in Ottawa was committed to helping shape the future international order.[13]

A belief was growing in Canada (and abroad) that, with the help of a system of collective security and international cooperation in postwar reconstruction, the world to emerge from the war could be a better place than the one that had come before. Unlike the situation two years earlier, when such thoughts were shared almost exclusively among members of the intellectual elite, as 1943 approached, almost every element of Canadian society was involved. Among the media, the *Winnipeg Free Press* still led the way, but it now had wide support. Slowly, the national magazines began to run editorials on similar themes. A writer in *Saturday Night* complained that Canada was "dull and lacking in pride" and encouraged a greater focus on external relations. Blair Fraser echoed this message in *Maclean's*. By November 1942 even the traditionally isolationist *Le Devoir* was publishing articles that spread hope and faith in the future.[14] At the nongovernmental level, a number of Canadian legal scholars joined a North American working group that developed a series of "postulates for the international law of the future" and a set of proposals to substantiate them.[15] And in Parliament the Co-operative Commonwealth Federation (CCF) leader, M.J. Coldwell, began a personal campaign for greater Canadian involvement in world affairs.

In December he attended what he called a "very valuable" conference at Mont Tremblant, Quebec. It was sponsored by the Institute of Pacific Relations (IPR), an affiliate of the CIIA.[16] The meeting included representatives from a number of smaller countries that, like Canada, were growing more interested in and capable of contributing to the future world order. The experience left the parliamentarian even more committed to ensuring that the new world organization not be developed exclusively by the great powers. In January 1943 he implored the Liberal government to think seriously about the postwar period. "The smaller nations," he declared, "have an important contribution to make." It was time to mobilize the Canadian public.[17]

For a change, his political opponents did not disagree. The platform of the new Progressive Conservative Party emphasized the need to foster "a common pride in Canadian achievement and institutions and ... to achieve that profound sense of the importance of national interests which will ensure harmony and co-operation and the future for our country."[18] In Parliament the Social Credit Party's leader, John Blackmore, expressed anxiety about the lack of attention "being paid to the problem of winning the peace."[19]

The combination of the WIB's advice, public interest in world affairs, and pressure in the House of Commons had a profound impact on the content of the throne speech that opened 1943. On 29 January the Liberals promised to move reconstruction to the forefront of the Canadian policy agenda.[20] Responses to the new direction varied. Coldwell's support for greater internationalism could have been predicted, but the Quebec nationalist P.J.A. Cardin, who had recently resigned from the Cabinet over the plebiscite on conscription, spoke cautiously: "We must keep our feet on the ground," he argued, "and not lose our heads in the clouds of excitement and exaggerated pride. Let us not exaggerate the importance and the extent of the contribution we can make in this struggle."[21] Others were not so timid. Howard Green, a proud and vocal Conservative imperialist from British Columbia, rejected Cardin's prudence as a sign of what he called "a small power complex" – a feeling that Canada was obliged to follow the lead of Great Britain and the United States. Green believed that, as a fast-growing economic power, his country had the opportunity to develop into one of the most influential states in the world and to exert influence far beyond its perceived capacity. This would only happen, however, if it spoke loudly on postwar matters.[22]

Among all of the divergent views, one common theme emerged: Canada had to refine, clarify, and publicize its views on foreign policy, particularly as they related to the postwar period. At first, the government was unresponsive, but its inaction could not halt the momentum. On 28 February 1943 the Canadian Broadcasting Corporation (CBC) launched a Sunday-evening multipart radio series on reconstruction called "Of Things to Come: Inquiry into the Post-War World." The early episodes were hosted by the popular novelist Morley Callaghan and focused on international organization. J.W. Dafoe and Norman Mackenzie were among the first panellists. The series stimulated ordinary Canadians to develop and discuss their ideas about the future of the world more openly.[23]

On Parliament Hill also, frustration with the Liberals' apparent inaction spread quickly. In mid-March the Conservatives challenged Mackenzie King to explain Canada's foreign policy. The prime minister responded only vaguely, reiterating a noncommittal statement that he had made to the House in 1938.[24] A week later, a Social Credit member of Parliament, Eric Hansell, demanded more information about the prospective new world order.[25] Normally, King would not have taken any statement made by Hansell or the rest of his party particularly seriously, but this time it was corroborated by more influential voices. First, in Quebec *Le Devoir* criticized the prime minister's vague comments in the House. Then, the Wartime Information Board submitted a detailed, confidential report advising the government to promote past and present Canadian achievements more actively at home and to speak enthusiastically about Canada's future potential.[26]

The WIB's recommendations coincided almost exactly with Anthony Eden's trip to Ottawa. For both Mackenzie King and the Canadian public, it could not have come at a better time. The Americans had not yet made a significant impact in what remained a frustrating war in Europe, and the CCF was gaining support in the polls. The Liberals – and Canadians more generally – needed inspiration, and Eden's charisma, and the mesmerizing effect that it could have on an audience, was virtually unmatched. His visit was anticipated eagerly in both the English- and the French-language press.[27] It was Eden, many thought, who would help bring Canada into the postwar planning process.

In the midst of the excitement and anticipation, however, neither the political leadership nor the Canadian public seemed to realize how far along this process had already come. In Washington, Franklin Roosevelt had begun to think strategically about the postwar order within weeks of the attack on Pearl Harbor. As one biographer has explained: "Once the United States entered the war, [the president's] wartime policies shifted dramatically. Active participation meant a chance for active leadership, and that was an opportunity not to be missed."[28] On 22 December 1941 Roosevelt quietly ordered Cordell Hull to form what became his advisory committee on postwar foreign policy. Chaired by the secretary of state himself, its job was "to translate into a program of specific policies and measures the broad principles enunciated in the Atlantic Charter."[29] To support the new committee, the State Department enlarged its Division of Special Research. By the time Roosevelt and Churchill met in Washington in June 1942, Sumner Welles's increasingly important subcommittee on political problems (which would later spawn the special subcommittee on international organization) had already set down a series of first thoughts on the future international organization, all of which stressed the dominance of the great powers.[30]

At the June meeting, the president invited the United Kingdom to share ideas about the postwar order. In response, the British set to work on their own plans. In early October 1942 Gladwyn Jebb's Economic and Reconstruction Department completed a draft proposal for a future world organization. Eden called it "The Four-Power Plan." Like the American scheme, it too assumed that the great powers would share control.[31]

Although Winston Churchill was too absorbed with the war itself to offer Eden any support, by the end of November the British Cabinet had expressed its approval in principle.[32] On 16 January 1943 Eden produced a twenty-eight-point "United Nations Plan." Implicitly acknowledging Great Britain's decline as a leading force in world affairs, it foresaw the British Commonwealth as one of four great powers sitting on an executive committee of the United Nations designed to police the postwar world. It also mapped out a series of six regional councils, a British imperial conference, a pan-American union, and an economic world council, all of which would report to the executive.[33]

One month later, after the United States Congress introduced six separate motions relating to international organization, Eden responded to Roosevelt's invitation by drafting a letter from Churchill entitled "Morning Thoughts." It described "a world organization based upon the conceptions of freedom and justice and the revival of prosperity" and then summarized the "United Nations Plan." With Churchill's approval, Lord Halifax delivered the note to the president the following day.[34]

On 10 February the foreign secretary prepared another message, this time inviting himself and Undersecretary Cadogan to Washington to begin a formal dialogue with Cordell Hull. The Soviets, through Maisky, would be kept informed of any progress.[35] Hull was open to the suggestion. In March 1943, while Congress was discussing a bipartisan senate resolution that explicitly supported the creation of an organization of the United Nations to maintain peace after the war, Eden arrived in Washington ready to cooperate.

The talks culminated in a meeting with the president that also included Hull, Welles, Winant, and Hopkins. Roosevelt, who had kept himself informed of the work of the State Department, sketched an outline of the future world order that was slightly different from Eden's. Instead of a council and a general assembly, his organization was made up of three layers. At the top was a four-power executive committee ("the four policemen"). It would "take all the important decisions and wield [the] police powers of the United Nations." Below it was an advisory council, made up of the four great powers and between six and eight regional members from the smaller states. Finally, there was a general assembly representing all of the participating countries. It would meet approximately once per year to, in Eden's words, "enable representatives of the smaller powers to blow off steam."[36] The British responded almost too positively. Just before Eden left for Ottawa, Roosevelt warned him of the dangers that could arise if it appeared that the great powers had begun to remake the world order without consulting the smaller states. The foreign secretary assured him that he would not let this happen.[37]

The combination of Roosevelt's insistence that the lesser powers feel included in all future planning and the need to finalize the UNRRA issue explains why Eden, never himself a leading supporter of greater dominion autonomy, came north to Canada. He did not expect to learn much about the future world order from his Canadian colleagues and might not have even known that, in December, Roosevelt had spoken briefly to Mackenzie King about his "four policemen" idea.[38]

Nevertheless, according to the British high commissioner to Canada, Malcolm MacDonald, the visit was "an unqualified success."[39] On 31 March, Eden introduced the Cabinet war committee to his (not Roosevelt's) recently revised view of the future world order. At the top sat an executive body made up of the most powerful states and selected additional members. Below it was a general assembly. In response to a question about the role of the great powers, Eden conceded that while the authority of the world organization had to derive from all of its members, the four most powerful states would take the lead on security issues.[40]

The next day, he made a similar statement to the House of Commons. It would take time and cooperation to plan and sustain an effective international organization. Certainly, the great powers had to lead, but all of the United Nations had a role to play. He concluded with an expression of determination: "Together," he said, "we can win the war and win the peace, and nothing else shall content us. It is our duty to hand on to our children a world in which freedom can live and a man command his soul, free from that constant dread which shadows our own time. Let us give this pledge this afternoon: We will neither falter nor fail until we have redeemed our world and opened to future generations a peace and promise that we have never known."[41]

The speech was received positively by the national media and galvanized Canada's postwar planning process. In his report, Blair Fraser of *Maclean's* wrote that Eden had shown "a significant understanding of the viewpoint of the smaller countries in the United Nations fraternity."[42] At least one senior Cabinet minister emerged convinced that Canada would have "an important but not the final voice" in developing "a sensible plan for postwar world security."[43] Thanks in large part to Eden, Canadians were becoming more confident and willing to participate actively in international affairs.

To the foreign secretary himself, the trip had meant something entirely different. Eden had anticipated a more difficult battle on the UNRRA issue. After some initial complications, Mackenzie King's willingness to compromise left the impression that Canada would be comfortable with the great powers making most of the significant relief and rehabilitation decisions. On the future international organization, the Canadian government's response had hardly been more forceful – thanks perhaps to its own lack of planning – as it only objected politely to a scheme based on Anglo-American dominance.

When Eden returned to London, he felt confident that Mackenzie King would support a new world order centred on the primacy of the great powers. Since the Canadians showed no signs of being overly demanding, the Foreign Office could now focus its attention on the USSR and the United States. The balance of power among the three states was changing, and the British were justifiably worried that they would be left behind.[44] Managing Canadian input into the future world organization became the responsibility of the relatively unimportant Dominions Office (DO), then headed by Clement Attlee.

Although the Foreign Office never gave it much respect, Attlee's group took its job seriously. Almost immediately, the DO inquired as to the feasibility of a meeting of the Commonwealth prime ministers to discuss postwar planning.[45] Since Mackenzie King did not wish to risk provoking French Canadian nationalism by travelling to London, he avoided committing to the gathering for over a year. At the same time, however, he understood the political benefits of appearing active and important. When Churchill and Roosevelt met in Washington to discuss war strategy in May, King joined them.

They would not fully include him in the military talks, but both leaders were happy to speak informally with the Canadian prime minister about the future world organization. Unfortunately, neither accurately represented the planning that was actually taking place in their respective countries. Even though he knew that in devising the "United Nations Plan," the Foreign Office had already considered and rejected his three-power regional system, Churchill's personal desire to reestablish the image of British prominence in world affairs caused him to revive his "three councils" proposal. He even suggested that Canada might represent the Commonwealth in North America.[46] Roosevelt reiterated his "four policemen" idea (which had recently been discarded by Sumner Welles's group in favour of a world council of eleven) and then implied that King himself might become the organization's first secretary general. The Canadian prime minister, who seemed to be overwhelmed by all of the attention and flattery, said very little.[47]

As a result, King left Washington misinformed about the state of Anglo-American postwar thinking. First, since he was excluded from the military talks, he did not notice what the historians Lloyd Gardner and Warren Kimball have called the significant "shift in the balance of power within

the Anglo-American alliance" that took place when Washington committed London to an invasion of France.[48] Second, because of the frankness of
his conversations with the two leaders, he wrongly assumed that he would
be consulted before any additional significant decisions, or at least those
that concerned Canada, were made. Finally, he seemed convinced that the
vision of the future world order to which he had been privy was actually the
one that would be taken to the Soviets.

The reality was quite different. While the British and American planning
processes went forward in anticipation of a meeting with the USSR, Eden
explicitly stated that the "smaller allies" would not be included again until
the Soviets had been fully briefed.[49] Furthermore, over the next four months,
London and Washington revised their postwar plans – in the American case,
to the point that the Department of State developed two actual draft UN
charters – and reaffirmed their commitment to a system dominated by the
great powers.[50]

If he had known the extent to which Anglo-American planning had progressed, Mackenzie King would have been shocked. His trip to Washington
had left him with the impression that thinking about the new international
organization was in its formative stages. After all, Churchill and Roosevelt
had only been speculating.

At home, speculation continued to surround the extent to which Canada
might be able to influence the future peace. *Canadian Forum*, a leading
leftist national magazine, had just recently added a monthly section on
the postwar years. "Slowly we have come to realize," began the first article,
"that what we, as democratic peoples, propose to do about the post-war
world has a profound bearing on our chances for success against the forces
opposed to us." It finished: "The spirit in which we plan *now* for a post-war
Canada will largely determine the spirit in which we approach the larger
problems of international security and justice which we must help to
solve."[51] The WIB had made a similar argument just before King's trip. While
the prime minister was away, the board began work on a brief that reaffirmed the importance of explaining the government's postwar goals to
Canadians.[52]

King received the analysis in mid-June just as the Canadian public's enthusiasm for active participation in world affairs was reaching a new high.
A published report on the CIIA's 1943 study conference, *Canada and the
World Tomorrow*, concluded that Canada was the only state capable of taking the lead "in eliciting and harmonizing the views of small power members of the United Nations."[53] In June an article in the *Economist* declared:
"If Canada is prevented by the smallness of her population from taking
rank with the Great Powers, she has in the last three years made a category
for herself all of her own. Relative to her resources her effort is second to
none. In absolute terms the distance which separates Canada from the Great

Powers is less than that between her own achievements and that of any other of the small powers."[54]

On Dominion Day, 1 July 1943, King himself got caught up in the patriotic atmosphere and proclaimed: "In the course of the present war, we have seen Canada emerge from nationhood into a position generally recognized as that of a world power." John Blackmore of the Social Credit Party added: "It is a cause for satisfaction to all Canadians that Canada has attained national status; that she has become a world power." Angus MacInnis made a similar statement on behalf of the CCF.[55]

With these thoughts in mind, the prime minister joined the supply debate in the House of Commons on 9 July to defend the allocation for external affairs. His speech, so often quoted in national histories of the Second World War, marked the first time that Canada's functional principle had been articulated publicly. "Even before victory is won," he remarked, "the concept of the united nations will have to be embodied into some form of international organization." While all countries had the right to be heard, for the body to work, representation at the highest levels would have to be limited. An effective compromise could be achieved, "especially in economic matters, by the adoption of the functional principle of representation."[56]

King's statement was noticed around the world. It was received positively, for example, by most of the medium-sized nations, including exiled representatives from the governments of Poland and Yugoslavia.[57] Washington also paid attention. Jack Hickerson of the Office of European Affairs made a full report on functional representation at the end of the month. In a follow-up analysis two weeks later, his office concluded that Canada was "emerging as the champion of the small nations" and would not hesitate "to voice purely Canadian views."[58]

At home, in a debate on external relations that lasted for almost a week, the prime minister was alternately praised and criticized. Naturally, the Liberals supported his stance. Generally, the Conservatives and the CCF argued that he had not said enough. The Social Credit Party could not decide whether it stood for or against a Canadian commitment abroad. And Quebec members of Parliament counselled greater caution.[59] Almost every report in the national media, however, was favourable.[60]

Despite all the coverage, no mention seems to have been made of King's crucial caveat. The phrase, "especially in economic matters," actually said far more about the prime minister's vision of Canada's position in world affairs than did the rest of his speech (which was drafted for him by Hume Wrong). The additional words were not derived from the thinking in External Affairs; rather, they came from King's experience at the UNRRA discussions in late March. He had listened carefully when Anthony Eden proposed that a differentiation might be made between nongreat-power representation on economic bodies versus those dealing with security issues. King agreed and foresaw a future for Canada as a major international player on socio-economic or, to draw from his book *Industry and Humanity*, industrial issues. There is no evidence that he sought special status for his country on questions of military security. In fact, in a Cabinet meeting the following month, he argued that "the necessity for rapid action might compel certain decisions to be taken [by the great powers] without there being time for consultation."[61]

The prime minister understood the functional principle differently from his officials in the Department of External Affairs. While Hume Wrong, Norman Robertson, and Lester Pearson believed that it might be applied to any aspect of foreign policy (so long as its applicability was always judged on a case-by-case basis), perhaps thanks to King's aversion to military conflict, he downplayed the possibility that it could be invoked with reference to security issues.

This last suggestion frustrated the officials in the East Block and convinced them to examine postwar questions on their own in greater detail. In late July, Norman Robertson used a December 1942 Dominions Office request for greater input from Canada into postwar (military) thinking as justification to initiate what would become two working groups on post-hostilities problems (PHP): an advisory committee, eventually called the post-hostilities (advisory) committee, chaired by the undersecretary himself, and a smaller working committee, chaired by Wrong. Robertson's group was policy-oriented; Wrong's focused on detail. The British had a similar structure in place, and their post-hostilities committees supplied the documents that served as templates for the Canadian planners.[62]

In evaluating the importance of the department's work, one official concluded that "the PHP papers in themselves had no impact."[63] There was some truth to this statement. Mackenzie King did remain generally uninterested in the planners' findings and relied primarily on the WIB for policy direction; moreover, the philosophy underpinning the functional principle never influenced King's thinking on security issues. That said, the more general impact of the committees should not be discounted. The planning process itself was evidence of the increasingly sophisticated way that Canadian policy makers were coming to think about the postwar world. More practically, the discussions among Canada's most senior civil servants formed the basis of the talking points that King often brought with him to meetings with other international leaders.

This latter point was particularly evident when Quebec hosted an Anglo-American military conference in August 1943. Even though he knew that he would not be included in the serious strategic discussions, King looked at his presence at the meeting as an opportunity to demonstrate Canada's importance to the general war effort. He even convinced Churchill to bring his chiefs of staff to Ottawa for a joint meeting of the British War Cabinet and the Canadian Cabinet war committee before the Quebec Conference began. This too would prove that Canada was being consulted.[64]

For Hume Wrong, the meeting presented an ideal opportunity for Canada to promote its vision of the future world order to the great powers. On 7 August 1943 he drafted a memorandum called "Post-War International Organization," in which he advised King to put forward Canada's view on the role of the smaller states firmly. He also warned his prime minister that if Canada did not learn more about British and American plans soon, it might lose its chance to have any impact on the structure of the postwar international system.[65]

The instructions were extremely helpful. On 21 August, King joined Churchill and Roosevelt for a late-evening conversation that dealt almost exclusively with global reconstruction. The British prime minister ignored the wishes of his Foreign Office and once again brought up his regional-councils idea. The well-prepared American president had been warned that this might happen. He therefore avoided a confrontation by immediately introducing a new four-power declaration that had been drafted for him by the State Department. It committed the United States, the United Kingdom, the Soviet Union, and China to working together to create "a permanent international organization, based upon the principle of the sovereign equality of all nations, and open to membership by all nations, for the maintenance of international peace and security, and for such other purposes as may be agreed upon." Until this body was established, the signatory states would also "consult and act jointly on behalf of the community of nations in maintaining international peace and security." The statement confirmed Wrong's worst fears. Planning had indeed continued without any consideration of the interests of the smaller powers.[66]

Mackenzie King was noticeably upset. The dominions in particular, he warned, would resent the implication that the Big Four planned to dominate the new order. This approach, he noted in his diary, "was contrary to [the] conception for which this war was being fought."[67] Churchill, who, like King, had only just seen the American document for the first time, made no immediate reply, but subsequent British actions suggest that there was some sympathy for the Canadian position.

The dominions secretary showed the document to the high commissioners a few days later. He regretted that the draft had ignored the small powers; nevertheless, the British felt obligated to accept it because it ensured that the United States would remain actively involved in world affairs after the war.[68] When Churchill spoke to Canada's Cabinet war committee again on 31 August, he too was conciliatory. He downplayed the discussions at Quebec as "tentative" and "exploratory," stressed that he himself did not agree with the American four-power plan, and promised that the dominions would have the opportunity to comment fully on the proposals before they went forward to the Soviets and the Chinese.[69] Clearly, however, Churchill and his staff were losing their influence. As one historian has explained: "The war acted like an x-ray, penetrating the Empire's ermine robes to expose the malignancies in its extremities and the weaknesses of its heart."[70]

Perhaps sensing Britain's weakness, King remained firm, reiterating his warning that even just the impression of great-power dominance among the small states would lead to "grave results." "It had been possible," he argued, "to leave the supreme direction of the war largely in the hands of the U.K. and U.S. governments, but the same conditions would not obtain in times of peace."[71] His assertiveness had little effect on the British Foreign Office, which continued to focus exclusively on setting the terms for a three-power meeting of foreign ministers in Moscow; however, it did seem to resonate with the Dominions Office, which kept Ottawa amply informed of any new developments. On 6 September, for example, the DO conveyed the good news that the Soviets had agreed with Canada's opposition to a regional system of security. The following week, it sent Robertson a copy of the proposed four-power declaration with a request for comments.[72]

The Canadians responded quickly. They immediately recommended additional, more explicit references to the smaller nations throughout the document. Vincent Massey presented the revisions in London, and nearly all of them were well taken. The Foreign Office then forwarded the changes to the United States, where they were also accepted.[73]

Ottawa communicated exclusively through London (rather than Washington) for a number of reasons. First, and most important, thanks largely to Malcolm MacDonald, whose advocacy for the dominions' rights had been recognized across North America, the British diplomats were more effective than were the Canadians.[74] Second, the staff in Washington had additional priorities. On 12 September 1943 Cordell Hull addressed the country and finally revealed the full extent to which the State Department had been planning for the future. Shortly afterward, the American Congress passed two resolutions committing the United States to participation in the immediate establishment of an international organization.[75] The fallout from the speech and the congressional resolutions made what one official called "exacting demands" upon the staff at the State Department. This generally inhibited them from dealing with the smaller countries even if at least some members acknowledged that "the time [was] coming when we shall have to give them the feeling of having been consulted."[76]

Finally, Canada's most effective representative in the United States, Lester Pearson, was not kept properly informed of the negotiations. In fact, presumably with Norman Robertson's approval, Hume Wrong waited until 18 October 1943, the day before the Moscow Conference was set to begin, to send him a package of telegrams summarizing the last six weeks of discussion. The documents were for Pearson's information, and no request was made for his comments.[77] The Canadian mission was therefore left to learn about the meeting through the press.

Even though Pearson probably relied on the *New York Times*, in Canada both the English- and French-language newspapers covered the Moscow Conference in detail.[78] The talks between 19 and 30 October were newsworthy because they introduced much of the Western world to its newest significant ally: the Soviet Union. Not only did the foreign minister, Vyacheslav Molotov, meet with his British and American equivalents, but, as host, Joseph Stalin also appeared.

Stalin was an intimidating man. Moscow's ambassador to the United States in the mid-1940s, Andrei Gromyko, wrote of him: "On the one hand, he was a man of powerful intellect, a leader with the unshakeable determination of the revolutionary, and also the ability to find common understanding with our wartime allies. On the other hand, he was a harsh man who did not count the human cost of achieving his aims, and who created a monstrously arbitrary state machine that sent multitudes of innocent Soviet peoples to their deaths."[79] "Ruthless," was what Anthony Eden said.[80] One who respected him far less went so far as to call him "a monster."[81] Fortunately, Stalin needed military support in 1943, and he was therefore prepared to cooperate with his great-power allies.

Thanks in large part to the Soviet Union, the Moscow Conference was one of the most successful summit meetings of the war. Molotov, who had initially been hesitant to discuss the postwar period at all, let alone support a statement that would be cosigned by the Chinese, demonstrated his eagerness to cooperate from the very beginning. On the first day, he withdrew his objection to discussing America's proposed declaration and consented to adding it to the meeting's agenda.[82]

On 21 October the trio reviewed the four-power statement in detail. After a long introduction by Hull, Eden brought up the Canadian amendments. Most important, he suggested that what had previously read "the signatory states agree to consult and act jointly on behalf of the community of nations in maintaining international peace and security" be changed to "they will consult with one another and as occasion requires with other members of the United Nations with a view to joint action on behalf of the community of nations." Eden specifically noted that it was the government in Ottawa that was most seriously concerned about the need to avoid any implications of a four-power dictatorship.[83] The revision was adopted without difficulty.

Over the next two days, Canada's representative in Moscow, Dana Wilgress, was fully briefed on the three-power discussions by a representative from the Dominions Office and by Cordell Hull himself.[84] On 23 October the British provided Wilgress with a revised draft of the declaration and requested additional comments. The Canadian government was satisfied with what it saw, and the proceedings continued relatively amiably, with Molotov even agreeing to include the Chinese in the declaration on 26 October.[85]

The three foreign ministers, along with the Chinese ambassador to Moscow, Foo Ping-sheung, signed a four-nation declaration on 30 October 1943. It included two significant Canadian contributions. One came from the 21 October meeting. The other added the phrase "large and small" to a provision stating that membership in the organization was to be open to all states.[86] Both additions emphasized the role of the small powers in the future world order.

On 1 November, Mackenzie King issued a press release expressing his approval of the results of the conference.[87] Reports from other countries also emphasized "the reassurance given to the small nations."[88] In his memoirs Cordell Hull noted that, in Moscow, Eden and his staff "were immeasurably aided by the British Dominions, in particular Canada."[89]

The end of the Moscow discussions marked one of the highest points in Canada's involvement in the creation of the United Nations. Anthony Eden's visit to Ottawa provided Canadians with information on the postwar world that had previously been shared only between the United Kingdom and the United States. Four months later Mackenzie King's presence at Quebec allowed his government to learn about and respond to America's four-power declaration at the same time as Great Britain. Consequently, Canada was able to make a tangible contribution to the subsequent meetings even without being present. In October 1943 it acted as the most authoritative voice of the nongreat powers.

Perhaps more significant, at least from the standpoint of domestic politics, is that Canadians felt important. Talk of the postwar period dominated discussions in the press and on Parliament Hill. The functional principle caught the attention of small states around the world. A tighter relationship was established between External Affairs and the Dominions Office. And even Mackenzie King began to argue more forcefully against greatpower dominance in future world affairs. To many, it seemed that Canada's international role had only just begun to grow.

After Moscow, however, with the Soviets more actively involved in postwar planning and America's dominance over Great Britain confirmed, Canada's capacity for greater global influence decreased considerably. Anthony Eden had indeed brought the Canadians into the great-power discussions, but in his focus on Anglo-American relations, he had also effectively shut them out of the truly important debates. For the officials in Ottawa, this meant that it was time to determine the most effective way for Canada to exert influence in the future negotiations: either individually as an independent state or collectively as a contributing member of the British Commonwealth of Nations. Neither choice would prove ideal.

5
Canada, the British Commonwealth, and the New World Order (February 1943–March 1944)

In the October 1943 edition of the American journal *Foreign Affairs*, Judith Robinson argued that it was "Canada's tragedy that this, the one country placed by history and geography in a position to show the way out of suicidal nationalism into sane internationalism, [could] not find its own way out of its own confusion of spirit."[1] The comment captured a Canadian dilemma that originated in the First World War era and reappeared as the Second World War headed toward its successful conclusion. Canada had supposedly emerged from the Paris Peace Conference of 1919 with independent international standing. It had signed the Treaty of Versailles and held its own seat at the League of Nations. Nevertheless, until the passage of the Statute of Westminster in 1931, it was legally still a British colony. And even eight years later, it had taken hardly more than a week for Canadians to decide to join the empire in what most in the United States felt was a European conflict. In the early phases of the Second World War, therefore, Canada's international status remained undefined. Was it a British ally or a British dominion? Could it be both? And how would this affect the Commonwealth's role in the future world organization?

Such questions made Mackenzie King cringe. His role model, Sir Wilfrid Laurier, had seen his government defeated by opportunistic imperialists, and King had spent twenty years distancing his country from the United Kingdom so that he would never succumb to the same fate.

For the most part, the British had not objected to his posturing. In 1943, however, the government in London felt threatened by the power of the United States and the Soviet Union. It saw a unified Commonwealth under its direction as the best way to maintain Britain's world standing. In April, Clement Attlee proposed a marginally necessary imperial conference to discuss some of the questions that had arisen out of the United Nations Relief and Rehabilitation Administration negotiations. Mackenzie King avoided giving him a straight answer. He reacted similarly in May when Winston Churchill pressured him to come to London for a conference of Commonwealth prime ministers. "All was going smoothly now," King wrote in his diary. With the conscription issue temporarily settled, Quebec seemed united behind the war effort. A formal Commonwealth meeting at this point could only reignite a French-English conflict and divide Canadians once again.[2]

Unfortunately for him, King could hold off a public discussion of Canada's place in the world only for so long. In June, on his own initiative, the prime minister's new parliamentary assistant, Brooke Claxton, began to direct a campaign to assert Canadian independence from Great Britain. This was the only way, he felt, that his country could be assured a leading, constructive role in the new world organization. The combination of Claxton's outspokenness, his position in Parliament, and his ties to the press and the nongovernmental sector (he had been an active member of the Canadian Institute of International Affairs) helped to propel the old imperialism-versus-nationalism debate over Canada's place in the world back to the forefront of the national political agenda.

Through it all, Canadians truly believed that the results of their internal discussions would have a direct impact on the shape of postwar peace. In this case, however, they were wrong. By late 1943 the future international order was almost set. The main organs of the new world organization had been outlined, and the primacy of the great powers had been affirmed. This had never been hidden from the government in Ottawa, but for a number of reasons, Canadians had yet to come to grips with their relatively minor role in postwar reconstruction. Nonetheless, the discussions of Canada's changing international status were crucial to the development of a new national image. By rejecting imperialism, Canada positioned itself as a leading proponent of a just world system founded on the principle of collective security.

During the early months of 1943, while Canadians were anticipating Anthony Eden's springtime visit, Malcolm MacDonald concluded a memorandum to the British war Cabinet rather bleakly. Without the Commonwealth behind it, he predicted, Great Britain would "gradually sink to a position of a second class power" after the war. To maintain London's international position, the dominions would have to be looked upon as "true partners," or "allies," and be treated as such. His analysis was corroborated by the Dominions Office, but it had virtually no impact on his prime minister. Despite Great Britain's increasing dependence on Canadian military and financial aid, Winston Churchill still refused to differentiate between the old empire and the new Commonwealth.[3]

This attitude was too much for the Canadian Liberal member of Parliament Brooke Claxton. On 14 June he vented his frustration to friend Lionel Curtis, editor of the British journal *The Round Table*: "Churchill's inability or unwillingness to see the Commonwealth in its true light is just like all the other efforts of the 'imperialists'; by refusing to accept association on terms of equality, he makes association more difficult and hastens the day when it will end."[4] Curtis, who held his own imperialist beliefs, did not wholly agree but did concede that the concept of "dominion status" did little but create "a façade of national sovereignty" while leaving the real decisions to Great Britain. Furthermore, the idea that imperial conferences could develop Commonwealth policy was, to him, "sheer poppy-cock." It was not feasible to gather the dominion leaders often enough to formulate a consistent foreign-relations strategy, nor was it realistic to expect the government in London to be capable of shouldering the burden of world peace on its own.[5]

Only days later Claxton took these ideas with him to a well-attended meeting of the Empire Parliamentary Association, a group of political representatives from Canada, Australia, New Zealand, Newfoundland, South Africa, and Great Britain. At the opening session, he spoke about the importance of international institutions to postwar stability. To him, the alternative, a revival of the old great-power blocs, could only lead to another conflict. M.J. Coldwell, who was also present, agreed. "It seems to me," he said, "that the policy of the Commonwealth should be in the direction of more international co-operation ... We want to see, I take it, certainly all of us in Canada, the closest co-operation within the British Commonwealth, but it must be a commonwealth in which we share."[6] The dialogue continued for seven days, and reports indicate that the conference was generally considered to have been a success. While it did not produce changes in policy, the delegates left with a better understanding of each other's points of view.[7]

Members of Canada's Progressive Conservative Party, many of whom had played leading roles in organizing the conference, almost immediately applied their findings in the supply debate. Howard Green criticized the government's lack of direction and proposed six guiding foreign-policy principles for the future. The third was a firm commitment to the British Empire. "It should be made clear," he argued, "that Canada believes that the British family should speak with one voice in foreign affairs. That is what the United States and the other nations of the world expect; that is what the Canadian people want." Green anticipated that Ottawa would eventually take over the leadership of the Commonwealth and believed that only as part of such a group could it gain greater influence in world affairs. Another Conservative, John Diefenbaker, corroborated the importance of Canada's role within the Commonwealth and advocated participation in an imperial war cabinet.[8]

These comments enraged Claxton even more. The Conservatives "were oblivious" and "out of step with the times," he recalled in his memoirs.[9] When Mackenzie King encouraged him to join the debate, he spoke extemporaneously, accusing the opposition of having "a mistaken conception of the British empire, a conception which is not in accord with reality." While Diefenbaker maintained that closer Commonwealth relations would foster national pride and reduce internal tensions, Claxton countered that "the best way to get the unity of feeling among our own people, which is the necessary basis of a foreign policy, is that it should be a foreign policy which is based on Canada's interests and appeal to Canadians as Canadians." As a small nation, Canada would need to work with all countries, not just the Commonwealth, to maintain international security and promote prosperity. In response to the old imperialists, Claxton was beginning to articulate a new vision of Canada's role in the postwar world.[10]

While Mackenzie King must have been pleased that the Conservatives had apparently lost the debate, he was probably less excited about Claxton's internationalist spirit. The ever-cautious prime minister therefore closed the discussion with his usual noncommittal vagueness. He referred to the Commonwealth as "a pattern on which the world might well seek to organize itself" but ignored the proposal for an imperial war cabinet. As minister of external affairs, King also never solicited his civil servants' advice on this issue. Fortunately for him, nearly the entire department was on his side; they too wanted to avoid commitments to the empire.[11]

Just one month later, representatives from Australia reintroduced the Commonwealth question. They were led by Prime Minister John Curtin, who, at 58, was still a proud, bold man always ready and able to speak loudly. In the midst of his campaign for greater influence over Great Britain's Pacific policy, he proclaimed: "I believe some Imperial authority must be evolved so that the British Commonwealth of Nations will have, if not an executive body, at least a standing consultative body." He foresaw it meeting frequently to ensure adequate consultation between Britain and its dominions on urgent matters.[12] As he explained at a press conference in Australia three weeks later, the Commonwealth needed an empire council to maintain its influence during the war and into the postwar period.[13]

As a first step, Curtin recommended that London sign the Moscow Declaration on behalf of the entire Commonwealth. This suggestion was greeted favourably in Australia and New Zealand. In Great Britain, *The Round Table* urged a full meeting of the imperial prime ministers to formulate a more unified approach to the postwar discussions.[14] In Canada, apart from its successful rejection of Curtin's proposal for the Moscow Declaration, the response from the Department of External Affairs to the new Commonwealth debate was consciously subdued. Hume Wrong favoured what he called "the education of the free world in the realities of the Commonwealth"[15] but also respected Mackenzie King's insistence that public debates on imperialism be avoided whenever possible. Therefore, when Gwendolen Carter of the American Foreign Policy Association requested background information for an article about postwar planning in the dominions, the department framed its response as a technical comment on appropriate terminology. "I wish that editors would not ask you or any one else to write about the 'Dominions,'" wrote Hugh Keenleyside. "The individual nations making up the Commonwealth are almost as distinct in character and interest as any countries in the world and much more distinct than some. The mere fact of their association in the Commonwealth is not sufficient to justify their being treated as a unit."[16]

To King's dismay, the East Block's efforts to minimize the issue were unsuccessful. By October the imperialist *Globe and Mail* had taken up Curtin's cause in earnest. After noting a surge of support across Britain for the Australian's proposal, the *Globe* declared itself in favour of a more unified Commonwealth foreign policy. Imperial cooperation was crucial to ensuring Canadian influence in the future peace negotiations.[17]

At about the same time, while the great powers were still meeting in Moscow, a controversial debate was taking place in the American Senate. The trouble began when a Democratic senator from Iowa, Guy M. Gillette, suggested that because of their affiliation with the United Kingdom, the nations of the British Empire could not be considered fully independent. According to the *Winnipeg Free Press*, Senator Carl Hatch of New Mexico then added: "The members of the British Commonwealth of Nations occupy a peculiar status. It is something short of what we recognize as complete independence of action, such as is exercised by the United States or by any other free and sovereign nation."[18]

By the time Anthony Eden returned from Moscow, the controversy had spread to the British House of Lords. On 2 November, in response to a motion to create a more permanent organization for Commonwealth consultation, the new secretary of state for dominion affairs, Lord Cranborne, spoke firmly: "There is no sphere where it is more important that there should be complete unanimity between the nations of the British Commonwealth than in the sphere of foreign affairs." Cranborne did not regard the current methods of consultation as perfect and was open to suggestions for improvements, but it would be up to the respective legislatures to make this decision together. He concluded: "We recognize fully that it is only if the British Commonwealth is of one mind about the many problems which will face the world after this war, and only if we can work closely and confidently together, that we shall be able to play that great part to which our long traditions and our wide interests entitle us."[19]

A Canadian Institute of Public Opinion (CIPO) poll in early November suggested that the general public agreed with Britain's dominions secretary. When asked whether it would support the formation of an imperial council, 54 percent answered "yes," and only 26 percent said "no." Even in Quebec more were in favour than opposed.[20]

Feelings were different in the civil service. Like most of his colleagues at External Affairs, Norman Robertson did not support any form of imperial council. His greatest concern, he told Canada's former representative to the League of Nations, Walter Riddell, was that if the Commonwealth spoke with a single voice, the dominions would lose their independent standing internationally. It followed that if Canada had bound itself to Great Britain's signature on the four-power declaration, it would have been forced to sacrifice representation on the future world organization.[21] Riddell responded that since the Moscow Declaration pledged to recognize the sovereign equality of all peace-loving states, there was no need for the Commonwealth to have spoken with one voice; however, to maintain international peace and security after the war, the countries of the new world organization would have to achieve something close to unanimity on all controversial issues. At Geneva, he suggested, this was best reached through extensive group consultation, and one of those groups was the Commonwealth.[22]

Malcolm MacDonald echoed Riddell in a speech to the Alumni Federation of the University of Toronto. "Let us pool our experiences and opinions," he proposed. "Let us all influence each other. I do not suggest that after consulting together the various nations of the Commonwealth will always agree precisely on policy ... But generally there will be agreement for on the whole our minds, our intentions and our ideas are similar."[23]

Robertson had no time to consider the compromise. Even before he received Riddell's reply, the prime minister of South Africa, Field-Marshal Jan Christiaan Smuts, attempted to boost his chances for reelection through a provocative Curtin-like speech to the Empire Parliamentary Association on 25 November. The postwar world, he maintained, would be controlled by three great powers: the Soviet Union, the United States, and Great Britain. For the United Kingdom to compete with the other two, it would need the support of both the Commonwealth and the empire. The dominions themselves might therefore have to become "sharers and partners" in British colonialism.[24]

The text of the address was released to the press on 3 December. At first, the Canadian response was low-key. In Vancouver, Bruce Hutchison drafted an editorial that found the Smuts proposal "in so vague a form that any final opinion on it [was] impossible."[25] The editors at the *Winnipeg Free Press*, evidently drawing from this analysis, agreed. The *Globe*, which was always anxious to defend proponents of the empire even when there was nothing to defend, lashed out at the *Free Press* two days later.[26]

Although the *Globe* editorial said little of consequence, it did keep the issue in the public domain, which helps to explain how questions about the future of the Commonwealth came to overwhelm perhaps the most significant Canadian Institute of International Affairs (CIIA) conference of the

Second World War. Back in February 1943, Brooke Claxton had suggested that the CIIA sponsor a two-day gathering of the country's elite to contemplate Canada's future prospects. Over the next six months, the idea grew into something more ambitious. Invitations were eventually sent out to over 100 representatives of the civil service, parliamentarians, prominent journalists, and academics.[27] As a basis for the discussion, Grant Dexter was hired to write a book on the future peace. He framed his analysis around collective security, but by late September it was clear to at least one of the conference organizers, Edgar J. Tarr, that the implications of Canada's position within the Commonwealth would supersede all others in importance.[28] On behalf of the Department of External Affairs, Hume Wrong concurred. Even Canada's chief post-hostilities planner had to concede that discussions of the future world organization now seemed less important than the postwar position of the British Commonwealth.[29]

In the end, the conference at the Seigniory Club in Montebello, Quebec, was more significant for what it spawned than for what it covered. Primarily because a number of prominent imperialists failed to attend, the discussants spent less time than was anticipated on the question of Commonwealth organization. Instead, there was general agreement that Canada was "among the greatest of the small powers," whose special relationships with Britain, the United States, and the Soviet Union (geographically) would allow it "to exert a considerable influence and to perform an important function in a world system." As a nongreat state, "Canada had an interest in supporting the principle of a world organization in which the small powers had an appropriate voice." Brooke Claxton's view of the future – one that he had been developing since the supply debate – clearly prevailed. There was no change in thinking at the policy level.[30]

In between roundtables, Tarr met with Wrong and the secretary to the Cabinet, Arnold Heeney. Together, they discussed Chatham House's plans for a third unofficial Commonwealth conference then scheduled for London in the summer of 1944. Tarr, who was on the agenda committee, emerged from their talk disturbed that the next meeting would likely attempt to bring about greater imperial centralization. In response, he worked with historian Edgar McInnis to draft an alternative agenda. On 30 December, Tarr sent an outline of his thoughts to Claxton, Robertson, Wrong, Keenleyside, and two officers from the Department of Finance. The proposal was subsequently copied to all of the leading members of the CIIA and stimulated an intense debate over the role of the Commonwealth in the new international organization.[31]

Through the first three weeks of January, at least ten prominent Canadians commented on the Tarr-McInnis paper. Clifford Sifton of the *Winnipeg Free Press* feared that "the reconstruction of the British Empire as a 'power unit' would tend to lead to balance of power arrangements, race for armaments and war." He suggested that future Commonwealth meetings be open to guests from non-Commonwealth countries.[32] John Holmes and Brooke Claxton agreed. The University of Toronto professor Alexander Brady (among others), on the other hand, still felt that there was room for private Commonwealth discussions to contribute positively to postwar reconstruction.[33]

The Chatham House committee on arrangements and agenda approved a preliminary conference schedule on 18 January 1944. The meeting would investigate Commonwealth relations generally and "the relation of the Commonwealth and its member nations to a world system." A decision on the list of invitees seems to have been postponed.[34]

Not surprisingly, given the links between the CIIA and the national media, the academic debate was followed by a heated dispute in the press. After the Empire Parliamentary Association Conference, the *Globe and Mail* and the *Free Press* increased the volume of their editorials dedicated to the question of Commonwealth unity. While the *Globe* stressed the benefits of greater imperial consultation, the *Free Press* warned that a common Commonwealth foreign policy would sacrifice Canadian independence.[35]

As it gathered momentum, the clash moved into government circles. Claxton, who was still close to Dexter and the *Free Press*, wrote to Vincent Massey, whom many considered to be one of Canada's most loyal imperialists, proclaiming that he had no sentimental attachment to the empire. He saw it as an organization that could serve the national interest if handled properly.[36] Privately, Massey and his old friend Lord Cranborne deplored what they considered to be a Canadian obsession with independence and prestige. Ottawa had misinterpreted Curtin's, Cranborne's, and Smuts's public comments as part of "a conspiracy to set the hands of the clock back in terms of Empire relationships." All of this, they felt, was simply "nonsense."[37]

At this point, with the academic community, the press, the Department of External Affairs, and the Canadian government all thinking and talking about the Commonwealth, the situation exploded. In late January 1944 Lord Halifax, fast becoming "the most widely respected figure among the foreign diplomats accredited to Washington," grudgingly agreed to come north to Ontario. The British Cabinet minister and ambassador to the United States was scheduled to speak at the centennial dinner of one of the hubs of Conservative support in Canada, the Toronto Board of Trade. The topic of his speech would be the Commonwealth and world affairs.[38]

Attendance at the address was overwhelming. Approximately 1,100 people packed into the hall. According to one report, hundreds more were turned away. The Conservative and imperialist premier of Ontario, George Drew, and the leader of the federal Progressive Conservatives, John Bracken, sat at the head table. From the very beginning, there was no question of where the sympathies of the crowd would lie.[39]

The speech itself began harmlessly. "I often think," pondered Halifax, "that to the outsider the British Commonwealth must surely appear an almost inexplicable freak of nature. We can imagine the bewilderment of an intelligent visitor from another planet on being confronted with its manifest contradictions." As he reviewed the history of the development of dominion status, he added: "The right of each member [of the Commonwealth] to determine its own external affairs may mean a gain or it may mean a loss. It is plainly a loss if, with our essential unity of ideal, the responsibility for action which represents that unity is not visibly shared by all. It is an immeasurable gain if on vital issues we can achieve a common foreign policy expressed *not by a single voice* but by the unison of many" (italics added).

He briefly examined the dilemma that the dominions perpetually encountered. While technically independent, whenever a major international crisis occurred, they were faced with a choice: sacrifice a degree of sovereignty and "conform to a policy which they had had only partial share in framing" or "stand aside and see the unity of the Commonwealth broken, perhaps fatally and for ever." The solution, argued Halifax, was not a return to the isolationism that had brought about the Second World War but rather for the entire Commonwealth to work together more equally and more effectively in the common fields of foreign policy, defence, economic affairs, colonial questions, and communication. He did not make any specific proposals to these ends; rather, he suggested that the leaders of Great Britain and the dominions work them out cooperatively at their next meeting.

Like Curtin and Smuts, Halifax had come to feel that after the war, Britain would not be able to maintain its position as a great power without the rest of the Commonwealth and empire. "To say this," he finished, "is to make no selfish claim. The unity of the Commonwealth is no mere British interest. So far from being an obstacle, it is a condition necessary to that working partnership with the United States, Russia, and China to which we look. If we are to play our rightful part in the preservation of peace, we can play it as a Commonwealth, united, vital, and coherent." The speech concluded to tremendous applause.[40]

Little did Halifax know that this seemingly innocent address – one that had in fact been cleared with Stephen Holmes of the Dominions Office in advance, and the topic of which had been suggested by Canada's own ambassador to the United States, Leighton McCarthy – would become the top story in just about every major Canadian newspaper. Nevertheless, because of the tension that had been brewing across the country, the comments, which were actually less inflammatory than those of Smuts, Curtin, or even Cranborne, became the target of significant criticism and praise.[41]

The subheading in *Le Devoir* made that paper's position clear: "L'ouverture d'une nouvelle et formidable campagne impérialist – Il faut accepter le défi."[42] The editors of the *Winnipeg Free Press* were equally upset, accusing Halifax of campaigning to deprive the dominions of their independence. They rejected the idea that the postwar world would be dominated by great-power blocs, arguing instead for the establishment of a cooperative "community of nations" along the lines suggested by the American secretary of state, Cordell Hull. For the group in Winnipeg, the debate was about more than just the Commonwealth: it would help determine the shape of the future world organization.[43] Predictably, the *Globe* was sympathetic, arguing that it was the duty of the Canadian government "to examine dispassionately all sane and reasonable proposals for strengthening it."[44] The *Ottawa Journal* went further. Its editorial asked: "Can any sane person, looking at the world realities, believe that when peace comes [the four-power system] will be otherwise? That, in a world of turmoil and dislocation, with quick and decisive action vital, and with power necessary to enforce decisions, the small nations will have much voice in shaping events?" The proposal for a more unified Commonwealth was Canada's best chance for influence on the international stage.[45]

Halifax's comments, and more important the controversy that they caused, enraged Mackenzie King. The day after the speech, he explained in his diary that he was "simply dumbfounded." Just as Massey had speculated, King saw the ambassador's talk as part of "a conspiracy on the part of Imperialists to win their own victory in the middle of the war" by further centralizing the machinery of the Commonwealth.[46]

On 31 January, in Parliament, King responded to Halifax directly. "By all means," he began, "let us within the British Commonwealth be as united as we possibly can in thought and action, but let us seek in regard to other countries also to effect a closer co-operation and coordination of policies, which will make for the sort of world organization we hope to see prevail in [the] future in this world ... In meeting world issues of security ... we must join not only with Commonwealth countries but with all likeminded states, if our purposes and ideals are to prevail. Our commitments on these great issues must be part of a general scheme, whether they be on a world basis or regional in nature."[47] The Conservatives, who were anxious to capitalize on the speech, predictably answered with a series of arguments in favour of greater Commonwealth integration.[48]

After Malcolm MacDonald alerted him to the trouble that he had created in Ottawa, Halifax wrote back, regretting "the annoyance" he had "unwittingly caused" but also defending his comments. Specifically, he reminded the high commissioner that he had "deliberately rejected the idea of a 'single voice' to which Claxton had referred [in July 1943]."[49] The ambassador then sent a letter of apology to the dominions secretary, Lord Cranborne: "I feel I owe you a word of explanation," he wrote, "and perhaps apology, for having, as I suppose, caused you a slight head-ache with my wretched speech at Toronto last week. Nobody was more bored than I was in having to go there at all ... [but I] honestly thought that I was ... pretty well in line with what Mackenzie King's Parliamentary Assistant, or whatever he calls him, Brooke Claxton, had said in the Ottawa House of Commons last July ... I suppose I ought to have confined myself to the usual review of the war! Forgive me."[50]

Cranborne's reply, which was, he admitted, "a very pompous epistle," was likely the best indicator of feelings in the British government toward Canada's place in the postwar world. "I can assure you," he wrote, "that the headache has not agonised us. Indeed, we all read your speech with admiration and agreement, in my case coupled with a little envy that you could put things so much better than I am able to do." Cranborne, who was and would continue to be one of the staunchest supporters of the rights of lesser powers in the future world order, went on: "Mackenzie King must know perfectly well that in the modern world small nations cannot stand on their own two feet. They must attach themselves to some great power, if they are to have any influence ... By taking this present line, he runs great risk of entirely upsetting the balance on which future peace and security must depend ... To my mind, the continued strength of the British Empire is essential to the preservation of the peace, and that Mackenzie King should repudiate it to get a temporary political advantage seems deplorable."[51]

Vincent Massey recorded his first response to the speech in his diary: "Edward Halifax has made a speech in Toronto on Empire relationships which I am sure will cause trouble, although what he said was moderate and to my way of thinking pretty sound. Whether it should have been said when it was by him is another matter."[52] The next day, Massey summarized the situation to Cranborne as "unfortunate." Halifax had chosen the wrong venue to express his thoughts, and their implications had then been exaggerated by Canada's Conservative press. To Massey, "the whole thing [seemed] to have been badly handled."[53]

Charles Ritchie, who was also in London, felt similarly. "Our minds," he wrote on 27 January, "are occupied with the incident of Lord Halifax's speech in Toronto. It was not a speech calculated in terms which could appeal in Canada. It was ineptly put and showed no understanding of our psychology. It ought to have been argued in terms of Canadian self-interest ... it is important that the loyalty theme, making sacrifices for the Home Country, should not be stressed – they are preaching to the converted and enraging the unconverted. Also the combination of Lord Halifax [and] Tory Toronto ... is so unfortunate as a starting point for a debate over the future of Canada."[54]

Back at home, the Canadian press resumed its petty bickering. For the most part, the *Globe* and the *Free Press* volleyed insults back and forth, as did *Le Devoir* and *Saturday Night*.[55] The articles and editorials added little of substance, but they did keep the issue alive. This is probably why the Canadian Association for Adult Education's travelling radio series, "Citizens' Forum," which had been designed to discuss postwar issues, soon began a series of broadcasts on Canada and the Empire. After an inconclusive debate in Winnipeg, an on-air discussion in Edmonton on 29 February determined that Canada was more important in the world because of its imperial affiliation.[56]

These comments were consistent with the findings of the Canadian Institute of Public Opinion. A poll in late March 1944 showed that a small majority in English Canada continued to favour a joint imperial foreign policy. In Quebec, as could have been expected, a full 70 percent responded that Canada should make external commitments on its own.[57] Despite the potential for even greater controversy, Mackenzie King managed the situation effectively. By the spring, thanks in large part to the Conservatives' lack of leadership and direction, Halifax's speech had become, in the words of Vincent Massey, "a dead issue."[58]

In London the deputy prime minister, Clement Attlee, made a brief statement in the House of Commons emphasizing that now was not the time to discuss the structure of the Commonwealth. As a public relations gesture, Anthony Eden reprimanded Lord Halifax ever so slightly and asked that he clear any subsequent speeches with a Foreign Office representative. Afterward, Malcolm MacDonald summarized the Canadian position for the Dominions Office in a fifteen-page memorandum that likely was not read in any great detail. His conclusion, that Canada could be independent and a Commonwealth partner at the same time, said nothing that the government in London had not heard before.[59]

This was also the basic feeling in the United States. The first American reaction to the Halifax speech was that the composition of the Commonwealth was an internal matter with which the United States would not interfere.[60] About two weeks later, the Department of State sent the ambassador in Ottawa, Ray Atherton, a second summary of the situation. Support for Halifax extended beyond Conservative circles, but it would never translate into policy; the Canadian public was "too ignorant of and indifferent to the issues of European politics to enable Canada to assume the responsibility of arriving at positive concerted policies with Great Britain on these issues."[61] As for the thesis itself, another State Department analyst concluded that it was "lacking in originality" and "fit into the dominant traditional pattern of British thinking."[62]

In the end, the controversy was rather typical of the Canadian experience in planning for the postwar period. The question of Canada's role in world affairs captured national attention among all levels of society. It caused Canadians to think back to the League of Nations and to contemplate their position in the international hierarchy. It was initiated by members of the United Kingdom government. And it had almost no impact on the creation of the United Nations.

The problem of dominion representation at postwar conferences was never truly solved; the UK remained the great power. For the King government to keep abreast of the most current plans for reconstruction, it had to continue to consult with the Dominions (or Foreign) Office. Paradoxically, in doing so, it tacitly acknowledged its dependence on Great Britain in world affairs. Even if it had truly wanted to, in planning for the new international order, Canada could never fully break free from the bonds of empire.

Nevertheless, the fallout from the Halifax speech was crucial to the development of a Canadian identity in world affairs. It made the general public more interested in and vocal about Canada's postwar prospects and encouraged Brooke Claxton to elaborate on his view of the future. Canadians began to identify with his vision of their country as "the greatest of the free small nations, an Atlantic and Pacific power, geographically tied to the United States, traditionally to Britain, French and English and everything else, immense in resources, decent and dull in character." In a letter to Lionel Curtis, Claxton explained with pride: "More than most other countries, [Canada] can act in its own interest in the sure knowledge that our interest is everyone's interest; we have no other."[63]

This was likely the first coherent articulation of what scholars have since called the "voluntarist world view" of foreign policy, a style which favours "enlightened diplomacy," and "pragmatic idealism."[64] This allegedly Canadian approach to world affairs was not based on an "idealist impulse"[65] so much as it was a reaction against a perceived imperialist threat. Claxton's new definition of the national attitude toward world affairs was also not backed by a domestic consensus. Public opinion polls suggested that Canadians were generally much more comfortable with imperial cooperation than he was. Nevertheless, as one historian has noted in a study of the development of what she calls a "colonial ideology," quite often "the presumption that some conscious system of beliefs must exist becomes, on examination, a self-fulfilling prophesy."[66] Ironically, in countering the imperialists, Claxton was acting just as they had one generation earlier. His goal was not to create a new authentically Canadian identity; he already knew what his country stood for. Instead, just as Great Britain had sought to impose imperial values upon its colonies, he sought to do the same to the Canadian people. He was successful, and this new national worldview contributed significantly to Canada's subsequent approach to planning the United Nations. But on this front, there was still much work to be done.

6
Forked Roads
(November 1943–July 1944)

When Mackenzie King looked forward to 1944, he saw Canada playing an increasingly important role in the future world organization in collaboration with its British and American allies. Public enthusiasm for postwar planning continued to increase, and his officers in the Department of External Affairs were growing restless. King's decision in late 1943 to turn the Canadian legation in Washington into an embassy was therefore welcomed across the country as a symbol of Canada's increased standing, and activity, in international affairs. For the prime minister himself, along with the symbolism came practical benefits: "I feel it important," he wrote in late October 1943, "in view of further conferences in Britain, and conferences that have to do with settlement of war and post-war problems that Canada ... should not hold in the eyes of the world a subordinate place to that of other much less important countries." When it came time to conclude the peace, Canada would need "a standing of her own at the side of the United Kingdom."[1]

His reasoning reflected his country's still strong ties to Great Britain. Throughout the early months of 1944, the Canadian government relied almost exclusively on British intelligence as a basis for its still cautious formal postwar planning exercises. It did so for three reasons. First, in an attempt to secure greater Commonwealth unity, the government in London made an active and deliberate effort to integrate the dominions into its reconstruction efforts. Second, thanks in part to disappointing work at the new Canadian Embassy, the Department of External Affairs did not receive sufficient information on the state of postwar thinking in Washington. Finally, personal animosities between the pragmatists in Ottawa and the more forward-thinking, if not idealistic, officers in Washington caused an overworked Department of External Affairs to ignore its United States representatives during their planning exercises.

The combination of King's caution, the department's small size, and the inability of its leading officials to work effectively together meant that Canada

had few opportunities to make a substantive contribution to postwar thinking in the period leading up to the great-power meetings at Dumbarton
Oaks in August 1944. Clearly, however, the country was finally preparing
itself to participate more actively in the future.

The public response to the announcement that there would be a new Canadian Embassy in Washington was overwhelmingly positive. Even *Le Devoir*,
a paper that was forever critical of Liberal foreign policy, could not help but
concede, "C'est quelque chose." The prominent anti-imperialist Léopold
Richer was not satisfied with Canada's continued ties to Great Britain, but
he also recognized that the prime minister had made a significant declaration of Canadian independence in world affairs.[2]

Opinion polls showed nationwide support for Canada's enhanced international role. On 20 November 1943 the Canadian Institute of Public Opinion (CIPO) asked whether Canadians would be willing "to take an active
part in maintaining world peace after the war even if that meant sending ...
soldiers, sailors or airmen to help keep the peace in other parts of the world."
The answer was an overwhelming "yes." Even in Quebec 56 percent of those
surveyed responded in favour, and only 34 percent were opposed.[3] A week
later, another poll suggested that Canadians were growing more optimistic
about the prospects for a successful world organization.[4]

According to the Wartime Information Board (WIB), when it came to
postwar planning, the government could not do enough. In December 1943
it found that two-thirds of Canadians expected "great change." This increasingly activist spirit was evenly distributed across the country. Individual
Quebecers might have been less willing to admit their interest, but educational and economic status, not ethnic background, were the most important determinants of attitudes toward world affairs. According to the WIB,
the government now had to shift its focus to the less educated; the elite had
already embraced internationalism.[5]

The alliances that had been formed among the upper classes to promote
postwar security were unprecedented. In June 1943 Toronto hosted a meeting of religious leaders that resulted in a joint declaration of principles for a
new world order. The document was signed by leading Roman Catholic,
Protestant, Orthodox, and Jewish representatives.[6]

Throughout the fall, Canada's League of Nations Society busied itself by
lobbying the major political parties. Its president, Walter D. Jones, praised
the recent attention that had been given to postwar planning in advance of
the end of the military hostilities. On behalf of his members, he proposed a
series of "fundamental features" of an effective world organization.[7] M.J.
Coldwell of the Co-operative Commonwealth Foundation (CCF) responded
first, citing Canada as "the first among the smaller nations of the world"
and encouraging Jones and his membership to continue their "efforts to

awaken public opinion to the necessity for vigorous and constructive action in the interests of peace." Mackenzie King followed four days later. The prime minister reserved his comments on the content of the organization's proposals but did promise that Canada would do its utmost to promote a spirit of tolerance and cooperation in the postwar period.[8]

At the Canadian Institute of International Affairs (CIIA), Charlotte Whitton was leading a campaign to grant women who were concerned with postwar problems membership at large in the institute. She hoped to use the CIIA's resources to create a network of women's groups, such as the Canadian Women's Committee on International Affairs, to study global-security issues. Despite its original objections, the CIIA's national executive recommended the admission of female members to male branches in late October 1944.[9]

A number of CIIA representatives continued to participate in the Canadian-American legal working group on what they called the "International Law of the Future." In April 1944 both the *Canadian Bar Review* and its American counterpart simultaneously published the results of some thirty conferences among judges, lawyers, professors, and officials. "With the United Nations playing the dominant role at the end of a second world war," the Canadian journal began, "a world situation may exist in which the further progress of organized effort can be assured. To this end, departures will have to be made, new methods will have to be tried, new institutions will have to be created, and sound legal foundations will have to be laid." The 100 pages of text that followed set the framework for a new international organization, implicitly stressing the importance of the principle of functional representation.[10]

The internationalist momentum was compounded by the success of the first United Nations Relief and Rehabilitation Administration (UNRRA) meeting. The Department of External Affairs reported that the smaller powers had been able to play an active role in the deliberations thanks in large part to the widespread acceptance of Canadian functionalism as a basis for representation. In a letter to J.W. Dafoe, Brooke Claxton, who was present in Atlantic City, reflected: "I was impressed more than ever with the opportunity of Canada to affect the main movement of events."[11] The *Winnipeg Free Press* later described this achievement and others as part of "a revolution in foreign policy."[12]

Back in London, Vincent Massey proclaimed that Canada had "entered a new chapter in the story of [its] existence as a community." The war had made his country more internationally aware. "She has been impelled," he said, "to play an increasingly active part among nations. Her *status* of course was already clearly defined ... but the growth of her *stature* continue[d]."[13]

At home, recognizing the need to maintain public support and improve domestic morale, the WIB's monthly publication, *Canada at War*, which until 1944 had focused almost exclusively on economic issues, now portrayed

Canada as a "fighting world power." "The government believes," wrote one contributor, "that the time has come when all the nations now united in the common purpose of winning the war should seek unitedly to ensure an enduring peace ... the dangers of future aggression can be removed and world security attained only by a general international organization of peace-loving nations."[14]

What the government believed and how it acted, however, were not quite the same. Back on 29 September 1943 the senior civil servant and chair of London's post-hostilities planning (PHP) subcommittee, Gladwyn Jebb, invited the high commissioners in London to participate directly in drafting Britain's PHP documents. According to the Dominions Office, the earlier that the rest of the Commonwealth joined the planning process, the "readier they [would] be to bear a share of the responsibility in executing it."[15]

On behalf of Canada, Charles Ritchie declined. "We have neither the time nor the experience," he explained in his report to Ottawa, "to assist in the drafting of highly technical documents of this kind, nor have we here in London any guidance as to the views of the Canadian authorities which might assist us in the day-to-day business of drafting documents." Instead, he arranged to have early outlines of the committee's findings sent back to Hume Wrong's post-hostilities working committee for comment as often as possible.[16]

In November the chair of Canada's more senior PHP advisory committee, Norman Robertson, reported the working group's findings to the Cabinet. Led by a still cautious Mackenzie King, the senior ministers seemed unwilling to accept the new state of public opinion. Only four days after the CIPO had found that Canadians accepted the need to continue to commit troops abroad once peace had been achieved, the political leadership concluded that "the Canadian people would not be prepared to maintain large military establishments after the war." The Cabinet still endorsed the work of the PHP committees, but it did so reluctantly, deferring consideration of more detailed postwar planning ideas indefinitely.[17]

In the meantime, Canadian policy makers turned their thoughts to the future of the Commonwealth. While a growing majority in Ottawa sought to reconcile collective security with imperial cooperation, the belief that Britain's future would be best assured within a Commonwealth power bloc remained strong in London. In response to what he saw as backward thinking, one frustrated Canadian representative abroad suggested that External Affairs shift its focus to "behind-the-scenes prodding in Washington."[18] The idea was clearly unrealistic. The department was being inundated with material from the PHP subcommittee in Great Britain, and there was no information coming in from the United States.[19] Moreover, the Canadian Cabinet was unwilling to make specific commitments. As a result, in February 1944, in the aftermath of the fallout from the Halifax speech, Charles Ritchie was left to inform Gladwyn Jebb that Canada would continue to respond to the British PHP proposals but that its comments would be nonbinding.[20]

Already frustrated with his government's lack of progress, Hume Wrong could not contain himself any longer. On 23 February 1944 he announced that Canada had to begin a comprehensive study of the postwar period immediately. "It would be a wasted effort," he suggested, "to attempt to plan from the foundation upwards, since as a secondary country we have not a great enough influence to make our views prevail. We should, however, be in a position at least to decide what is not acceptable and to advocate changes or additions to fit our particular interests." The following week, the Cabinet finally ordered a series of special studies on postwar problems.[21]

After a number of preparatory meetings, Canada's PHP advisory committee approved a plan of work for Wrong's subcommittee on 31 March. It included two studies related to international organization: the benefits of regional versus universal world systems and postwar defence arrangements with the United States.[22] Clearly influenced both by its genuine belief in collective security and by its desire to discourage any thoughts of greater Commonwealth unity, the working group rejected schemes for organizing the new world order on a regional basis.[23] On defence, the committee concluded that Canada could not rely on the United States for protection. Canadian interests would be better served through a multilateral international security organization in which all nations accepted "a fair share of responsibility." A world body might also help to minimize potential conflict between the United States and the Soviet Union.[24]

During these deliberations, it became clear that officers in the department held two distinct visions of their country's proper place in world affairs. Those from what John Holmes has called "the more utopian wing of officialdom," like Escott Reid, foresaw Canada making a significant contribution to shaping the postwar order.[25] To them, Canada had become what *La Presse* had recently called "l'une des principales puissances secondaires du monde."[26] It did not take long for such thinking to spawn a revitalization of the concept of middle power. On 1 February 1944, in the midst of grappling with how to reconcile his country's growing international stature with its preestablished position as a small state and active member of the Commonwealth, Reid's mentor at the time, Lester Pearson, became the first Canadian official to formally refer to Canada as a "middle power" in the context of external relations when he drafted a memorandum for Norman Robertson:

> Canada is achieving, I think, a very considerable position as a leader, if not *the* leader, among a group of States which are important enough to be necessary to the Big Four but not important enough to be accepted as one of

that quartet. As a matter of fact, the position of a "little Big Power" or "big Little Power" is a very difficult one, especially if the "little Big Power" is also a "big Dominion." The big fellows have power and responsibility, but they also have control. The little fellows have no power and responsibility; therefore [they] are not interested in control. We "in between" States sometimes get, it seems, the worst of both worlds. We are necessary but not necessary enough! ... There is, I think, an opportunity for Canada, if we desire to take it, to become the leader of this group ... [of] middle powers.[27]

There was political support for this argument, but most of it came from those who were also overly optimistic about Canada's international potential. In April 1944 Stanley Knowles of the CCF argued that "as the largest of the small nations," Canada had to take a leadership role in ensuring that world councils were not dominated by the great powers.[28] Like Pearson, rather than considering his country's real capabilities, Knowles based its deserved global influence on a relatively subjective interpretation of its standing in the world. By allowing national pride to overwhelm his assessment of Canada's international position, he exemplified how the sense of entitlement inherent in the middle power idea was gradually overtaking Canada's formerly pragmatic, defensible, and functional approach to world affairs.

Not everyone agreed with the middle power approach. The architect of Ottawa's functional principle, Hume Wrong, for example, noted the increasing references to Canada's world standing with disdain. In a long memorandum on policy at the UNRRA meetings, he remarked: "This emphasis on status has often led to a completely unreal division of the world between Great and Small Powers. It is to be hoped that the absurdity of labelling indiscriminately as Small Powers diminutive states like Afghanistan or Paraguay, satellite states such as Panama or Slovakia, and intermediate states like the Netherlands or Brazil will gradually disappear." Canada was certainly "a leading secondary power among the United Nations," but its contribution to the war and the peace to follow, not its ranking in an international hierarchy, justified its influence in the future world organization.[29] For Wrong, the functional principle and the middle power concept served separate purposes. While the former was meant to determine the distribution of influence in international affairs, the latter appeared to be specifically designed to make Canadians feel good about themselves. Moreover, argued Wrong supporter Maurice Pope, the success of the future world order was contingent upon the cooperation of the great powers. Rather than asserting itself and risking conflict among its allies, Canada's role, Pope wrote to Pearson, would "be to sit back like good little boys and take our lead from those ... who are directing the war."[30]

The only point on which both sides agreed was that, in planning the future world order, Canada had to avoid closer integration with the United

States. The government in Ottawa therefore continued to cooperate with its counterpart in London. At the opening of the long-delayed Conference of the Commonwealth Prime Ministers in May 1944, Mackenzie King reaffirmed Canada's commitment to "the solidarity of the Commonwealth." The war, he declared, had "brought Canada closer than ever to Britain's side." It was London, not Washington, that his country turned to in a time of crisis.[31]

The conference allowed the United Kingdom to provide the dominions with their first comprehensive planning update since Moscow. Over the winter, the great powers had agreed to an informal exchange of notes on their visions of the future. This first step anticipated an official meeting in Washington to discuss more detailed proposals that would be developed over the first half of 1944. These findings would eventually be presented to the rest of the United Nations. By the end of February the Americans and the British had agreed on a set of topics that could be discussed at the next great-power meeting,[32] from which Gladwyn Jebb's interdepartmental committee produced a series of five memoranda accompanied by an explanatory note. Great Britain's newly formed armistice and postwar committee made minor changes to the documents and then circulated them to the war Cabinet on 22 April. The Cabinet agreed to seek feedback on the proposals at the Conference of the Commonwealth Prime Ministers and to bring the results to the great-power talks.[33]

The sixteen-day conference began on 1 May 1944. Almost immediately, Canada faced criticism in the British and Australian press. Many felt that Mackenzie King's noncommittal attitude was preventing greater imperial unity.[34] Privately, Blair Fraser, who was covering the meeting for *Maclean's*, suggested that the critics simply did not understand the Canadian emphasis on collective security. "I really don't think they have the foggiest idea," he wrote.[35] By 4 May the fog had begun to lift. In comments that, according to Grant Dexter (who was also in London), "made for confusion and uncertainty," the Australian prime minister, John Curtin, seemingly backed off his insistence that the conference create a Commonwealth council. Two days later, it was clear to Dexter that Australia was actually moving toward greater independence. Without Curtin's leadership, the quest for imperial unity was all but over.[36]

Although Winston Churchill himself was disappointed, his Foreign Office seems to have expected this result. Anthony Eden was therefore able to present his proposal for a new, dominion-friendly international organization without delay. It began with a world council composed of the four great powers and a number of smaller states. Great Britain would strive to ensure that one of these additional members would always come from one of the Commonwealth countries. This council would be responsible for all matters of international security. Beneath it would be a less important general assembly.

The nineteen-page document covered five major issues: the scope and nature of the permanent organization; questions surrounding the pacific settlement of disputes; the military aspect of postwar security (which explicitly rejected Churchill's regional-councils idea); coordination of political and economic machinery; and the method and procedure for establishing the new world body.[37] It was formally discussed by the dominion prime ministers on 11 May. To Eden's delight, Mackenzie King called the plan "forward-looking" and praised it for promoting the principle of functional representation. He reminded the British that after the Washington talks, it would be crucial to consult with the smaller powers "to avoid any appearance of presenting to them a fait accompli to which they can do little more than sign their names." Nevertheless, he refused to commit his government formally, citing the need to study the document at home in greater detail.[38]

Later that day, in what Churchill publicly called "the great climax of the development and demonstration of the power of Canada,"[39] King addressed the British Parliament. His speech contained nothing particularly new, but its importance was, to Grant Dexter, "beyond all exaggeration."[40] Blair Fraser later referred to it as "possibly one of the momentous utterances of his long political career."[41] King endorsed the concept of collective security and presented the success of the Commonwealth as an example of what could be achieved through international cooperation. The prime minister also reaffirmed Canada's loyalty to the British Empire. Although he had rejected the thesis that the Commonwealth should speak with one voice in world affairs, King continued to support "close co-operation and coordination of policies" between Great Britain and its dominions.[42]

The conference's official conclusion was unremarkable. On 16 May the prime ministers released the text of a joint declaration:

> We affirm that after the war a World Organization to maintain peace and security should be set up and endowed with the necessary power and authority to prevent aggression and violence.
>
> In a world torn by strife, we have met here in unity. That unity finds its strength, not in any formal bond but in the hidden springs from which human action flows. We rejoice in our inheritance of loyalties and ideals, and proclaim our sense of kinship to one another. Our system of free association has enabled us, each and all, to claim a full share of the common burden. Although spread across the globe, we have stood together through the stresses of two World Wars, and have been welded strongly thereby. We believe that when victory is won and peace returns, the same free association, this inherent unity of purpose, will make us able to do further service to mankind.[43]

Speaking publicly, Winston Churchill declared the meeting "one of the important milestones in the history of our united association."[44] It was, according to one journalist, a definitive victory for collective-security advocates.[45] A Canadian Cabinet minister, T.A. Crerar, called it "the clearest, strongest note which has been struck, so far as the organization of the post-war world is concerned."[46] Because of King's expressed commitment to Commonwealth cooperation, the imperialist *Globe and Mail* also approved.[47]

The *Globe*'s support was consistent with the general state of public opinion. Despite a concerted government campaign against greater imperial unity, a CIPO poll taken on 17 May found that 81 percent of the country still believed that the dominions and Britain should send delegates to a council of the empire. The number of Canadians outside of Quebec who wanted to abide by such a council's decisions on foreign policy continued to exceed those who preferred that Canada act independently. Even with Quebec included, 40 percent supported a unified Commonwealth foreign policy, while 50 percent were opposed.[48]

When Mackenzie King returned to Ottawa, he tried to please both sides: "I was never more proud to be a Canadian than I am at this hour," he began, "and I was never more proud to be a citizen of the British Commonwealth."[49] Nevertheless, reminded a leading Canadian internationalist in a public speech two days later, "it is as well to keep clear in mind that other great aspect of Canadian life – that, although within the fabric of the British Commonwealth, we *are* a North American nation ... We should feel happy, as Canadians, that we are able to be a member nation of the British Commonwealth, proud of our British heritage, and at the same time, as a North American nation, with North American personality and orientation be proud of the intimacy of our friendship with the great power to the south."[50] Theodore Newton's comment was fitting. For six months, Canadian planning for the future world organization had all but neglected the increasingly important role of the United States.

Ever since a meeting with Churchill and Chiang Kai-shek in Cairo in November 1943, even most British officials had been forced to concede that President Roosevelt had taken over the leadership of the (Western) United Nations. At the end of the month, in Teheran, it was Roosevelt's vision of a future world order led by four great-power policemen that was presented to Joseph Stalin. The Soviet dictator seemed more attuned to the mood of the times than did either of his colleagues and responded that he doubted whether "the small nations of Europe" would approve of such an elite organization. Later, he also rejected Churchill's regional-councils idea.[51]

The Canadian government would have been pleased with Stalin's reaction – if it had been made aware of it. However, unlike the situation back in Moscow, information on the great-power discussions seemed to be unavailable in Teheran. Even updates from London to the high commissioners were delayed by almost two weeks.[52] In Washington, Jack Hickerson of the Office of European Affairs reported to Secretary of State Cordell Hull that "relations with Canada continue excellent," but neither he nor anyone else tried to replicate Hull's Moscow communications with Dana Wilgress.[53]

When it came to involving Canada in America's more general postwar planning, the results were also disappointing. Part of the problem was the State Department. Until Edward R. Stettinius, Junior, took over as undersecretary from Sumner Welles, it remained poorly organized and did not effectively communicate with its missions abroad. Canada's representation in Washington also played a role. On 13 December 1943 Hume Wrong asked Lester Pearson to determine whether the Americans had established a group similar to Britain's subcommittee on post-hostilities planning.[54] Pearson might have referred him to the State Department's Division of International Conferences or to the new Division of Political Studies. He might even have noted what was becoming known as the informal agenda group, the unit that took over the work of Welles's defunct special subcommittee on international organization. Instead, he made no response at all.

When Wrong asked again one month later, Pearson wrote back: "General Pope and I have both made inquiries and cannot find anything comparable to the Post-Hostilities Planning Sub-Committee in London. There appears to be no interdepartmental group charged with the general task of preparing for the immediate post-hostilities period in enemy and liberated territories. There are doubtless many people in the War and State Departments respectively who are studying various parts of the problem, but no coordinating body."[55] There was clearly a lack of communication between Pearson and the State Department; within days, Stettinius formally announced the creation of a new Division of Territorial Studies.[56]

There was a third factor. Presumably with Norman Robertson's knowledge, Hume Wrong made almost no effort to integrate Canada's US representatives into the department's planning process. For example, he hardly consulted with Pearson or Reid while developing the first PHP papers.[57] Then, in June, he refused to send the Canadian Embassy in Washington a copy of the United Kingdom's draft paper on the organization of world security that had been discussed at the Conference of the Commonwealth Prime Ministers. "There are only 2 or 3 copies in Ottawa," he explained, "and we cannot spare one at present." Perhaps recognizing that his behaviour verged on offensive, Wrong did offer to telegraph a draft analysis on postwar Canadian-American defence relations to Washington for comments within a few weeks, but even here his tone was less than enthusiastic.[58]

Wrong, among others, seems to have been particularly unimpressed by Escott Reid and his idealistic hopes for the future. As he later privately told Pearson, an American representative had "expressed an exact opposite opinion" in response to Reid's most recent analysis of world affairs.[59] As a result, Wrong refused to allow the junior counsellor to promote his idea for an international police force to the US State Department after the latter had pronounced itself against it.[60]

During this period, along with sharing Wrong's wariness of the staff at the embassy in Washington, Norman Robertson was preoccupied with the notion that Lester Pearson was headed for a promotion that would place him above Wrong in the department's hierarchy. When he learned that Pearson was going to succeed Leighton McCarthy as Canadian ambassador to the United States, Robertson immediately arranged for Wrong to be elevated to a newly established position of associate undersecretary of state for external affairs. Wrong's salary was increased to that of an ambassador, and in what Malcolm MacDonald found to be a "somewhat curious" move, the announcement of Pearson's appointment was preceded by one regarding Wrong's advancement.[61]

This is just one of many reasons why Robertson too might have ignored Pearson's request for more information about the Conference of Commonwealth Prime Ministers. Ottawa's report, which was completed in early June, still had not been delivered at the end of the month when an almost desperate Lester Pearson pleaded with the undersecretary a second time.[62] Robertson was also "non-committal" on Escott Reid's suggestion that he send additional staff to Washington after the next planned great-power meeting to gather more information on the American reaction.[63] This decision was in many ways the right one – Reid grossly overestimated America's willingness to share intelligence with Canada – but it still seems to have been motivated as much by mistrust as by anything else.

Mackenzie King was not informed of his staff's uneasy relations with the embassy, nor, as minister of external affairs, did he make any effort to learn about them. Left to themselves, Robertson and Wrong generally excluded Pearson and Reid from the postwar discussions, while the latter two, in part because of their lack of access to information, underperformed in Washington. Canada never knew that Franklin Roosevelt received a draft of the planned future world organization for the first time in December 1943, nor did it learn of the president's initiative to bring the three great powers together for a formal meeting in Washington until much later.[64] Most important, neither the King government nor the Department of External Affairs was ever informed or consulted before a meeting of the Office of Special Political Affairs that dealt specifically with the concept of functionalism.

On 25 February 1944 the State Department held a detailed discussion about representation and voting in international organizations. The dialogue produced a realistic interpretation of the functional principle. "Consideration must be given," the Americans concluded, "both to the importance of the matter to the country desiring to participate and to the importance of a given country's concurrence for a workable solution to the matter." This reasoning justified the positions of the Soviet Union and China on the United Nations Relief and Rehabilitation Administration's policy committee. It also helped to explain why Canada had been excluded.

A distinction also had to be made "between international discussions on matters of urgent political importance such as threats to the peace, and on other matters." Understandably, therefore, the new international security organization would have "a council dominated by the great powers, with perhaps elected representation of smaller powers and the practice of admitting other states to discuss matters on which they have a direct interest; and an assembly of universal membership but with very limited executive and legislative powers." Subsidiary, functional organizations could handle the less important problems, and membership in these minor groups could be determined according to a state's "interest in and competence to deal with the particular subject."

The State Department officials had thought about, and even accepted, the functional principle so long as it was restricted to nonsecurity issues. And the United States appeared to support nongreat-power representation on an international security council when matters directly affecting the state in question were being discussed. In emergencies, however, the great powers would maintain the right to consult and determine policy among themselves. They might later seek the consent of the smaller countries whose interests were at stake, but such consultation would be perfunctory.[65]

If members of the Canadian government (along with Wrong and Robertson) had been aware of this meeting, they would have been more confident that their views were being considered and that, at times despite themselves, their representatives in Washington were communicating the Canadian position at least somewhat effectively. Perhaps this would have given them the confidence to provide Pearson and Reid with more timely information. But they did not know of the meeting, and without greater guidance from Ottawa, the staff in Washington could have no real sense of the Canadian position. This left them with little choice but to speak for themselves, further undermining their government's credibility.

At the same time, it was almost too easy to forget that the office in Washington was still quite capable. On 11 July, Pearson submitted a persuasive analysis of current US foreign-policy aims. The document concluded: "A consciousness of growing national strength and pride in the prowess of the armed forces has strengthened a tendency to disregard intermediate and small powers and, indeed, treat them with an impatience which will cause even more resentment than during the war ... during the next six months, we must be prepared for a good deal of confusion, controversy, timidity and evasion, of narrow parochial politics on the one hand and grandiloquent but meaningless international platitudes on the other."[66] The memorandum was well received in Ottawa. Norman Robertson circulated it widely in the Department of External Affairs and to the Canadian missions abroad.[67] Despite their differences – which centred around the issue of trust – Canada's most important civil servants sincerely respected one another and could still cooperate.

But cooperate was really all that they could do. In the first half of 1944 the national public certainly believed that Canada was playing an increasingly important role in world affairs; however, when it came to international organization, the reality of this crucial planning period was rather different. By rejecting closer ties to the empire while at the same time failing to cultivate more effective relations with the United States, the Canadian government had left itself in a state of virtual limbo. It was neither a great power nor a particularly small one. It could not be considered a British dependency, nor was it an entirely North American country. This dilemma would reveal itself most clearly as the planning for the future world order reached its most important stage later that fall.

7
Disappointment at Dumbarton Oaks (April–October 1944)

In the spring and summer of 1944, most Canadians believed that, in the international community, their country had achieved a position of prominence that would allow it to play an influential role in the shaping of the new world order. Canada was not a great power, they conceded, but it deserved a more significant place in the next world organization than some of the less consequential participants in the Second World War. The great-power meetings in August and September tested this belief. With the help of their British colleagues, Canadian officials attempted to differentiate the position of the so-called middle powers on the United Nations Security Council (UNSC). Their efforts did not succeed. The middle power argument was vague, complicated, and insufficiently thought out. The staff in Ottawa and Washington continued to struggle to work effectively together, and the political leadership, once again faced with controversy over conscription at home, was hardly engaged. By the time the Dumbarton Oaks Conference ended, the efforts to promote national independence on the world stage in mid-1944 had made Canada appear more closely tied to Great Britain than ever before.

On 19 April 1944 the Dominions Office notified Ottawa that Great Britain hoped to meet with the United States and the Soviet Union to discuss specific plans for a "United Nations organisation" in early June.[1] Among the issues that they would cover was the composition of the executive, or security council. As had been made clear before, the great powers would be permanent members and would have the right to veto major military decisions. The role of nongreat states was apparently still open to debate. This consideration provided the first testing ground for the middle power argument. As Hume Wrong explained, "it [was] unreasonable and undesirable that all states without permanent seats should have the same chance of selection for a non-permanent seat no matter what their size or importance may be."[2]

While the Canadian planners formulated a negotiating strategy to recognize the middle states, the great powers struggled to set a firm meeting date. First, the British called for a postponement until early August so that all sides could exchange more detailed notes. Further difficulties ensued when the Soviets objected to the American request to include the Chinese. Eventually, the Big Three agreed to gather on 21 August in Washington at Dumbarton Oaks, the former Georgetown estate of Robert Woods Bliss, the US special assistant to the secretary of state. After the negotiations, the US and the UK planned to meet separately with the Chinese. The results of these discussions would be taken back to the Soviets to produce a four-power declaration.[3]

Like every other small state, Canada was not invited to the great-power meeting. Apart from the usual criticisms from the Conservative Party and the French Canadian nationalist press, reaction to the country's exclusion was understandably subdued.[4] Instead of complaining, the Department of External Affairs contemplated means by which it might influence the discussions from the outside. Canada, argued Hume Wrong, would have to work pragmatically. "The main outlines of the new organization will be agreed upon by the three Great Powers and we shall have to accept their decisions," he explained. Using the British memoranda from the recent Conference of Commonwealth Prime Ministers as a basis, the department had to generate a list of subjects upon which "a Canadian view might exercise a considerable influence" and then focus on them exclusively.[5]

Naturally, the department concentrated on the place of the smaller states on the security council. This was not only crucial to the middle power argument, but also essential because, to this point, the British position on the issue had been rather vague. Originally, the planners in London had argued that the security-council question was "a matter for grave consideration." Each region of the world had to be fairly represented, but it also made sense in principle that when a state's interests were at stake, it should have the right to be heard.[6] Anthony Eden, whose ideas were likely to form the basis of the British approach to the meetings, personally hoped that the council could be made up of between nine and twelve states. France could join the Big Four as a full-fledged great power, and one of the nonpermanent seats could potentially be held exclusively for the dominions.[7]

However convenient this reserved position might have been, when he was asked to consider it, Dana Wilgress did not hesitate to reiterate the by now well-known Canadian position that proposals for a regionally based international security organization had to be avoided at all costs. Canada could never choose between loyalty to either the United States or Great Britain. Moreover, its interests were best assured through great-power harmony, which was more likely to be achieved within a genuinely multilateral world system.[8]

When it came time to suggest an alternative to regional representation – one that might have ensured that the so-called middle powers held a position of preference – Hume Wrong's senior assistant, John Holmes, could not offer anything specific. There was, of course, the functional principle, but its criteria – capacity and contribution – were not clear. Recognizing how challenging it would be to measure and compare individual countries along functionalist lines, Holmes concluded that it might well be up to the general assembly to conduct an election. In that case, the preponderance of small states among the United Nations would make it even more difficult for the middle powers to assert themselves.[9]

According to Charles Ritchie, Canada might have been able to handle undifferentiated treatment so long as all states had the right to representation, and indeed voting power, on the security council when their national interests were at stake. He anticipated that Great Britain would oppose such a proposal out of fear that fluctuation in the size of the council could diminish its credibility and authority. No matter, he insisted. As "a question of principle," it was worth fighting for.[10]

In late June, having reviewed the British memoranda in detail, the Department of External Affairs began to seek information about the US and Soviet proposals. Washington and Moscow were not particularly forthcoming so, on 18 July the British Foreign Office (FO) secretly provided Pearson and Reid with access to the most recent American planning documents. The Canadians could not remove the materials from the embassy and were observed closely while they took detailed notes. Pearson and Reid also explicitly agreed not to reveal the FO's actions to anyone beyond their government, particularly not to anyone in Washington.[11]

If the Canadians had kept their promise, it is doubtful that the Americans could have realized what the British had done. As the most powerful country in the West, the United States instinctively took the smaller states' views on the new world order less than seriously and therefore paid them little attention. In March 1944, for example, without directly consulting any of the lesser powers, the State Department's Division of International Security and Organization had concluded that the executive council should be made up of the Big Four and just four others. The US, UK, USSR, and China would be permanent members, and the additional countries would serve annual terms with no opportunity for immediate reelection.

The Americans had thought it best to grant states not sitting on the council the right to participate in decisions affecting them directly. At the same time, however, by limiting the size of the UNSC so stringently, and by restricting the terms of nonpermanent members to a single year, they had effectively nullified the capacity for nongreat powers to make an extended impact. The United States' willingness to admit nonmembers to discussions also hinged prohibitively on the vote of the council itself (on which the great powers had a veto). Finally, the planning document made adamant its refusal to grant the invitees the right to vote.[12]

Fortunately, the US proposal was widely criticized internally. In mid-July the planners therefore reconsidered. A recast document enlarged the executive council to eleven, although nonpermanent states would continue to serve one-year terms with no possibility for immediate reelection. The United States also assigned responsibility for choosing the temporary members to the general assembly , but no criteria were mentioned for governing these elections.[13]

For information on Moscow's thinking, Canada had to rely on an article published in late July by an N. Malinin[14] in an obscure paper called *Zvezda*. The Soviet approach emphasized great-power control and leadership. It proposed to divorce the technical functions of the former League of Nations from the areas of responsibility of the new body. A separate organization could be created to deal with social and economic matters.[15] This final point stood in stark contrast to the British plan. Thinking in London favoured "the betterment of world-wide economic conditions and the removal of social wrongs" by actively supporting institutions that served these purposes.[16] Officers in Ottawa (and Washington) favoured the British position.

On 2 August, having now considered all three plans, and with the conference just weeks away, Robertson urged a once again domestically preoccupied Mackenzie King to approve an official Canadian response that could be sent to London immediately. "Perhaps the point of chief importance in the draft," he wrote the prime minister, "is the argument that the functional idea of representation should be applied in the Council so that States other than the Great Powers, which have a role of real importance in world security, would not be treated on a basis of equality with small States whose role is insignificant." "If weight is to be given to our views," he added, "we are perhaps most likely to make progress before the Four Powers have agreed on an outline scheme."[17]

King, who was at this point thinking almost exclusively about a sudden and dramatic increase in Canadian casualties in Europe following the Normandy invasion (which had the potential to ignite another conscription controversy and thus to have an adverse effect on his reelection campaign), followed his undersecretary's advice. That day, External Affairs cabled the Dominions Office. The message warned the British not to take the views of the more important "secondary states" for granted. Regional representation on the executive body of the new world organization was important, but there were other factors that had to be considered more seriously. When it came to security, for example, a state's relative military power was crucial. Finally, in Mackenzie King's typically understated fashion, the note concluded: "The views put forward in this telegram are intended rather to be an amplification of the United Kingdom proposals, with special reference to the situation of secondary states, than in criticism of them."[18]

King reported to Parliament on the official Canadian position going into Dumbarton Oaks on 4 August. "The simple division of the world between great powers and the rest is unreal and even dangerous," he began, repeating the Robertson-Wrong document almost verbatim. "The great powers are called by that name simply because they possess great power. The other states of the world possess power – and, therefore, the capacity to use it for the maintenance of peace – in varying degrees ranging from almost zero in the case of the smallest and weakest states up to a military potential not very far behind that of the greatest powers." In the interests of fairness and international stability, he suggested, the United Nations ought to apply the functional principle in determining which states should stand alongside the great powers on the security council.

King then moved on to an issue that was closely tied to his book *Industry and Humanity*, one for which he might have written his own text. "If the new world system is conceived in terms of power alone," he said, "peace may be kept for a time, but not for long. If it is to last and broaden out from precedent to precedent it must embody a dynamic idea and ideal. The concentration on security, and on the need to marshal overwhelming force to meet threats to security, is not enough. Security from war is indeed essential, but real security requires international action and organization in many other fields – in social welfare, in trade, in technical progress, in transportation, and in economic development." He concluded by emphasizing Canada's independence from Great Britain and its growing status in world affairs.[19]

His comments were poorly received by the Conservatives. Member of Parliament Howard Green condemned the prime minister for refusing to see the country as anything more than "one of the leaders in kicking the shins of the bigger nations." He then warned the House: "If the Canadian people, if even any large portion of the people aim no higher than for Canada to be a small nation, she will never be anything more, and the result will be that she will end up under the thumb of the United States."

Green's solution was, paradoxically, both antiquated and yet entirely reasonable. Rejecting the functional principle as ineffective, he revived the traditional Conservative argument that Canada should serve on a greater imperial council. According to opinion polls, the idea no longer resonated strongly with the general public, but the reasoning should have. Whether Canadians cared to admit it, when the great powers met at Dumbarton Oaks, the British representative would be seen by the rest of the world as speaking for the entire Commonwealth. "We will find that we are more or less bound by what he says," Green predicted, "whether we have a representative there or not."[20]

Nevertheless, as M.J. Coldwell pointed out, Green's belief that Canada was set to become a great power in the near future was ludicrous. The Cooperative Commonwealth Federation (CCF) leader argued that given its relatively small population, Canada had no choice but to assume the role for which it was best suited, "as at least one of the spokesmen for that group of nations which within the united nations can be described as the lesser powers."[21] Mackenzie King agreed. Canada would not attend the great-power meetings, but Canadians could be assured that the British would be "fully aware" of their views and would present them responsibly.[22]

Both arguments were flawed. Green underestimated the willingness of Great Britain to promote dominion interests and was therefore wrong to assume that Canada's agenda could not be put forward without Canadian representatives being present. But Mackenzie King's assumption that allowing British negotiators to establish the Canadian position would not come at a price was equally short-sighted. As a number of officials predicted, when Great Britain expressed Canadian concerns to the United States and the Soviet Union, both the American and Soviet leadership assumed that it had been granted permission to speak on Canada's behalf. It therefore became more difficult to see Canada as truly independent.[23]

Nevertheless, even if in not demanding representation at Dumbarton Oaks, the King government had conceded a degree of sovereignty, the Liberal approach was not necessarily the wrong one. The Soviets had no interest in the opinions of the lesser powers, and while the State Department's advisory committee did think it best to court some of the more powerful secondary countries, it had also concluded that so long as the great powers were careful, and did not appear arrogant or dominating, the smaller states would eventually accept their inferior position.[24] Put simply, there was absolutely no chance that Canada could have presented its views at Dumbarton Oaks independently.

Moreover, ever since the meeting of the Commonwealth prime ministers, the British attitude toward the dominions had appeared to be growing increasingly sympathetic. In the middle of June the Foreign Office had recommended that its delegation to Dumbarton Oaks include a representative from the Dominions Office. The individual – Stephen Holmes was eventually chosen – would have three duties: to keep "in close touch with the progress of discussions and the papers produced at the Conference so as to be able to call the attention of the Delegation to any points' raised which might affect Dominion interests or ... relations with the Dominions; to ensure that as frequently as can conveniently be arranged information as to the progress of the conversations is supplied to London for communication to Dominion Governments; [and] to maintain such informal liaison with the Dominion Missions in Washington on the subject as may prove convenient and desirable."[25] To many in London, the dominions had become Britain's final hope for genuine great-power standing in the postwar world.

On 15 August, with these thoughts in mind, the United Kingdom's permanent undersecretary of state, Alexander Cadogan, led the British delegation to Washington. Cadogan had spent ten years as his government's primary representative to the League of Nations and had been present during the Atlantic Charter deliberations of 1941. A confidential American report commented on his thoughtfulness, his skill as a negotiator, and his personal integrity. "He is a true Government official," it concluded, "who does the job required of him, and who represents the British Government to the best of his ability." Because he was a regular at Cabinet meetings and was in close contact with Eden and Churchill, his views could be interpreted as authoritative. Indeed, he was "the best informed man in the foreign service on British foreign policy" and particularly well briefed on the world organization.[26]

Cadogan was instructed to issue daily reports to the Commonwealth representatives in Washington. He was also advised to refuse to commit to any specific proposals while "making it plain" that the British would keep "an open mind" in considering all of the dominions' ideas.[27] Unfortunately, this did not always translate into advocacy. At the official opening of the conference on 21 August, for example, when Lester Pearson requested assurance that the British would defend the right of nonmember states to participate in security-council discussions when their interests were at stake, Cadogan was what Pearson called "sticky."[28] To compound this lack of support, the dominions secretary, Lord Cranborne, formally rejected the Canadian middle power idea. The principles of functional and regional representation on the security council were sound; however, he maintained in a letter of explanation to the government in Ottawa, his government felt that "any system that attempted to classify secondary powers in different categories might arouse antagonism to the organisation at the outset."[29]

Preliminary talks with the Americans were even more disappointing. On 17 August, Escott Reid criticized the implications of the wide-ranging great-power veto. In response, Leo Pasvolsky, whose tolerance for Reid was about equal to that of Hume Wrong's and who had spent the previous week dealing with what he felt to be petty concerns coming from Latin America, insisted rather angrily that Dumbarton Oaks was a Big Four meeting and that without great-power agreement, there would not be an international organization. If the Canadian was not satisfied, it was simply too bad.[30]

Always resilient, Reid might normally have appealed beyond Pasvolsky. In this case, however, he did not really have that option. The leader of the American delegation to Dumbarton Oaks was another government official, the new undersecretary of state, Edward R. Stettinius, Junior. The good-looking, forty-three-year-old former lend-lease administrator had replaced Sumner Welles in September 1943. Nicknamed "the tooth" (because of his ever-present smile), he was, in one Canadian's words, "a glad-hander."[31] More fairly, Gladwyn Jebb recalled, "he was a splendid man, but he wasn't very effective."[32] His strengths were in organization and compromise; Stettinius had a way of making people get along regardless of their feelings for one another. But his background in foreign relations was limited, and he was rarely able to fully grasp the issues before him. He therefore gave Pasvolsky full charge of the technical aspects of the Dumbarton Oaks negotiations, and the civil servant's response to Escott Reid was all but final.

Whether the Soviet representative to the meetings, the ambassador to Washington, A.A. Gromyko, understood the intricacies of the debates at Dumbarton Oaks will probably never be known. A "young but hard-working and able diplomat," Gromyko served as a mouthpiece for his superiors, and the State Department doubted whether he had any real influence on Soviet policy.[33] As the US ambassador to Moscow explained: "It would be a serious mistake ... to assume that the statements and actions of the Soviet delegates at the talks might be influenced to any appreciable extent by the personalities or individual views of any of the members of the Soviet delegation. Soviet policy on these matters will be decided almost exclusively in Moscow and in these decisions no personalities are likely to be of obvious importance except those of the party leaders of the Kremlin."[34]

Together, the three officials at Dumbarton Oaks understood their limitations. In their opening remarks on 21 August 1944, each one mentioned that the meetings were purely provisional. After that, their statements diverged, particularly with regard to the small powers. Cadogan was the most inclusive. "Individual nations, small and great," he said, "must be the basis of our new World Organization; and our problem is to construct a machine which will give to each of them the responsibilities commensurate with its power." Great-power unity was crucial to an effective organization, but no one wished "to impose a Great Power dictatorship on the rest of the world."[35] Stettinius and Cordell Hull spoke as though there were no small states,[36] and Gromyko stressed the importance of the "nations which bear the main brunt of the present war, and which possess the necessary resources and power to maintain peace and security."[37]

Once again, Great Britain was Canada's best option for influence. Lester Pearson, who seemed to feel that the British were not working hard enough to support the smaller states, pressured Cadogan's team rather aggressively to limit the Big Four's veto power and to insist that nonmembers of the council have the right to be heard before committing their troops abroad. Without this provision, he threatened, "it would clearly be difficult to get many secondary Powers to join the organization."[38] His apparent irritation was misplaced. As Stettinius would reflect later, it was "the British group" that continuously showed "concern with the sensibilities of the smaller powers."[39]

Despite Pearson's doubts, Cadogan's work did pay off. Three days into the conference, the parties agreed in principle that those excluded from the security council should have the right to "attend and be heard on matters affecting them."[40] The following week, they reached a formal compromise. A state that did not have a seat on the UNSC could always be present at meetings to resolve disputes in which it was directly involved. The council alone would decide whether that state would be invited when its interests were affected only indirectly. Nonpermanent members would now be allowed to serve terms longer than one year. And both Cadogan and Stettinius urged the Soviets to consider economic and social matters more seriously.[41]

For Hume Wrong, while these results were not ideal, they were, for the time being, sufficient. In his first report to the working committee on post-hostilities problems (PHP), rather than dwelling on the lack of influence that Canada might have had at Dumbarton Oaks, he stressed the "special position" that the dominion governments had held as "the only governments aside from the great powers to know what was going on." "Canada," he explained, "had two points of view to consider. We did not want to throw a monkey-wrench into the harmony among the Great Powers but, on the other hand, we wanted to protect the Canadian position as well as that of other small countries. Canada had expressed her views firmly and was inclined now to let some of the other countries carry the argument for a while."[42]

Robertson's advisory committee agreed. On 31 August the undersecretary of state for external affairs led a discussion that focused on the unwillingness of the Big Three to officially designate certain contributing states as middle powers and then recognize them in the selection of nonpermanent members of the security council. At the end, the committee decided that "no attempt [would] be made in the present instrument to establish criteria for membership and that the first election to the Council should be ad hoc." Later, the organization could establish a policy that considered the nonpermanent members' military and financial contributions to international security. "In general," the committee concluded, "it was hoped that ways might be found to emphasize the responsibilities and obligations rather than the prestige which should be associated with membership on the Council."[43]

Later that day, the Cabinet war committee accepted the PHP report. Ottawa committed itself to three long-term, general goals that it would pursue aggressively once the preliminary discussions had ended: expanding the responsibilities of the security council to include nonmilitary obligations; developing an accountable method for electing nonpermanent council members; and reducing the impact of the great-power veto. Canada would continue to communicate its concerns through Great Britain.[44]

Lester Pearson was left unimpressed and disappointed. He therefore ignored Hume Wrong's instructions to accept the decision not to pursue the middle power idea and approached the Americans on his own. Against the expressed orders of the British government, he revealed to Jack Hickerson that the Foreign Office had provided him and Escott Reid with access to the US proposal and then pleaded his case for the rights of the middle powers.[45] Pearson reported his conversation to Ottawa the next day but did not mention his revelation. Instead, he asked permission to speak in greater detail, wrongly suggesting that the Americans were more sympathetic than the British to the position of the nongreat states.[46]

Regrettably, Pearson had misjudged the situation. While he was accusing the British of neglect, Alexander Cadogan was seeking permission from the Foreign Office to promote the Canadian cause more aggressively. He personally doubted whether "any satisfactory formula" could be devised to delineate the so-called middle powers, but "in view of the Canadian Government's attitude," he wrote to Lord Halifax, "I suggest that I make an effort to insert [in the United Nations Charter] after the words 'nonpermanent seat' ... [the] words 'due regard being paid to their contribution to the maintenance of peace and security.' This would enable Canada (for instance) to plead that she had inherently a better right to be elected to Council than e.g. Costa Rica."[47]

The Foreign Office was pleasantly receptive. Rather than considering military contributions exclusively, it agreed instead to accept Cadogan's suggestion, adding to the end of his suggested insertion the words: "and towards the other purposes of the Organisation." This concession came with its own conditions. As an imperial power, Great Britain still considered geography important and remained reluctant to differentiate the secondary states formally in the United Nations Charter. The British could accept functionalism but not the arbitrary and divisive nature of the middle power idea.[48]

On 9 September the Dumbarton Oaks joint steering committee discussed the selection criteria for nonpermanent executive members. As they had promised, the British argued that preferential treatment should be given to states that contributed to the work of the security council. Gromyko supported them in principle, but concerns about restricting the freedom of the general assembly caused him to hesitate to formalize his position in writing. The Americans were adamantly opposed. With Leo Pasvolsky standing firmly behind him, James Dunn argued "that such a provision would, in effect, set up three ... categories of powers – the great powers, those who made [a] special contribution, and the remainder." This violated "the principle of sovereign equality," which had been so important to ensuring wide international support for the United Nations. Dunn might have been willing to reconsider his position once the organization had been established, but as things stood, he did not believe that the proposal would meet with general acceptance.[49]

Stettinius, who hated to see the delegations in conflict, referred the matter to Cordell Hull. Perhaps Britain's obstinacy would cause the secretary of state to overrule his civil servants. Instead, Hull stood behind Dunn. The combination of his resistance and the Soviet Union's unwillingness to compromise any further caused the British to give in. On 19 September they withdrew their proposed qualification for the selection of nonpermanent council members.[50]

From this point on, the talks at Dumbarton Oaks focused on whether the great powers would be allowed to veto discussions of international disputes to which they were a party. The United States and Great Britain argued that the smaller states would view such clout as evidence of a Big Four dictatorship. The Soviets insisted that the veto was necessary to preserve "the principle of unanimity." Great-power consistency had been the basis of Stalin's willingness to allow Gromyko to participate in the negotiations. He would not give this up. Cadogan and Stettinius personally pleaded with Gromyko, but he remained resolute.[51]

Faced with a potentially fatal deadlock, the negotiators appealed to their superiors. This decision was a risk, particularly since Churchill and Roosevelt had hardly been taking Dumbarton Oaks seriously. The British prime minister continued to obsess about the war itself, while the American president, who was focused primarily on the upcoming national election, had frustrated his bureaucrats with repeated unrealistic and unsuccessful attempts to obtain great-power status for Brazil. Stalin, naturally enough, had the least sympathy for the smaller states.

During the Dumbarton Oaks meetings, Churchill and Roosevelt had spent most of their time at the Chateau Frontenac Hotel in Quebec discussing military matters. While there, the British prime minister received a message from South Africa's Jan Smuts suggesting that, considering the importance of Soviet participation to the success of the new world organization, "the smaller powers should be prepared to make a concession to Russia's amour propre and should not on this matter insist on theoretical equality of status ... and [the] United Kingdom and United States should use their influence in favour of common sense and safety first rather than status for the smaller countries." Churchill was sympathetic. Roosevelt was not, but he was most concerned that the matter disappear so that he could announce a full-dress meeting of the United Nations before the election.[52]

Mackenzie King, who was hosting this second Quebec Conference, disagreed with both of them. The middle countries had to be taken more seriously, and the world was not yet ready for an official large-scale meeting. The prime minister's first plea had no impact – Canadian views did not play a role in British or American policy toward the Soviet Union – but King was helpful in convincing Roosevelt that the international conference would have to be delayed.[53]

The delay became inevitable when, back in Washington, the Soviet representatives remained immovable on the veto question. The delegation left without a complete agreement on 28 September. The following day, the Chinese arrived for a week of inconsequential meetings.[54] When these talks ended, Stephen Holmes wrote a review of the British delegation's overall attitude toward the Commonwealth. His report documented the lengths to which Cadogan had gone to promote recognition of the intermediate-sized powers and to ensure that their voices had been heard on military, economic, and social questions. "In some cases," he concluded, "these attempts have been successful, in other cases not, but some credit may be due to the United Kingdom even when success has not attended their efforts."[55]

The Canadian government was less optimistic. Mackenzie King was disappointed with the disparity between the powers of the Big Four and the middle states. The prime minister was also particularly concerned that the veto issue had not been settled. He went so far as to encourage Churchill, unsuccessfully, to delay the publication of the proposals until some of the issues with the Soviets could be resolved.[56]

Hume Wrong's report to the PHP working committee suggested similar disenchantment. The associate undersecretary doubted that the Canadian people would ever support a policy that forced states to act on a security issue without necessarily having been consulted in advance. To him, the results of the Dumbarton Oaks talks suggested that the great powers had been trying to transform their tripartite alliance into the world organization. This might have been a good idea in theory, but such a partnership would serve as an announcement to the rest of the international community that the new world order would not respect "the principle of sovereign equality of nations."[57] Privately, he told Norman Robertson that as the great powers became more powerful, Canada's position in international affairs was "becoming still more subordinate to the United Kingdom."[58]

Publicly, the initial response of the *Winnipeg Free Press* was more optimistic. The British had fought hard for the smaller powers, and the editors anticipated that additional discussions would provide the Canadians with greater influence. "We have passed the stage," they claimed, "when a single power, or group of powers, no matter how powerful it may be, can safely afford to ignore the aspirations and desires of the lesser states."[59] Two days later, Grant Dexter and Bruce Hutchison lunched with a frustrated Hume Wrong. After hearing that, in his opinion, the agreement was "so unsatisfactory in its present form" that the Canadian Parliament might not ratify it, they began to portray the meetings differently. The settlement reached at Dumbarton Oaks became "only a draft" that was "subject to change," and

Canada would continue to fight for "a better deal for the little powers." The proposals would "grow and develop as time and experience suggest."[60]

Back in Washington, Escott Reid could not wait for this growth and development. On his own initiative, he drafted an aggressive statement opposing the Dumbarton Oaks proposals. The memorandum emphasized the role of morality in international relations and argued in favour of a global police force, a world government, and limits to the power of the Big Four.[61] The document was never released. Instead, on 10 October Mackenzie King made a more moderate statement. Using notes prepared for him by Hume Wrong, the prime minister emphasized the opportunities that the Canadian people would have to revise the proposals before they would be considered by Parliament.[62] The next day, Wrong justified his decision to replace Reid's statement with his own:

> I feel that we should keep our hands as free as possible during the current phase of negotiations, and avoid public commitment in support of amendments, the inclusion of which we may not be able to secure. The wisdom of this course is supported not only by these general considerations but also because it would be unfortunate if the Canadian Government were to take a position which might figure in the election campaign of the United States. Hence, as you know, it was decided that all [that] should be done was to issue promptly a much more general statement, and I hope that we shall be able to refrain from any detailed comment, at any rate until after the elections have taken place, if not longer.[63]

The feelings of the United States were crucial, and, Wrong seemed to imply, Reid had not considered them sufficiently.

In this case, the associate undersecretary could not have been more correct. Reid and, indeed, Pearson seem to have been working on the mistaken assumption that Great Britain had been the most significant impediment to Canadian influence on the Big Three. The Canadian Embassy had misinterpreted the attitude of the United States. Pearson's revelation that the Foreign Office had granted him access to the American planning documents, and that it was continuing to liaise with the dominions throughout the Dumbarton Oaks meetings, had caught the staff in Washington by surprise. Surely, the Americans had "understood that the British Delegation would from time to time confer" with the Commonwealth "in regard to the broad phases of discussions." They were also aware that countries such as Canada might receive periodic "general informational telegrams." But the consultation had been much closer than that.[64]

A shocked Edward Stettinius felt that the best solution would have been to follow London's lead and forward all of the important American documents to the Canadian Embassy; however, after confirming Pearson's comments with a member of the British delegation in Washington, Jack Hickerson was not as sympathetic.[65] "In the Dumbarton Oaks discussion," he argued to his colleagues, "the U.K. gave the Dominions everything thus putting them in a favored position over the other United Nations. Brazil and other countries whose soldiers are actually fighting in the war received no information about the discussions. Canada had everything. This simply isn't fair." This led him to question Canada's credibility as an independent state. Perhaps, for example, if it were allowed to join the inter-American system, it might act as "the camel's nose under the edge of the tent for the entire Commonwealth."[66]

Hickerson was not alone. An American representative who was observing preparations for an international civil-aviation conference in Montreal wrote home: "Canada wants to be treated as an independent nation and yet, at the same time, profit from the British connection … She has succeeded rather well so far as witness, for example, how closely she was informed of the Dumbarton Oaks Conference, but some day her efforts to be two things at once may cause resentment that will make her course as an independent nation more difficult." From his next comment, it seems that the difficulties had already begun. "We like to think that Canada is expressing her own views when she speaks," he continued, "but when we know that she is being fed by Britain with a constant stream of information strongly colored by the British point of view it is only reasonable to wonder sometimes whether she speaks from the basis of Canadian interests."[67]

Subsequent actions by Canada's representatives in Washington compounded the problem. Because he underestimated the impact of his loose speaking on American attitudes, Pearson sent home misguided advice. In October, while resentment toward the Canadian government was growing, he informed Robertson that Canada was in an ideal position to "modify" the American position on Dumbarton Oaks, adding that his embassy might be the best communicator with the decision makers at the State Department.[68]

If the response to Pearson's prior actions had not already proven him wrong, Escott Reid's activities the following week certainly did. According to an American report, at a lunch with members of the State Department, Reid "spoke unusually frankly and forcefully," never stopping to entertain a response and suggesting that his views were particularly authoritative. He lamented that too many people "had the erroneous idea that Canada always followed the British lead in international affairs" and suggested that most representatives at the State Department failed to recognize his country's independent status. He went on to suggest that the Canadian Parliament would not pass the Dumbarton Oaks proposals as presented and that the national media were only holding back their criticism because of the pending American election. In November, he warned, "all hell may break loose."[69]

The United States was clearly unimpressed, as Norman Robertson learned in what he called a "rather irritating" discussion that he and Hume Wrong had with Ray Atherton a few days later. He found the American ambassador ungracious and frowned at his accusation that Canada had not effectively kept in touch with the State Department. Robertson ended the conversation by questioning a recent US decision to offer to consult fully on Dumbarton Oaks with the Latin American countries while making no similar proposition to Canada.[70]

When Pearson heard of what had happened, he responded defensively, attributing any problems in the Canadian-American relationship to the ambassador, Leighton McCarthy. "The top people in State," he explained, "rarely saw him either at the Department or at the Embassy." Communication would be more effective if Canada had enough qualified senior officers to liaise with their American counterparts. He and Escott Reid were working as hard as they could, and indeed Reid's "reporting activities" had been "extensive and valuable," but there was only so much that the two of them could do.

When it came to America's failure to consult with Canada on Dumbarton Oaks, Pearson commented:

> The rejoinder to it would be that the British had already told us everything and that they, in turn, got our views from the British. That, of course, is a most unsatisfactory rebuttal from our point of view, and, indeed, from theirs as well. I have discussed this matter more than once with Hickerson, and he himself is very disturbed by the tendency among certain of the very top people in the State Department (and in the White House) to accept, and, indeed, to promote the doctrine that on general political questions the views of the British Commonwealth should be co-ordinated and received through the United Kingdom. That being the case, they probably do not feel the same necessity (quite apart from other considerations) of discussing their own views with the separate parts of the British Commonwealth as they do in the case of, say, Guatemala and Bolivia.[71]

Pearson accurately assessed the US attitude, but his depiction of Hickerson was misleading. America's leading Commonwealth-relations representative was disturbed, but his frustration at this time was with Canada's own Escott Reid. In a memorandum to the State Department, Hickerson called his comments on America's decision to consult with the Latin American republics and failure to speak with the Canadians "intemperate" and then went on: "In effect Mr. Reid's attitude resembles that of an individual who is hurt at not receiving the privileges of a club [the inter-American system] while his name is still pending on the waiting list." Representatives from New Zealand and Belgium had not felt the need for a special invitation to present their views to the United States; moreover, Hickerson and Pearson had already spoken about this issue three times.[72]

Another member of the Office of British Commonwealth Affairs regarded Reid's representations with similar disdain:

> The Canadians in this matter are evidently faced with unpalatable conse-
> quences of their policy of expediency which at one moment leads them to
> take advantage of their association in the Commonwealth and at another
> moment leads them to seek the advantage of an independent position. The
> United States on the other hand is faced with the alternatives of allowing
> Canada to assume that the United States, like the British, favors a *bloc* orga-
> nization of the world and does not intend to deal with Canada directly on
> world matters, or, of reminding the Canadians that our policy is interna-
> tional in the broad sense and that in consequence we are ready to talk with
> them frankly as with other Western Hemisphere nations.
>
> A further factor which must be taken into consideration is the undoubted
> reappearance of the Canadian inferiority complex now that the unifying
> pressure of necessary wartime policies is wearing thin.

Nevertheless, the memorandum ended optimistically. Canadian-American relations had traditionally been frank and positive, and the United States "would be glad to see an autonomous, mature Canadian attitude emerge." Moreover, "there was a place" for an independent Canada in the new international organization. Unfortunately, the Canadians had yet to decide if this was what they truly wanted.[73]

One could not really fault the indecision. Over the previous five years, Canada had evolved from a relatively insignificant former colony into a noteworthy, contributing middle-sized power. It had done so in such a short period of time that there had been few opportunities to formulate a consistent foreign-policy direction. The middle power idea was perhaps a start, but it had yet to be considered in sufficient detail.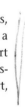

Some Canadians had become impatient. The imprudent and overzealous tendencies of Lester Pearson and Escott Reid, when left unchecked, were more harmful than helpful in an environment of great-power domination. This was particularly true when combined with an inaccurate assessment of British and American attitudes toward the appropriate role for the smaller powers in the future world organization. Furthermore, in retrospect, Pearson's unprofessionalism in his attempt to blame Leighton McCarthy for his own failings was, at best, disheartening. Nevertheless, he and Reid were the most talented officers available for work in Washington, and Pearson's charm and international reputation remained significant assets to the Department of External Affairs. Canadians would have to find a way to balance their British ties with their independent aspirations. And they would have to figure out what they wanted the middle power idea to mean. They had six months.

8
Middle Power Politics
(October 1944–April 1945)

After the Dumbarton Oaks Conference, the national campaign to anoint Canada a so-called middle power accelerated. Writing for the Canadian Institute of International Affairs' *Behind the Headlines* series, the historian Lionel Gelber argued that during the war, Canada had "moved up from her old status to a new stature." No longer in the same class as Mexico or Sweden, the country had to "figure as a Middle Power."[1] At about the same time, the Wartime Information Board proclaimed that Ottawa's twenty-four missions abroad represented "proof positive of Canada's growth of importance as a 'middle' power and sobering evidence of the increased responsibility which Canada must be prepared to assume in the post-war world."[2] Others, both on the radio and in the press, made similar arguments. Canada was not a great power, but it was clearly not a small one either. In fact, according to the *Winnipeg Free Press*, it had become the leader of the middle power cause.[3]

Although the value of middle power advocacy was, and has since been, disputed, even the most critical have allowed that it had "at least one good purpose, and that was to give Canadians a sense of proportion, to convince them that they need not be mere ciphers in the international community, and to warn them against assuming that they could model their tactics on those of the great powers."[4] It typified, "the nationalistic (yet defensive) thinking that prevailed in Ottawa towards the end of the war [and] was employed by the Mackenzie King government to attempt to carve out for Canada a special position in the hierarchy of international power."[5] But the middle power idea was also rather vague, complicated, and insufficiently thought out.

The expectations attached to Canada's new status were unrealistic. In the period leading up to the United Nations' founding conference in San Francisco, the King government was neither willing nor able to extend its global obligations unconditionally. Moreover, increasing tension among the great powers relegated the interests of all of the small states to the background. While some might have seen this situation as an ideal opportunity for Canada to assume a leadership role among the secondary countries, the officials in Ottawa simply did not have the resources to do so: most of their diplomatic missions were new, insufficiently staffed, and generally incapable of building effective coalitions with other middle-sized states. It is also unlikely that Mackenzie King would have sought middle power status for Canada even if the opportunity had been there. When members of the Dominions Office expressed measured sympathy for the idea in early 1945, Canada refused to participate in a joint Commonwealth proposal out of fear that cooperation with Great Britain would sacrifice national autonomy.

In retrospect, what Canadian officials wanted was inherently contradictory. The Department of External Affairs envisioned a special position for the "middle powers" on the United Nations Security Council (UNSC). It acknowledged that with such standing Canada's international obligations might increase. At the same time, it followed King's orders and fought to limit the country's global commitments when it was not represented on the council. Tension and miscommunication among the leading civil servants further complicated matters. While some became caught up in the public's excitement and encouraged an activist approach to planning for the new world organization, others preferred the prime minister's more cautious attitude. In the end, regardless of whether the opportunity to create a tier of middle powers ever really existed, Canada had not yet reached the point in its national development that would have allowed it to take this step.

On 30 October 1944 Hume Wrong sent Norman Robertson a pessimistic briefing on the British view of the Dumbarton Oaks Conference. It appeared that the government in London was so concerned with keeping the Americans committed to postwar reconstruction that it had begun to downplay the importance of the middle-sized states. The report, along with Lester Pearson's and Escott Reid's insistence that Canada's best hope to alter the proposals lay in Washington, caused Robertson to arrange a meeting with the US ambassador, Ray Atherton. His case was straightforward: countries such as Canada, which would be called upon to make a substantial military contribution to the new world organization, were underrepresented on the proposed security council.

An apparently sympathetic Atherton asked for more detail. Did this mean, for example, that the six nonpermanent seats should be reserved for states with the capacity to provide military assistance? Robertson was noncommittal. The American secretary to the meeting, Charles Bohlen, recalled "that he was speaking in terms of general considerations rather than of a specific solution but ... he did feel that the proposals as now drafted did not take into account sufficiently the role of the countries which lay between the great powers and those like Guatemala, for example, which possessed no military strength whatsoever."

When Bohlen accused the Canadian undersecretary of compromising the premise that all states should be treated equally, Robertson did not disagree. In his opinion, since the great powers had differentiated themselves from the outset, "it would perhaps have been better to have left unstated in the document the principle of sovereign equality of all nations." The State Department was unimpressed; the Canadian government, which had opposed the great-power veto on the grounds that it promoted inequality, was now demanding such treatment for itself.[6]

A disappointed Atherton forwarded a memorandum of his conversation to the Division of International Security and Organization (ISO). The staff in Washington were surprised at what they read. Escott Reid's persistent advocacy on behalf of the middle states had given the ISO what it believed to be a clear understanding of the Canadian point of view. Atherton's report made the officials less certain. While both Canadians expressed concerns about Dumbarton Oaks, Reid had gone so much "further" that their views did not appear to be entirely consistent.[7]

The observation was astute. Divisions between the more prudent civil servants in Ottawa and the less restrained officials in Washington had once again been growing. The tension increased significantly through the final weeks of 1944 primarily because Reid overestimated the Canadian delegation's achievements at an international civil-aviation conference in Chicago.

The meeting, which took place from 1 November to 7 December, included representatives from fifty-two United Nations, making it the largest and most inclusive of all of the wartime conferences. It was greeted with anticipation by the Canadian press, and media coverage throughout was favourable. Reid in particular was cited by the chief American delegate, Adolf Berle, as having become "one of the foremost experts in the field of aviation policy."[8]

Canada came to Chicago particularly well prepared. Thanks mainly to Reid, it was the only delegation to have brought with it a thorough draft convention. Upon their arrival, the Canadian representatives worked effectively throughout the meetings to alter and adjust their proposal to satisfy the concerns of the other states. "Praise for Canada's role at the conference," wrote one Canadian historian, "was universal ... The greatest praise was reserved for Canada's role as mediator, or honest broker between the superpowers."[9]

Although the conference did produce an interim agreement, overall, most observers and later analysts considered it a disappointment. The delegates failed to resolve differences over basic regulations governing air-traffic rights, nor could they agree on a variety of fundamental economic issues. Moreover, throughout the meetings, the Latin American states set a dangerous precedent by negotiating as a bloc. In a letter to Mackenzie King on 13

December, Norman Robertson warned that if the Latin Americans voted together at the conference to establish the United Nations, they could possibly secure half of the nonpermanent security-council seats for themselves. Canada had to be careful lest it be "confronted with a solid block of Latin-Americans plus the United States."[10]

Sure enough, by January 1945 Washington had arranged an inter-American conference of foreign ministers. The potential impact of the talks on the middle power campaign was significant. The overwhelming size of the Latin American contingent made it more likely to favour open elections for the six nonpermanent seats on the security council. This approach, of course, would require that all nongreat states be treated equally. When Wrong asked whether the Mexico City meetings would compromise US support for the Canadian middle power idea, this time it was Atherton who was noncommittal. The ambassador had been placed in a difficult position. He did not want to disillusion an American ally, but President Roosevelt himself had made Latin America a distinct priority.[11]

Ever the optimist, Reid saw things differently. In a letter to Robertson in January 1945, he argued that the results of Chicago had proven that, with proper and detailed preparation, Canada could effect significant change at any international negotiation. With effort, the terms of the interim agreement on civil aviation might even be applied to the new world organization.[12]

In Chicago the conference had agreed to create an assembly governed by a twenty-one-member provisional council. Its composition would be based, first, on each member's involvement in the aviation industry; second, on the state's willingness to provide international civil air-navigation facilities; and only lastly on the need to respect regional diversity. A supplementary section read: "Any member State not a member of the Council may participate in the deliberations of the Council whenever a decision is to be taken which especially concerns such member states."[13]

Lester Pearson shared Reid's optimism. When an unexpected and accidental misrepresentation of the Canadian view on Dumbarton Oaks appeared in the *New York Times* and raised questions about Canada's commitment to the world organization, he urged his government to proceed aggressively and present a detailed statement of its problems with the great-power proposals.[14] In his reply, Norman Robertson counselled caution. On 20 December 1944 he reported to Pearson that the Canadian government was indeed preparing a public response to Dumbarton Oaks. It would stress "the position of important secondary states" by focusing specifically on "the necessity of associating with Council decisions states not represented on the Council which are required to participate actively in their execution" and "the desirability of establishing standards for selection of non-permanent Council members."[15]

The undersecretary divulged this confidential information to make Pearson – who had been left out of much of the policy-planning process – feel included. He hoped that, this way, his colleague would delay commenting publicly until the department had released its own statement. In Washington, Robertson's message was interpreted instead as permission to speak openly on these themes. On 28 December, at the Winnipeg Canadian Club, Pearson preempted the official Canadian response to Dumbarton Oaks. After acknowledging the supremacy of the great powers, he proposed that "function, rather than status [determine] membership on international executive agencies."[16] The general assembly's authority had to be enhanced, and the great-power veto had to be limited. Finally, he formally introduced what John Holmes has described as "the right of consent,"[17] the idea that security-council decisions should initially be binding only on its current members. The speech was reprinted in the *Winnipeg Free Press* the next day and commented on extensively in Washington.

When he found out what Pearson had done, Robertson was furious. According to one member of the US Office of European Affairs, "he said he would have to tell Mr. Pearson that Ambassadors just can't sound off at will on such subjects." The King government was not prepared to see Canada acting so assertively in the public eye.[18] More cynically, but equally convincingly, Jack Hickerson later wrote: "Pearson's pretty frank comments in this speech disturbed his bosses in the Department of External Affairs somewhat. I think this was due chiefly to their feeling that he would steal the thunder of their memorandum to us."[19]

What probably frustrated Robertson most was that the memorandum was on its way. Just two days after the speech in Winnipeg, Hume Wrong completed a draft Canadian response to the Dumbarton Oaks proposals. The similarities between it and Pearson's comments were overwhelming. On middle powers, Wrong wrote, "the proposals recognize the primary responsibility of the great powers for the maintenance of peace by according them permanent membership in the Security Council and requiring their individual concurrence in certain classes of decisions. They do not, however, recognize any difference between the responsibilities of other members of the United Nations despite the fact that their power and capacity to use it for the maintenance of peace range from almost zero upwards to a point not very far behind the great powers." Wrong also articulated the same two key elements of the Canadian middle power campaign: states that were not represented on the UNSC could not be obligated to execute security-council resolutions, and a means had to be developed to distinguish the middle powers during the selection of nonpermanent members.[20]

The draft received enthusiastic approval across most of Ottawa. Only the meticulous legal mind of John Read foresaw difficulties. "The memorandum fails to put forward any satisfactory formula for determining the class of second preference share-holders in the New World," he wrote to Robertson. "I am inclined to the view that no formula can be found ... In these circumstances, I am wondering whether it might not be better to drop the second objective [to recognize middle powers as distinct], or, at any rate, to generalize it and weaken it so that it would not be likely to bring about a disruptive movement in a world conference which might lead to the loss of the first objective [to institutionalize the right of consent]."[21]

If Read had gotten his way, the Canadian proposal would have served only to limit Canada's international responsibilities, not to expand them. It is therefore revealing that his recommendation was rejected. Wrong and Robertson were clearly more cautious than Pearson, but they too were committed to greater national involvement in world affairs. The undersecretary took the proposal to the Cabinet war committee and received its tentative approval on 8 January 1945. After minor revisions, it was released to the great powers.[22]

When Lester Pearson and Escott Reid met with staff in the State Department two days later, they sought, on their own initiative, to respond to John Read's concerns. Without warning their superiors in Ottawa, they suggested a concrete middle power formula. Reid advocated that the United Nations be divided into three categories: the great states, between six and ten secondary powers, and the rest of the member countries. The states in the middle group would occupy four of the six nonpermanent seats on the security council and would be selected based on their ability and willingness to contribute military forces to UN activities. Reid committed his country to working with other interested allies to develop a draft proposal to this end.[23]

While the Americans found the idea intriguing, records of their conversation show that at least one official struggled with the relative value of a small state's willingness to provide the council with a strategic military base versus a direct troop contribution from a larger, more powerful one. To him, as John Read had predicted, it would be impossible to create a list of middle states. It was too difficult to differentiate fairly and consistently between the medium and the small. In response, Pearson reiterated that the Canadian government felt that "the contribution of actual military forces" should be the key criterion, but his comment was not received enthusiastically.[24]

In his report to Ottawa, Pearson wrote optimistically that the State Department officials had been "interested" in Reid's suggestion. When the Americans received the official response from Ottawa on 12 January, however, their new undersecretary of state, Joseph Grew, reiterated the practical and logistical problems that would arise from any attempts to differentiate the nongreat powers.[25]

This did not stop the tenacious Escott Reid. On 23 January he drafted a formal list of fifteen potential middle powers and divided them into three categories: current United Nations (Canada, India, the Netherlands, Brazil, Belgium, Australia, Mexico, Poland, Yugoslavia); neutrals (Spain, Turkey, Argentina); and enemies who would acquire middle power status after a probationary period (Germany, Italy, Japan). But the lack of effective communication between Washington and Ottawa continued. Hume Wrong did not bring Reid's proposal to the Cabinet war committee the next day.[26]

He did, however, travel to Washington himself in February, just prior to the Mexico City Conference. The results of his first meeting with officers from a well-prepared State Department were no different from those produced by Reid's meeting three weeks earlier. In the words of one American who was there:

> It appeared from the discussion that the Canadians were principally preoccupied with obtaining a system of election for the non-permanent members of the Council which would accord a special position to the so-called "middle powers." They felt that their potential contribution to security enforcement should be given recognition in determining the composition of the Security Council. They therefore insisted upon the proposal for a panel of secondary powers from which a certain number of the non-permanent members of the Council would be regularly elected. The effect of this on the remaining states, and the general difficulties as to the functioning of the Organization, were pointed out to them. As a result of this discussion, they became inclined to drop this proposal.[27]

Reid, who also attended the meeting, interpreted its results differently. He insisted that apart from Pasvolsky, Dunn, and Hickerson, "The other United States representatives present indicated, insofar as they took part in the discussion, a lack of understanding of the real nature of the special difficulties of Canada and other intermediate powers and of the solutions which we had tentatively suggested."[28]

Perhaps because he felt this way, Reid, along with Pearson, Wrong, and Arnold Heeney, met privately with Pasvolsky two days later. The American expert on international organization dismissed the middle power idea once more. If there had to be conditions for differentiating the nongreat states, in addition to the Canadian desire to recognize military capacity, they would also have to include "moral leadership" and regional representation. "Once we started spelling out criteria," he warned, "we would find it necessary to add more." Hume Wrong replied that the United Nations might consider excluding certain members from the security council altogether, but his suggestion did not seem to generate much enthusiasm.[29]

In his report to Mackenzie King, Wrong wrote realistically: "I was left with the impression that our memorandum had not been very seriously considered in the State Department but that at least some of our purposes might win their support." The Americans had completely opposed the middle power idea on the grounds that it contradicted the principle of the sovereign equality of all states. Wrong was hopeful that after consulting with the Latin American states in Mexico City the following week, the United States "would not oppose a minor addition to the Charter stating that in electing the non-permanent members of the Council the Assembly should pay due regard to the contribution to the purposes of the Organization of the states chosen." This, he suggested, "would be some improvement."[30]

The Inter-American Conference began on 21 February and lasted until 8 March, culminating in approval of the Act of Chapultepec. The US report explained that "steps were taken ... in developing machinery for united action by the American states in the face of aggression or threat of aggression, whether from within or without [the] hemisphere."[31] Nevertheless, the meeting did not create the "solid Latin American phalanx" that many in Canada and elsewhere had feared. Concerns that the United States might support a Brazilian claim for a permanent seat on the security council seemed unfounded, and no official agreement was reached on a united inter-American approach to the UNSC.[32]

The impact of the Latin American meetings was one of many things on Mackenzie King's mind when he travelled to the United States on 9 March to meet with Franklin Roosevelt. According to one well-informed US official, King was coming to Washington "tried by the animosities aroused by the conscription issue in Canada" and in the midst of planning a reelection campaign. A lack of willing volunteers had caused the prime minister to fully renege on his 1939 pledge not to invoke compulsory military service. While he had successfully forced the resignation of his minister of national defence to prevent an internal political crisis, his party had emerged from the ordeal profoundly shaken. King's visit to the White House was meant to allow him to shift the focus of the Canadian public to international issues on which they could "stand together under his leadership and demonstrate Canada's maturity and increased importance as a nation."[33]

Hume Wrong briefed the prime minister twice before his trip. The first time he spoke generally, stressing the need for the great powers to take the concerns of "the smaller responsible countries" more seriously.[34] Two days later, he was more specific: the proposals left too great a gap between the rights of the great powers and the other states that had made a significant contribution to the war. To remedy this problem, a means had to be devised to ensure that the "more important smaller states" would be elected to the security council more frequently than others like Liberia or El Salvador.[35]

King and Roosevelt seem to have gotten along effortlessly. The prime minister presented the middle power argument, and the president appeared to be sympathetic. Unfortunately, Roosevelt had been speaking, in Lester Pearson's words, "without the papers." The Canadian ambassador later told Gladwyn Jebb that he "did not believe for a moment that the official American attitude would be changed in the least as a result of Mr. Mackenzie King's visit."[36]

Pearson was certainly correct. On 10 April 1945 Leo Pasvolsky sought advice from the American delegation to San Francisco on a proposal to recognize the middle powers as distinct. After a brief discussion, he recommended that it be rejected. The question was brought up again the next day. Once more, America's leading expert on international organization urged that the selection process for nonpermanent security-council members be left to the general assembly. Only if the secondary countries exerted sufficient pressure in San Francisco would the United States consider a short list of criteria, among which would have to be regional representation. The issue arose again in subsequent meetings, but the response was always the same.[37]

On 12 April the US delegation discussed the second half of the Canadian middle power proposal. While one senator suggested that he sympathized with Ottawa's position on the right of consent, once again it was Pasvolsky who insisted that such a stipulation "would have the effect of limiting enforcement measures to the action of great powers." Moreover, when he had mentioned the argument to a number of Canadian representatives, they had been "somewhat shaken in their position," and there had been a similar response at Mexico City. Clearly, with Pasvolsky in charge, Canada would not be able to look to the United States for support on this issue.[38]

The middle power campaign in London was initially more promising. After the first Pearson-Reid discussions in Washington in December 1944, one member of the Dominions Office wrote: "In substance there is much to be said for their view and if it were possible without incredible embarrassment to draw up a list of States which could reasonably be regarded as competent for election to the Security Council to the exclusion of a third category who would not be so regarded as so competent there might be something to be said for this scheme." While the difficulty in devising the list was "probably insurmountable," the DO remained open to a Canadian proposal on the subject.[39]

Canada also had an ally in the Foreign Office. Gladwyn Jebb told John Holmes that "on the subject of the proper representation of the Middle Powers, [he] was in complete sympathy. He agreed that this was more than a question of the rights of the Middle Powers, and that their proper representation would actually strengthen the Security Organisation." Ironically, on the right of consent, an issue on which the Americans instinctively had more sympathy, Holmes found Jebb "less sympathetic."[40]

At the executive level, it was the dominions secretary, Lord Cranborne, who in January first reported to the British War Cabinet that Canada was asserting a strong claim for a category of middle-sized states. The armistice and postwar committee considered the views of the dominion governments in detail one month later. The group reviewed eight options for better recognizing the middle countries, including enlarging the security council to fifteen, drafting specific middle power criteria, assessing states' military capacities, and initiating a system of weighted voting. In the end, it decided that the best chance for a satisfactory agreement would be to create a short list of deserving middle powers and to dedicate four of the six nonpermanent seats on the security council to them.

On the second Canadian point, the right of nonmember states to recuse themselves from security-council decisions upon which they had not been consulted, the committee sided with Jebb. Assuming that the King government had made this request as insurance in case the middle power campaign failed, it concluded that if Canada could be assured consistent representation on the UNSC, this second stipulation would not be necessary. It therefore recommended that London promote the first Canadian proposal and "stand firm" against the second.[41]

After his experience in Washington, Hume Wrong would have preferred the opposite. When he heard of the British decision, he wrote Lester Pearson: "I have the gravest doubts that any such plan will be adopted although I would not be at all inclined to discourage such a plan."[42] In a discussion with Vincent Massey and members of the Dominions Office, he virtually abandoned the idea of specific middle power criteria, suggesting that Canada would have to rely on the general assembly to select the appropriate states to the security council. At San Francisco the Canadian delegates would concentrate on ensuring that non-UNSC members would have "nominally the free choice left to them as to whether or not they [would] take action, military or economic, in accordance with the Council's wishes on any given occasion." Recalling the situation at the old League of Nations, he noted that states whose interests were at stake were always invited to meetings of the executive; there was no reason for things to be different in the new organization.[43]

These comments would have absolutely no impact on the armistice and postwar committee's subsequent discussions. Faced with a world organization comprised of an overwhelming nineteen Latin American states, nine European countries (excluding the United Kingdom itself), and five dominions, the British felt more strongly than ever that the composition of the security council had to be tightly controlled.[44]

Over the next few weeks, both the Foreign and the Dominions Offices explored ways to ensure significant imperial representation on the council. Ideally, one seat would always be reserved for a dominion; however, noted one representative, this "would not satisfy Canada, who as a 'middle' Power would expect more frequent election." Perhaps, then, there could be three categories of states below the Big Four: middle powers, Latin American countries that did not qualify for middle power status, and the remainder. Two states from each group could sit on the security council. Of the dominions, Australia, Canada, and India belonged in the first category. Once again, however, the British realized that "to allot 2 seats only to the 'middle' Powers would not secure the objective, so strongly pressed by the Canadians and others, of securing adequate permanent representation of such Powers on the Council." Moreover, with Brazil and Mexico also classified as middle powers, Latin America would often have three, and perhaps even four, representatives on the UNSC. Finally, this proposal would diminish the positions of New Zealand and South Africa.

The committee considered enlarging the security council from eleven to thirteen. In this system, the number of middle power seats would increase to four. But the United States and Soviet Union had stood firmly against this idea at Dumbarton Oaks, and Anthony Eden himself felt that there were too many practical disadvantages to a larger executive body.

It also briefly discussed reserving half of the nonpermanent seats for the most significant military contributors to the council's activities. Admittedly, a similar process seemed to work effectively at the International Labour Organization (ILO), but the committee struggled to define "exact criteria of military importance," as the ILO had struggled to define criteria of industrial stature.

In the end, the armistice and postwar group recommended that the United Kingdom delegation at San Francisco use what influence it could to support the interests of the dominions, but it did not propose specific criteria for selecting nonpermanent members of the security council. Optimally, there would be three categories of states, and indeed thirteen members of the council, but this was unlikely. It therefore advised the war Cabinet that the United Kingdom should table a list of middle powers only if the entire Commonwealth developed such a proposal in advance. There would be an opportunity to do so at the next conference of Commonwealth leaders in London.[45]

By the time this meeting took place, two other factors had slowed down the middle power campaign. The first was Yalta. Back in the fall of 1944, the Dumbarton Oaks negotiators had not reached an agreement on the right of the Big Four to veto discussion of international disputes to which they were a party. The Soviet Union felt that, to ensure great-power unity, critical comments against any of the permanent members of the security council had to be avoided at all costs. Great Britain and the United States contended that such an affirmation of great-power superiority would cause some of the smaller nations to reject the proposed world organization entirely. Even if they could be convinced to join, warned the American official, James Dunn, they "would do it with a bad grace and would thus gravely injure the whole basic spirit of the organization, which [would have] to be built on the foundation of friendly international co-operation, if it [were] ever to be a success."[46]

In the end, the Anglo-American-Soviet meetings in the Crimea from 4 through 11 February were less important to Canada for solving the veto question than for reinforcing the relative equality of all of the smaller states in the eyes of the great-power leadership. According to the American conference secretary, throughout the negotiations, Churchill claimed to speak "on behalf of the British Commonwealth of Nations, the Empire and, he believed, the Self-Governing Dominions."[47] His attitude contributed to Stalin's insistence that in exchange for his concession on the veto issue, the Ukraine and Byelorussia[48] – two Soviet satellite states – would have to be admitted to the world organization as equal members. Churchill only made matters worse when, in what was likely meant to be a defence of dominion rights, he expressed "great sympathy for the Soviet request." To Stalin, who clearly expected the new entrants to function as Soviet appendages, this reinforced the notion that the United Kingdom maintained a similar relationship with its former colonies.[49]

Great Britain and the United States achieved their goal on the veto but also secretly conceded the membership of the two Soviet republics. While this did not concern Churchill, Franklin Roosevelt feared a possible public backlash against him for allowing both the UK and the USSR multiple votes in the new organization. On 10 February he covertly solicited support for additional representation in the assembly for the United States.[50]

Six weeks later, after rumours of the secret negotiations became public, Canada's ambassador to Moscow, Dana Wilgress, responded with anger and disappointment: "As one of the medium powers uncertain as of our chances of election to the Security Council," he explained, "we are desirous of seeing more authority and influence invested in the Assembly. We certainly do not wish to see it divested of respect by reason of the inclusion of members incapable of expressing a free opinion diverging to the slightest degree from one of the principal permanent members of the Security Council." Despite the risks that might be incurred by alienating the Soviet Union – and, indeed, the United States – at this point in the war, Canada had a moral obligation to object. Norman Robertson conveyed his government's disappointment to Ray Atherton later that week.[51] Nevertheless, on 29 March the White House announced that it would seek two additional votes in the general assembly. Some radical members of the American Senate even argued that Great Britain's six votes justified the decision.[52]

Although Mackenzie King was too busy planning for the upcoming federal election to respond seriously, in Washington an extremely disappointed Lord Halifax suggested that his government encourage public expressions of dominion autonomy throughout the United States. "The local tendency among the uninformed majority," he explained, was "still to regard the independence of Dominions as ... window dressing."[53] This could not help the empire in the future.

But Canada was hardly Great Britain's main concern. The British were adamant that India – a member of the Commonwealth that had not yet been granted independence – be permitted a seat in the assembly, and this claim was particularly vulnerable. To keep India, London would have to make concessions to the somewhat anxious government in Washington.[54]

Fortunately, the American people were divided on the question of additional votes, and the popular press was critical of the secretive nature of the great-power arrangement. Mindful of the importance of public opinion, on 5 April President Roosevelt ended the controversy at a press and radio conference in Georgia. "I am not awfully keen for three votes in the Assembly," he announced, "It is the little fellow who needs the vote in the Assembly." When asked if the inclusive body had any real power, the president – who thought that he was speaking off the record – answered bluntly, "No." Clearly, Roosevelt's position on the role of the small states had not changed. Nevertheless, the United States would have only one vote in the general assembly. The image of the United Nations as an inclusive, democratic body was preserved.[55]

Yalta had a significant impact on the middle power project. By equating its satellites with the British dominions, the Soviet Union officially pronounced its opposition to the concept of secondary states. To Stalin, there were the Big Four and then everyone else. Moreover, as Wilgress observed, the Soviets would "be suspicious of attempts on the part of the other two great powers to assure the election of countries [to the UNSC] likely to support the policies of that power."[56] The unwillingness of the leading Western allies to stand up to this declaration made the Canadian campaign that much more difficult.

The struggle was compounded by Canada's refusal, and also inability, to assume the role (that so many had already wrongly ascribed to it) of leader of the secondary states. Australia was the first country to look to Canada as the primary international spokesperson on small-state rights. In early November 1944, the day after a *Sydney Daily Telegraph* article had noted the failure of a series of independent Australian proposals to gain broad acceptance, Foreign Minister Herbert Evatt told Canada's high commissioner in

New Zealand, Walter Riddell, that he was depending on the King government to "continue to lead the fight for the Dominions." He promised his country's support for any initiative that might further the position of the Commonwealth states in a future international organization.[57] The Department of External Affairs did not issue a formal response.

On 27 December, Norman Robertson did report that Doctor Eelco van Kleffens, the able foreign minister from the Netherlands, had made a point of conveying his view that the Dumbarton Oaks proposals "did not make adequate provision for associating the Middle Powers with decisions of the Security Council, to which they would be expected to give effect." Van Kleffens even went so far as to propose that the Canadians, Dutch, Belgians, and Brazilians join forces to promote the middle power position. Mackenzie King noted, "I agree with him," but once again no formal action was taken.[58]

The problem was not necessarily that Canada was uninterested but rather that it lacked the resources to lead. It was not until mid-January 1945, for example, that Hume Wrong finally completed arrangements to allow the Canadian high commissioners complete access to documents travelling between Ottawa and their offices. Even then, he admitted, the letters would lack context. The additional material could not be included without Great Britain's expressed permission.[59]

The British were comfortable releasing such documentation to the rest of the Commonwealth, but over the next three to four months, the dominion officials were so busy becoming acquainted with one another's positions on Dumbarton Oaks that they had little time to develop any real sense of ideological unity. At first, for example, South Africa opposed the middle power idea in its entirety. It took until the end of January, with some good work from Lester Pearson, to bring Smuts on side. Poor communication also meant that a proposal from the Canadian high commissioner in Australia to create a list of middle powers was never passed on to Pearson or Escott Reid even though they were developing similar ideas at the same time. A plan from the office in New Zealand was similarly neglected in early March.[60]

Effective cooperation was even more tenuous with the Dutch and the Belgians, two peoples who aspired to middle power status at least as fervently as the Canadians. As he did with the national representatives in the other Commonwealth countries, in mid-January 1945 Hume Wrong finally obtained permission to grant the European foreign ministers access to Canadian memoranda on the Dumbarton Oaks proposals.[61] To follow up, his senior assistant, John Holmes, met with van Kleffens. The foreign minister told Holmes that "he could not see why some formula might not be achieved to provide proper representation for the Middle Powers." The Canadians seemed interested, but it would be two more weeks before Ottawa received the official Dutch memorandum. Throughout March, van Kleffens sought a meeting with senior level Canadian authorities to compare ideas, but the best External Affairs could do was to promise to arrange a discussion with Hume Wrong in April, just days before the San Francisco Conference was set to begin.[62]

Discussions with Belgium were even less fulfilling. The Department of External Affairs did not receive comments from Brussels on the Dumbarton Oaks proposals until 14 February. The report echoed the Canadian functionalist line almost verbatim, but it still took nearly three weeks to organize a meeting between the two countries' negotiators. On 5 March 1945 Charles Ritchie, not Vincent Massey, had lunch with the chargé d'affaires at the Belgian embassy. The two differed over the importance of regional organizations within the new global body, and no plans were made for a follow-up conversation. Norman Robertson was shown a final report on the state of public opinion in Belgium two weeks later, but nothing seems to have come of it.[63]

Communication with the Latin American countries was no better. On 18 February 1945 Robertson received a letter from the Chilean government proposing a specific formula to differentiate the middle powers. The plan was quite well thought out. Of the six nonpermanent members of the security council, three would be selected to serve fixed terms based exclusively on their capacity and willingness to contribute to international security. Canada, Brazil, and a European country would take the positions first. The other three members could be selected based on what were called "other considerations." Even though the proposal was quite thorough, Charles Ritchie scribbled on the document: "This is not much of a contribution to our thinking on the subject! I suppose it might be circulated as suggested and filed away unless you [Wrong] think that Robertson should see it."[64] With more staff and improved communication, Ritchie might have learned that the Americans had considered the Chilean proposals in considerable detail.[65] There is no evidence to suggest that this ever happened.

Moreover, even though External Affairs was conscious of the sympathies of the American leadership, particularly of President Roosevelt, toward Latin America, Canada paid no more, and perhaps even less, attention to proposals from Mexico, Brazil, and Cuba. Government officials generally relied on what were condescending and rather insensitive analyses provided by their British counterparts. Overall, as Norman Robertson told Ray Atherton, "there had been very little study in Canada and none in official circles of the Act of Chapultepec."[66]

There appeared to be another potentially meaningful opportunity for cooperation when France reached out to the small powers in early 1945. In a national interview, Minister of Foreign Affairs Georges Bidault asked rhetorically: "is it desirable, is it logical, that ... nations farthest removed from the danger under consideration, whose military and economic contribution is the least, should have exactly the same voice in the Council as those nations directly exposed, and those whose resources make them pre-eminently responsible for security? I do not think so."[67] In February, according to a British report, Paris accepted "the Canadian thesis that the more important secondary powers should have some sort of special position." External Affairs was aware of the French stance, but it appears that it lacked both the will and the capacity to respond proactively.[68]

Given America's lack of interest, the Soviet Union's lack of support, and Canada's lack of resources, the middle power campaign now hinged on the full backing of the Commonwealth, led by Great Britain. After Yalta, on 22 February the Dominions Office invited Canada and the rest of the dominions to London "to ensure fullest discussion and mutual understanding" of the goals of the Commonwealth in San Francisco.[69] Mackenzie King accepted the invitation but warned that the discussions would not commit his government to any joint Commonwealth position at the conference that was to follow. Moreover, with a federal election just months away and a foreign-policy debate set to begin in Parliament, the Canadian prime minister could not spare any members of his government. Vincent Massey and Hume Wrong were placed in charge.[70]

As might have been expected, the Conservative press viewed the conference as one last opportunity to form a unified imperial position on world organization. An editorial in the *Globe* read: "It would be calamitous if [the Commonwealth] representatives should enter the San Francisco conference without being able to demonstrate that commonality of outlook and purpose is possible, and without some arrangement for their close co-operation in the solution of issues." Clearly, however, King's unwillingness to send a Cabinet-level representative overseas was designed in part to show that Canada would be acting alone in San Francisco. To be certain that Canadian independence had been affirmed, Massey was instructed not to make any commitments.[71]

The British were also divided. Most of the staff in the Dominions Office believed that if the Commonwealth failed to cooperate at the meeting, its power and influence would decline significantly, as would Britain's international position. The Foreign Office, however, still felt that the United Kingdom could stand on its own as a great power. On 28 March, when the Department of State suggested that the four sponsoring powers present a united front at San Francisco by agreeing to clear any substantive changes to the Dumbarton Oaks proposals among themselves before bringing them forward to the rest of the conference, Eden's group was inclined to agree.[72]

The dispute between the Foreign and Dominions Offices was sent to the armistice and postwar committee. During its discussion, Cranborne and Eden reached a compromise: Great Britain would not put forth significant amendments to Dumbarton Oaks until it had "at least *tried to* [clear] them with the Americans and Russians."

The first major change that they planned to propose to the great powers divided the candidates for the six nonpermanent positions on the security council into three categories. Category "A" included eight states "provisionally selected on a rather arbitrary basis, but with regard to their population, their overseas possessions, and their trade." Canada and Australia represented the dominions. Four of the positions were reserved for these eight states at all times. Category "B" was made up of the remaining seventeen Latin American countries. One of these members would always sit on the security council. Finally, one member would be selected from the final seventeen United Nations. Cranborne acknowledged that this proposal would likely frustrate the representatives of both South Africa and New Zealand, which would be relegated to category "C"; however, the possibility that this arrangement could give the British leverage over Canada on other issues, including the right of consent, made it worthwhile.

Along with the plan came one caveat. Since the idea was controversial, and because it served Canada's interests more than any other country's, Cranborne suggested that it be up to the representatives from Ottawa to initiate the negotiations. Only after a Canadian middle power proposal had been considered by the entire Commonwealth would the British circulate their position paper, "modified as necessary in the light of the discussion."[73]

A somewhat reluctant Cranborne drafted a memorandum to this effect for the British War Cabinet. On 3 April, the day before the London meetings were set to begin, the war Cabinet rejected the briefing. The minutes of the meeting note that "it was suggested that a better basis for election to the non-permanent seats on the Security Council would be to provide that all members of the Organisation other than the five Great Powers [which included France] should be equally eligible, but that the six non-permanent seats should be filled by electing one Member State from each of the six main territorial groups, viz. Europe, Asia, Africa, Australasia, South America and North and Central America." The dominions secretary was also ordered to resist the Canadian proposal to limit the obligations of any United Nation not represented on the security council.[74]

The Cabinet's decision hardly mattered. From the very first Commonwealth meeting on 4 April, Canada's three-person delegation of Vincent Massey, Hume Wrong, and John Holmes made it clear that it had no intention of being part of a Commonwealth bloc.[75] The Canadians were also perfectly happy to allow the other dominions to dominate the discussion. When Massey failed to mention the middle power idea in his opening address, it was up to Herbert Evatt to introduce the concept of what he called "Security Powers," and it fell to Jan Smuts to express sympathy for Mackenzie King's public declarations that Canada was "not far from being one of the Great Powers."[76]

Massey and Wrong put forward their country's concerns on 5 April but did not offer any concrete suggestions on the middle power issue. The next day, Evatt reiterated his belief in the "need to recognise the distinctive position of the nations which are coming to be called the 'middle Powers,' but which, in effect, belong (like the five Great Powers) to what may be called the 'Security Powers.'" Again, he did not suggest any specific criteria to differentiate these states.[77]

On 9 April the conference discussed the middle power idea in greater detail. Lord Cranborne expressed the war Cabinet's position and then invited the Canadian government "to reopen the issue." Massey spoke in rather vague terms of the need to recognize middle, or "security," powers. "It was not a question of prestige or status," he explained. "The Canadian attitude was based upon the opinion that power and the ability of responsibility should be recognised." His government could not understand how "the view could be accepted that there should be parity between the Dominions and like states on the one hand, and countries like the smaller South American republics and Liberia on the other." Wrong added his government's second point: "Decisions of the Security Council should be binding in the first place only on Members of the Council and on such other states as had specifically undertaken to assist in carrying them out."

The Canadians received support from Evatt, but Smuts thought that it might be best to put off any restrictions to the power or composition of the UNSC. Britain's deputy prime minister, Clement Attlee, agreed and then formally proposed that representation be determined on a regional basis. This approach, which divided the seats by continent, would allow the states of the Commonwealth to occupy as many as four of the nonpermanent positions at one time. When further discussion failed to generate consensus, Cranborne referred Attlee's suggestion to a committee of experts.[78]

The smaller group leaned toward the ideas of the old armistice and postwar committee. When asked if there should be criteria for election to the security council, it concluded:

If power and responsibility are to be made to correspond to the maximum extent it seems that on the whole the best plan would be to adopt some criterion for the election of "middle Powers." A formula might be found on the following lines:

"The necessary qualifications for the six non-permanent seats on the Council should be the war potential of the member States, coupled with their willingness to place their military resources at the disposal of the Security Council and with their actual performance in this World War and the last."

This would lead to the drawing up of a list of states in order of qualification. This should be divided into a shorter and longer list, the former containing the States best qualified for membership on the Security Council; and it should be provided that not less than four of the six non-permanent members should be elected from the States in the shorter list. This solution, while giving a better chance of election to the better qualified States, would also not deprive the smaller and less important States of the possibility of ever being elected. It would, however, be necessary at each election to ensure that the various geographical areas of the world were as far as possible represented.[79]

Later that day, Cadogan reported back to the entire conference. After devoting "considerable time to the consideration of criteria for the purposes of qualifying for election to the Security Council," the committee had concluded that "no criteria offered a solution; a combination of criteria was necessary." Therefore, it was best to revert to the original United Kingdom line from Dumbarton Oaks: at San Francisco, the British representatives would argue once again that, in nominating members for the security council, "due regard should be paid to the contribution of members towards the maintenance of international peace and security"; they would also encourage the United Nations to establish "some body to consider ways and means of ensuring that suitable Powers were elected."

Later, Hume Wrong defended the rights of nonmember states to opt out of council decisions if they were not consulted one final time. Cranborne agreed that without the provision, the smaller countries would have to place a degree of faith in the decisions of the great powers; he argued, however, that if they did not do so, the world organization would fail, creating a real risk of another war. Wrong attempted to respond, but Evatt joined the dominions secretary in condemning what was coming across as a rather isolationist Canadian position. Fittingly, the meeting therefore ended without an agreement.

Upon reflection, Wrong was satisfied. The results of the conference were, he thought, "as good a proposal as I expected we could get."[80] And while *Le Devoir* still maintained that "Le conférence impériale ... constitue peut-être la meilleure preuve contre l'admission du Canada dans la société des nations,"[81] those who were there disagreed. One British secretary wrote to his Canadian counterpart, Arnold Heeney: "Our feeling is that they have been immensely worth while. The talk has been very frank and friendly, and while all differences have not been resolved, at least the delegations will all go to San Francisco with a much greater understanding and sympathy with each other's point of view than would otherwise have been the case ... we have got sufficient unity of outlook and ideals to be able to stand a ... few healthy difficulties without getting too much excited about it."[82] Vincent Massey's official report was similar. The meeting, he explained, "provided a useful example of Commonwealth machinery functioning for mutual advantage."[83] Moreover, there remained a hope that in the future, a middle power list would be developed.

This hope was the final relic of a campaign that never stood a real chance. When it came to international security, the Canadian government was far less committed to the middle power project than the general public would have ever believed, and the Department of External Affairs lacked both the will and the resources to translate the passion of its most optimistic and ambitious civil servants into a large-scale, policy-oriented small-state coalition. The Soviet Union did not tolerate lesser-power suggestions, and its great-power allies, while more sympathetic, were not prepared to sacrifice their own pressing interests for the sake of Canada and other like-minded states. Furthermore, as similar in approach as these states might have been, they still struggled to share and develop their ideas effectively. When it came to postwar thinking in Ottawa, there was a widening gap between the desirable and the achievable. As San Francisco drew closer, and as the general public's enthusiasm for Canadian leadership continued to increase, the discrepancy would grow even larger.

9

The Public Road to San Francisco (October 1944–April 1945)

On 6 January 1945 a Canadian Institute of Public Opinion (CIPO) poll showed that 90 percent of people nationwide, and even 79 percent of Quebec residents, believed that Canada should join the new international organization after the war.[1] Three days later, when Grant Dexter tried to discuss this finding with Mackenzie King, he found the Canadian prime minister disappointingly noncommittal. "Had a long talk with King," he wrote to his associate George Ferguson. "Unfortunately he got going on the conscription crisis and most of my time was spent listening to his account thereof. Mighty interesting and exceedingly frank but not helpful."[2] The *Winnipeg Free Press* journalist was not alone in his frustration. Earlier, Vincent Massey had complained that "the crisis in Ottawa" had "brought all postponeable activity at External Affairs to a dead standstill."[3]

The irritation was understandable; at a time when the Canadian public was more interested than ever in the future of the world, the prime minister seemed to be absorbed by domestic politics. The appearance, however, was deceiving. While the question of conscription did return to haunt the government in the late fall of 1944, King had in fact made a personal commitment to the new world organization in a Cabinet meeting just before the trouble began. He was deliberately "hold[ing] back information from the public," he admitted in his diary, in an attempt to manage the national enthusiasm.[4] Relations among the great powers, whose unity would determine the success of any global body, were deteriorating rapidly, and the popular middle power idea, fast becoming the rallying point for international activists across the country, was no longer the focus of the Canadian diplomatic campaign. Led by Hume Wrong, the more pragmatic element in the Department of External Affairs had begun to concentrate on the less glamorous task of increasing the strength of the new world organization's Economic and Social Council (ECOSOC).

When King finally addressed foreign policy in the House of Commons in March 1945, he did so with a cautious optimism that was hardly appreciated by the over sixty elected representatives who took part in the debate. Many of them, caught up in a wave of national pride that was reinforced by an equally idealistic news media, remained unshaken in their belief that Canada would play a leading role at the San Francisco Conference. With a national election pending, Mackenzie King saw little reason to correct them.[5]

In late 1944 the Canadian Institute of International Affairs (CIIA) recommitted itself to internationalist activism and launched a renewed effort to stimulate discussion of the postwar world. Gathering momentum from the publication of Grant Dexter's Montebello document, *Canada and the Building of Peace*, the institute's *Behind the Headlines* series published a set of pamphlets by noted scholars and journalists that discussed and evaluated the future world organization. Members and supporters also increased their public speaking engagements.[6]

To reach a wider audience, Malcolm W. Wallace, the new CIIA president, chaired a project co-managed by the Canadian Association for Adult Education and the Canadian Broadcasting Corporation. Using the now long-running "Citizens' Forum" radio program as its medium, in February 1945 the group presented a four-part series entitled "Can We Build a Lasting Peace?" During the final episode, citizens from British Columbia, Manitoba, Ontario, and Quebec all agreed that Canadians would have to cooperate actively with the rest of the international community to ensure the success of the new world organization.[7]

Canada's National Film Board (NFB) was making a similar point. By 1945 its two successful theatrical series, "World in Action" and "Canada Carries On," were playing in over 600 English-language and 60 French-language theatres. The films were so popular that they were eventually distributed throughout the United States, Great Britain, and Latin America. In Washington the new American assistant secretary of state, Archibald MacLeish, even requested that the NFB's commissioner, John Grierson, produce a film about Dumbarton Oaks for the United States government.[8]

The documentary was meant to present the negotiations as a great success, but the reality was more worrisome. Differences were emerging among the great powers, and many were beginning to wonder whether they could ever be reconciled. "The danger, as I see it," wrote one perceptive member of the American Council on Foreign Relations,

> is that policy will be defended on purely ideological grounds ... Obviously the Russians and the British and the Chinese and we Americans are not fighting for the same kind of postwar world. The Russians are thinking about the future of the proletariat; the British are concerned with the preservation of the monarchy at home and in as many other countries as possible; the Chinese Government wants to get rid of the Communists; and Americans

want to get the Germans and Japs defeated as quickly as possible so they can get back home and turn their attention to reconversion and full employment. The only aim, it seems to me, on which we are all agreed is the speedy defeat of the Germans.[9]

The Big Three attempted to resolve their differences at Yalta in February 1945. Although they did manage to set a firm date for a general conference of the United Nations on international organization, the Western allies left the Crimea as worried as they were relieved. In a personal letter to President Roosevelt in mid-March, Winston Churchill reflected: "When the war of the giants is over ... there will be a torn, ragged and hungry world to help to its feet; and what will U.J.[10] or his successor say to the way we should both like to do it?"[11]

The following week, Stalin announced that military responsibilities would preclude his internationally prominent and well-respected foreign minister, Vyacheslav Molotov, from leading the Soviet delegation to San Francisco. He would be replaced by the relatively junior ambassador to the United States, A.A. Gromyko. In London, Churchill worried that Molotov's absence would cause a "deplorable" public impression.[12] In Washington, Adolf Berle agreed, calling the situation "anything but promising." Without Molotov the Soviet delegation would lack the authority necessary to negotiate realistically, and the conference would likely deteriorate into "meaningless generalities about words, and actually become a sparring match for position in the great play-off."[13]

Among the well-informed, expectations of San Francisco were changing quickly. Britain's deputy prime minister, Clement Attlee, spoke publicly of the need for "compromise and mutual concession" as he warned a radio audience that the road to peace would not be as smooth as once thought. The *New York Times* published an article shortly afterward with the headline "San Francisco Issues Are Now Foreshadowed: Observers Question Whether the Public Realizes the Difficulties to Be Met."[14] While time might have helped to alleviate the tension among the great powers, to delay the meeting until some of their issues had been resolved was impossible. As Anthony Eden explained to the dominions in London that spring, while neither he nor Churchill wanted the conference to begin on 25 April, "the United States had set their heart on it and for obvious reasons it was very difficult to oppose them." Furthermore, he added, any delay at this point could have only a "lamentable effect on world public opinion."[15]

Nevertheless, the Canadian general public remained optimistic. Immediately following the announcement of the San Francisco Conference, the *Winnipeg Free Press* declared that Yalta had marked "a turning point in the world's history."[16] "The world organization now to be born," it claimed, "is destined, at least by the hopes of countless millions, to be the guardian of the future peace of the world."[17] For once the *Globe and Mail* agreed. "The conference at Yalta," the editors wrote, "has produced valuable fruits ... It has made further and promising progress toward laying the foundations of a new world order which will guarantee peace and security for the world."[18] In Quebec *La Presse* was also generally positive.[19]

Not everyone had been fooled. Even before Yalta, a leading member of the CIIA, Edgar J. Tarr, wrote a friend at Harvard University: "So far as the world in general is concerned, I find it increasingly difficult to remain optimistic. It seems to me that an attitude of defeatism regarding the postwar world is spreading, with the result that thought in most countries is being centred on second bests, and that this in itself makes less likely the development of a broadly based internationalism, political and economic. Unless this trend is reversed in the near future, I shudder to think of the consequences."[20] Lester Pearson was similarly worried. At San Francisco, he reported to Norman Robertson, it would be difficult to reconcile the Soviet and American approaches to world order.[21] Himself far less positive by nature, Hume Wrong had become openly pessimistic. The results of San Francisco, he told Dana Wilgress, would hinge on the freedom and the willingness of the Soviet delegation to compromise. If Molotov could not come, it would be "a long, quarrelsome and unproductive conference."[22]

All three did what they could to improve the situation. Tarr and the CIIA had some success reaching out to the academic elite. At the same time, Lester Pearson pressed on, relatively unsuccessfully, with the middle power campaign. Hume Wrong chose a less popular course. Unlike Pearson, who had told the US State Department that "the Economic and Social Council should not be too closely defined in the Charter," Wrong had come to believe that the ECOSOC discussions would be the best place for Canada to make a significant impact. In mid-January he sought permission to establish a group tasked specifically with developing proposals in response to the economic and social aspects of Dumbarton Oaks.[23]

His request was approved. On 2 February, Wrong met with Robertson, Charles Ritchie, and a number of Canada's most senior economic officials to discuss the future role of the Economic and Social Council in the new world organization. While the meeting did not reach any specific conclusions, it did leave Wrong with ideas to bring up in Washington the following week. During his discussions with members of the State Department, the associate undersecretary discovered that the Americans – who had shown less interest in economic and social problems – were willing to be more flexible on the provisions governing ECOSOC than they were on security matters. He therefore advised his government once again to spend more time on the nonmilitary issues as it prepared for San Francisco. When he returned home, Wrong acted upon his own recommendations by drafting a lengthy memorandum on the economic and social aspects of the future world organization.[24]

These issues were also being considered by Canada's most important allies. In March 1945 the British Foreign Office suggested that, unlike the rules governing representation on the security council, membership on ECOSOC might be determined by the same functional criteria that were used in the International Labour Organization. That same day, on behalf of Roosevelt and Stettinius, Churchill's old friend Bernard Baruch arrived in London to convince the hesitant British prime minister of the benefits of an economic and social council. Just seventy-two hours later, Lester Pearson reported that the State Department had begun to emphasize the work of ECOSOC in its radio broadcasts. And while the Canadian ambassador himself still felt that the council was "far too complicated a subject" to deal with in San Francisco, Lord Halifax reported that the normally recalcitrant United States was (grudgingly) prepared to discuss the proposal in detail.[25]

Mackenzie King must have been pleased. His book *Industry and Humanity* had stressed the importance of economic security to world order, and the Canadian public was supportive of all efforts at reconstruction, be they at home or abroad. Whatever pleasure he might have felt, however, he hid. After quietly tabling the Dumbarton Oaks proposals in Parliament on 5 December 1944, the prime minister turned his attention back to the question of conscription. The debate ended successfully on 8 December, but still, aside from a brief mention of the importance of winning the peace in the throne speech on 31 January 1945, King refused to discuss the new world order through much of February. In his analysis of the period, John Holmes suggests that the prime minister "preferred not to confuse Parliament or the public by provoking public debate on foreign policy."[26] It is more likely that King deliberately allowed the situation to remain unclear; knowing the truth about the great-power struggles could have provoked panic within a country still emerging from a divisive domestic debate. The Liberal leader was equally coy about the composition of the Canadian delegation to San Francisco. Although he confirmed Norman Robertson's list of suggested participants toward the end of February, he postponed announcing his choices, or even conceding that they had been made, until after the next House debate on external affairs.[27]

Anticipation of this debate began to build on 5 March when the government reported that it had received its invitation to San Francisco from the Big Four. The offer was accepted before Parliament, or even the Cabinet, was consulted. On 16 March, after a brief visit to Washington, King submitted a draft parliamentary resolution to his senior ministers. They approved it quickly.[28]

Three days later, the government introduced a motion in Parliament that launched what one historian has called "the most comprehensive and extended debate on foreign policy in Canadian history."[29] The resolution read:

1 that this house endorses the acceptance by the government of Canada of the invitation to send representatives to the conference;
2 that this house recognizes that the establishment of an effective international organization for the maintenance of international peace and security is of vital importance to Canada, and, indeed to the future well-being of man-kind; and that it is in the interests of Canada that Canada should become a member of such an organization;
3 that this house approves the purposes and principles set forth in the proposals of the four governments, and considers that these proposals constitute a satisfactory basis for a discussion of the charter of the proposed international organization;
4 that this house agrees that the representatives of Canada at the conference should use their best endeavours to further the preparation of an acceptable charter for an international organization for the maintenance of international peace and security;
5 that the charter establishing the international organization should, before ratification, be submitted to parliament for approval.[30]

While, only ten days earlier, King had expressed concern in his diary about "not beginning to know the things I ought to know in meeting Parliament in the coming weeks and being prepared for the San Francisco Conference,"[31] when he spoke to the motion on 20 March, he appeared far better informed, or at least more realistically so, than the vast majority of his colleagues.

"Next to winning the war," the prime minister began, "the supreme end to be achieved is the winning of the peace." He stressed the need to make the new organization palatable to the great powers. Without them, it would not survive. With them, however, unlike the League of Nations, the new global body would be able to act "instantly and effectively" in times of need.

King assured the House that Canada would have a prominent and useful role in the economic and social activities of the council. He then reminded his colleagues that "the humanitarian tradition which has played so worthy a part in our national life should give us a special interest in worldwide social betterment which the assembly and the economic and social council will seek to foster."

In his subsequent discussion of security, the prime minister was deliberately vague. Based on the functional principle, the great powers would be primarily responsible for military matters. That said, there was a difference between the smallest states and the "important secondary countries," and the Canadian representatives would work hard "to secure due recognition of their relative standing among the nations of the world." King refused to provide any detail on how they might do this, noting only, as had the British, that "some method of selection which would have due regard for the power and responsibility of secondary states would make the [security] council a more powerful and efficient body." He then added: "In considering this great plan for organizing peace, it is all-important that we think broadly and take a long view. The benefits which Canada may hope to gain from full participation in the organization are immense. They should not be weighted merely in terms of prestige. No country has a greater interest than ours in the prevention of another general war. That is our overriding consideration." Clearly, Canada's primary role at San Francisco would be to foster harmony among the great powers. Any other interests would be secondary.[32]

Caught somewhat unprepared, the Conservatives delayed their official response. It was therefore the Co-operative Commonwealth Federation (CCF) that offered the first detailed reply. Canada's social democratic party promised the government its full support. Like King, M.J. Coldwell was tentative about the possibility of establishing a concrete middle power formula and conceded that for the sake of world peace, Canada might "have to accept something short for the time being of what we desire." His conclusion, however, was far less reserved and launched a wave of Canadian nationalistic rhetoric that shifted the focus of the debate. Before sitting down, Coldwell proclaimed: "Canada is recognized as a leader – I almost said the leader – among the secondary nations."[33]

Paul Martin, soon to join the Cabinet as secretary of state, followed by calling Canada "one of the leading middle nations." Instead of echoing King's emphasis on the need for unity among the great powers, Martin concluded: "Canada, as a middle power, must be assured that it can bring its case before the world assembly or world council. We must be assured that settlement by the greater powers will not be made arbitrarily at our expense."[34]

This more assertive nationalistic tone was adopted by the majority of the English-speaking Liberal representatives who followed. On 22 March, Arthur Roebuck argued that Canadian support would be integral to any military action by the security council. The member from Toronto maintained that if France and China had earned great-power status, then Canada deserved it as well.[35] Later that day, J.J. McCann called Canada "a fighting world power" and "one of the most important nations of the world."[36] The Liberal member from Brant, Ontario, went even further, misconstruing the comments of his prime minister to suggest that King himself had supported calls for a permanent Canadian place on the security council.[37] Even Brooke Claxton seemed to misunderstand Mackenzie King when he suggested that for Canada "to serve humanity," it need not "sacrifice [its] own national interests."[38]

The Conservative House leader, Gordon Graydon, was slightly less inflated. He too argued that Canada stood "head and shoulders above all nations other than the great powers in her capacity to make a contribution to the maintenance of peace," but rather than using this claim to justify greater Canadian standing or influence, he proposed only that his country had a moral duty to increase its commitment to active participation in world affairs. Canadians could no longer pursue "an ostrich-like course in time of peace only to pull our heads out of the sand at the last minute and find that we are in a war."[39]

Unfortunately for King and the Liberals, Howard Green and most of the rest of the Conservatives had a different agenda. The imperialist member from Vancouver South decried the lack of permanent Canadian representation on the United Nations Security Council as "humiliating," given his country's military and economic contribution to the war. Instead of demanding independent representation, Green accused the King government of "dodging, twisting and turning to get away from a permanent Commonwealth seat, with the result that Canada is not to get her rightful place in this world organization." "The Canadian people," he argued, were "not interested in having Canada declared a middle-sized nation or a secondary state, but they [were] interested in Canada's developing into a great world power, standing beside Great Britain and the other dominions in the British empire." These views were echoed by a number of Green's Conservative colleagues and then refuted by some of King's Liberal front- and backbenchers.[40]

The smaller parliamentary parties were generally more cooperative. Fred Rose of the Labour Progressives[41] made a thoughtful speech in favour of greater Canadian independence and activism in world affairs. "Canada's new stature as a power," he said, "should find expression at San Francisco."[42] The comments of John Blackmore from the Social Credit Party were hardly comprehensible, but at least he promised that his group would vote in favour of the government resolution.[43]

Two female members of Parliament (MPs), Cora Casselman and Louise Nielson, spoke positively during the debate. Casselman, a Liberal, recounted the general public's extensive and increasing interest in world affairs. She then finished: "I do not speak officially for women; I cannot do that. But I do know that women throughout this land will feel that a world security organization is an answer in some measure to their longing to have done with war."[44]

A majority of members from French Canada also backed the government. The comments of the most idiosyncratic of the Quebec representatives, the Independent-Liberal Jean François Pouliot, were (for once) relatively typical. He condemned the prime minister for waiting so long to hold a debate on external relations, but eventually admitted that he would vote in favour of the resolution.[45]

Only five nationalist Quebec MPs, clearly scarred by the government's recent decision to impose conscription, opposed the motion. Liguori Lacombe argued unsuccessfully (and incorrectly) that since Parliament's legal term would end on 17 April, and the meeting of the United Nations was not set to begin until 25 April, any Canadian negotiating team in San Francisco would lack the necessary mandate to represent the country. Moreover, he added, it was time for Canada to turn its focus inward. Fellow Independent Frédéric Dorion agreed.[46]

J. Emmanuel d'Anjou, a Liberal, and J. Sasseville Roy, an Independent-Conservative, claimed that Canadians had no business at San Francisco because of their inexperience in world affairs and in peacemaking particularly. Liberal MP Wilfrid Lacroix was even more suspicious: "We shall see," he predicted, "after this war, communistic influence permeate the whole of Europe and if Canada approves the purposes and principles set forth in the proposals already framed at Yalta, it means for us a war in which we shall inevitably be involved within ten or fifteen years."[47] His comments, like those of his colleagues, were generally dismissed by all but the most radical and isolationist French Canadians.

Mackenzie King closed the lengthy debate on 28 March. In a two-hour address, he reiterated his plea for caution. Those who thought that Canada belonged with the great powers at Dumbarton Oaks were mistaken: "Too many cooks sometimes spoil the broth, and to have the representatives of the great powers meet in the first instance and see what they could do was I think the successful and wise way of proceeding," he explained. He also rejected the calls for formal Commonwealth cooperation, citing its potentially damaging impact on national unity. Finally, the prime minister addressed the middle power question. Any assumption of "an alleged desire on the part of the Canadian government to see Canada enrolled among the middle powers" was "unfounded." Indeed, the country had interests beyond its borders, but its contribution to the world order could not "be measured by counting heads."[48] When the House voted, 202 MPs supported the motion, and only the five Quebec nationalists stood against.

King's warnings could not dampen the ever-increasing expectations and enthusiasm that were being played up by the national media. The first article on the parliamentary debate in *La Presse* focused exclusively on functionalism and the prime minister's alleged "bel idéalisme." It made no mention of the Economic and Social Council.[49] The *Free Press* emphasized how Canada had "grown mightily in the eyes of her own people" and went so far as to say: "We are not a Great Power in the sense that we could hope to survive for even a few days in a war with the United States or Russia. But there is an element of greatness in Canada's power. It is an element compounded of tolerance, of sober confidence, of realistic understanding of the world, of a will to be friendly with all nations and of a quiet faith in the reasonableness of men."[50] In *Saturday Night,* Francis Flaherty argued that the debate "put on as convincing a display of internationalism as the most enthusiastic idealist could wish." Like the rest of the reporters, he too omitted any reference to ECOSOC.[51] The ever-critical *Globe and Mail* was certainly less positive, but this was mainly because its editors could not see past what they believed to be King's rejection of the empire.[52] And while Pierre Vigeant of *Le Devoir* noted accurately "qu'il nous faut constater que nos hommes politiques ne possèdent qu'une information superficielle sur la politique étrangère," once the leader of the nationalist Bloc Populaire, Maxime Raymond, declared that he supported a Canadian presence at San Francisco, criticism from the normally assertive nationalist paper all but disappeared.[53]

The only individual who seemed to truly understand Mackenzie King's message was the American counsellor at the embassy in Ottawa. In a letter to the State Department, he observed that the Liberal government had come to accept that the organization created at San Francisco would be far from perfect. He therefore concluded that while the Canadian delegation might campaign on behalf of the smaller states and emphasize the right of consent, in the end, it would sign the agreement regardless of its success.[54]

The composition of the Canadian delegation confirmed his analysis. First and foremost, Mackenzie King made himself chair of the group. From the Conservatives he added the moderate and cooperative Gordon Graydon. He also took M.J. Coldwell. He did not choose John Blackmore, whose comments would have been unpredictable. From French Canada King included his loyal minister of justice, Louis St. Laurent, and the relatively inconsequential Conservative senator, Lucien Moraud. Cora Casselman was selected to give Canadian women a voice,[55] and Robertson, Wrong, Pearson, Pope, Reid, and a number of others were added as advisers. Within a week, each delegate and adviser received a 153-page briefing book. Its content reflected King's cautious approach to world organization and encouraged greater Canadian activism primarily in the economic and social arenas.[56]

As the Canadians prepared, the American planners established the framework and structure for San Francisco. Along with four commissions and ten working committees, there would be a steering committee, consisting of the chairs of all of the delegations, as well as a smaller executive committee. Canadian representation on the latter group was never in doubt. According to one American planner, even those who expressed general concerns about its composition "thought it was essential that Canada should be a member."[57]

In the midst of this encouraging news, on 12 April Mackenzie King learned that Franklin Roosevelt had died of a cerebral haemorrhage while resting in Warm Springs, Georgia. The president's death had a profound impact around the world and touched King personally. Roosevelt had been "a great friend," he noted in his diary. The Canadian prime minister immediately ordered that flags on all federal buildings throughout the country be placed at half mast.[58]

In terms of the United Nations, while most justifiably viewed Roosevelt's passing with a combination of sadness and pessimism, it had at least one notable positive effect. The American ambassador to the Soviet Union, Averill Harriman, used the widespread feelings of grief as leverage in an attempt to convince Stalin to reconsider the decision to keep Molotov away from San Francisco. The Soviet leader, who was personally distraught by the loss of his colleague, took Harriman's plea to heart and committed Molotov to the world conference as an affirmation of the Soviet Union's dedication to international cooperation and world peace. At about the same time, back in the United States, the new president, Harry Truman, vowed to go ahead with the plans for the new world organization without any delay. In London the British also prepared for the negotiations to continue.[59]

With these ideas in mind, Mackenzie King wrote to his long-time friend and spiritual confidante Joan Patteson: "It is wonderful to think that these days at San Francisco may mark the period of transition between an old order that has been full of tyranny, strife and injustice, and the new order which may help to maintain peace and further good-will."[60] The prime minister's sense of hopefulness was, for him, understandable. His government's term in office had come to an end at an ideal time. The war was nearly over, and the Allies were headed to victory. While some of his civil servants might have remained pessimistic about the international situation, the Canadian public stood almost unanimously behind its delegation to San Francisco. Finally, regardless of what had been reported in the media, the prime minister had been given a mandate to pursue a policy of caution and moderation at the international discussions. If Canada was to take any sort of leadership role at the United Nations Conference on International Organization, it would come in the economic or social fields. For the most part, idealistic middle power advocacy would have to be someone else's project.

10
Growing Up: Canada at San Francisco (April–June 1945)

"The little nations all had their say and the big powers got their way," wrote the editors of *Canadian Forum* when the United Nations Conference on International Organization came to an end on 26 June 1945. "The final text, in so far as security provisions [were] concerned," hardly differed from the Dumbarton Oaks proposals. As for the group from Ottawa, it had "behaved with perfect decorum." The editorial was unapologetically realistic. Canada had done well, but it was still a "little nation."[1]

The Canadian delegation arrived in San Francisco in late April 1945 with mixed expectations. For most, the optimism that came naturally with the opportunity to reshape the world order was tempered by an understanding of the limitations of what they were hoping to accomplish. Led by a prime minister whose mind was admittedly divided between the conference and an upcoming national election, the delegation shunned the spotlight, allowing others to make the loud points and only adding its opinion when it felt that it was absolutely necessary. This approach disappointed some of the secondary states, but it pleased the great ones immensely.

Canada was not a leader on the middle power issues. Its voice was relatively muted on the election of nonpermanent members to the security council. And its impact on the question of the right of consent has been exaggerated in most historical accounts. It made its greatest contribution to the creation of the Economic and Social Council (ECOSOC). The new body was a substantial improvement over what had been anticipated by the Dumbarton Oaks proposals and was proof that, in nonsecurity areas, there was still room to recognize the functional principle. Security, however, was the domain of the great powers, and with Canada's help, clamouring among the lesser states for a more democratic security council was effectively curtailed.

The Canada that emerged from San Francisco was not the leader of the so-called middle powers. This title had been earned and assumed by Australia's Herbert Evatt. For the Canadian government, this was of little concern. The United Nations Charter served the national interest: it affirmed the unity of the great powers and broadened the meaning of international order to include nonmilitary issues. In all, Canada's performance at San Francisco mimicked the personality of its political leader: it was neither heroic nor particularly admirable, but it was composed, well thought-out, and successful.

On 19 April 1945 Mackenzie King left Ottawa for Chicago. He spent 20 April visiting Hull House, the University of Chicago, and an art gallery and then boarded a train for Oakland. On the morning of 23 April, he took a ferry from Oakland to San Francisco and then headed for the St. Francis Hotel. The Canadians had been assigned the sixth and seventh floors.[2] Maurice Pope, who travelled with King and the rest of the Ottawa contingent, noted the utter confusion that met the group when it arrived. The Americans had promised office space and typewriters, but neither were available. "When the complete lack of everything was made known to us," Pope wrote in his diary, "Hume Wrong immediately exploded like a bunch of crackers."[3]

An equally disgruntled Lester Pearson came in from Washington the next day. Since he had been excluded from many of the significant policy discussions over the recent months, Pearson doubted that he would play a meaningful role at the conference.[4] To make matters worse, he got a headache on the train, perhaps in part because an uninvited guest to his quarters, Herbert Evatt, chatted endlessly about the place of Australia within the new world organization. Pearson's assessment of the outspoken foreign minister was accurate: "He is an arrogant and aggressive fellow, but intelligent and well-informed. His views seem to me to be pretty sound, but his expression of them a little too forceful to make him popular." Evatt would have an impact at San Francisco, but not everyone would remember him fondly. When Pearson reached the St. Francis Hotel on 24 April (without his luggage, which had been lost) and noted the lack of orderliness, he was not surprised. Other recent events that he had attended as ambassador to the United States had been similarly disorganized. Dejected, he confided in his diary that he found the situation rather "hopeless."[5]

Later that day, the twenty-two-member Canadian delegation (seven delegates and fifteen advisers) held its first meeting in the prime minister's hotel room. King instructed his colleagues to refrain from proposing amendments or making loud comments until they had, together, developed a sense of how Canada might best contribute.[6] Some, like Maurice Pope, felt that this was the right decision. San Francisco was an inappropriate place for public grandstanding.[7] Others, like Escott Reid, were disappointed that they had been instructed merely "to be helpful."[8]

When King, Wrong, and Norman Robertson spoke to the press the next day, they reaffirmed that Canada's first interest was in the "success of the conference." The delegation had arrived in San Francisco with an open mind. It was "anxious to confer and cooperate with other countries and did not come as a special pleader." As for the term "middle power," it was "not [a] good one." A distinction might be made instead "between countries in respect of resources, extent of trade, geographical position, international influence and willingness to assume international responsibility."[9]

Under the circumstances, this rather unexciting approach was realistic and effective. Between 25 April and 4 May the great powers paid little attention to the concerns of the smaller states. Instead, while the representatives of all of the invited countries spoke in platitudes at the plenary sessions, the Big Four privately discussed their own proposed amendments to the Dumbarton Oaks proposals and developed a unified view of what changes they might be willing to accept.[10] During this period, members of the Canadian delegation, many of whom had all of a sudden taken ill, generally participated on the margins.[11]

Canada made its first formal public statement on 27 April at the second plenary session. In a preview of things to come, both the deputy prime minister of Australia, F.M. Forde, and Mackenzie King addressed the conference on the same day. The contrast between the two was immense. The Australian, noted Lester Pearson, "spoke for nearly three-quarters of an hour. He was too long, but was very good, vigorous and straight-hitting." "If there is to be any leader of the Middle Powers here," Pearson thought, "Australia is obviously making a bid for that position."[12]

King was brief. He quickly noted the importance of the meetings at San Francisco, expressed his regret over the passing of Franklin Roosevelt, and then made his country's position clear: "It is not the intention of the Canadian Delegation to put forth in plenary session special amendments to the proposal." "Our Delegation," he explained, "will express its point of view at an appropriate time and place on specific questions as they arise. Our sole preoccupation in any amendment which we may put forward or support at a later stage will be to help in creating an organization which over the years and decades to come will be strong enough and flexible enough to stand any strains to which it may be subjected."

King's last words referred back to his book *Industry and Humanity*. "In conclusion," he said, "may I express my firm conviction that the spirit in which we approach the great task of this Conference will determine the measure of its success. It is for each nation to remember that over all nations is humanity. It is for all to remember that justice is the common concern of mankind. The years of war have surely taught the supreme lesson that men and nations should not be made to serve selfish national ends, whether those ends be isolated self-defense or world domination. Nations everywhere must unite to save and serve humanity."[13]

For Canada, the next week focused on relationship building. A meeting with the rest of the Commonwealth representatives was, by all accounts, successful.[14] Hume Wrong and Norman Robertson considered the plenary speeches and began to strategize possible Canadian amendments.[15] Lester Pearson's spirits improved when he assumed the role of primary conduit between the delegation and the national and international media.[16] Escott Reid remained despondent that Canada was not doing enough, but the vast majority of the rest of the Canadian contingent settled in comfortably.[17] Mackenzie King, busy preparing his radio address to mark the end of the war and planning his return to Vancouver to begin his reelection campaign, did not interfere.

On 4 May 1945 Canada released its suggested amendments to the proposed charter. On the middle power question, it asked vaguely that the general assembly "adopt rules governing the choice of the non-permanent members, in order to ensure that due weight be given to the contribution of members to the maintenance of international peace and security and the performance of their obligations to the United Nations." On the right of consent, it made a number of similar proposals, the most important of which allowed members not represented on the United Nations Security Council (UNSC) to participate in council meetings if the use of their forces was under consideration. The Canadians virtually rewrote the proposed chapter on the Economic and Social Council, expanding its provisions and integrating some of the amendments that had already been raised in the plenary sessions by members of other delegations. Less significant references to the UN secretariat and to the revision of the charter followed.[18]

Over the next few days, the work of the conference accelerated. Thanks to the German surrender on 7 May and the great-power announcement that the Big Four had agreed to a series of amendments, there was a new hope evident among the delegates. The plenary sessions ended, and the working committees began to meet four times daily. The Canadian delegates added a fifth meeting for themselves by assembling each morning to plan their collective approach to the day's issues.[19]

The strategy when it came to the middle power idea was, quite simply, not to have one. Despite an erroneous *Winnipeg Free Press* article claiming that Canada was emerging as the "chief" secondary country at San Francisco, in discussions of the position of the nongreat states on the security council, the Canadian delegation allowed others to do the talking.[20] In this instance, it was up to the representatives of the United Kingdom to advance the middle power case.

At the first four-power consultative meeting on 2 May 1945, the British suggested modifications to Chapter VI, Section A, of the proposals, which stated that the general assembly would elect six states to fill the nonpermanent security-council seats. Making reference to Canada, Anthony Eden asked that the great powers add the clause: "due regard being paid to the contribution of members of the Organization towards the maintenance of international peace and security and towards the other purposes of the Organization." The proposal was well received by Molotov, and the Chinese also did not object. The United States, however, expressed significant reservations. One representative argued that the stipulation would infringe unfairly on the rights of the general assembly. Another worried that Eden's criteria would create conflict among the smallest states, which might construe them "as a build-up of another favored group." When the British refused to back down, Stettinius agreed to have his representatives study the issue.[21]

Later that day, the US delegation gathered in Stettinius's penthouse suite at the Fairmont Hotel. Leo Pasvolsky reiterated his profound dislike of the British proposal but noted that since it was acceptable to the Soviets, the United States had no choice but to go along. He then suggested that the proposition be amended to recognize the importance of geography. One delegate mentioned that Canada would object to this addition, but the Americans approved it nonetheless.[22]

When the Big Four met the next day, representatives from both the United States and China urged that the words "equitable geographical representation" be added to the British amendment. Eden grudgingly agreed, but Molotov objected to the implication that geography could rival military contribution in importance and insisted that the phrase "in the first instance" precede the statement on the contribution of members to the security of the international organization. Once again, members of the United States delegation responded negatively, but Stettinius took charge and imposed an agreement. The great powers approved a joint recommendation of the new wording.[23]

With the Big Four in accord, the debate moved to the first committee of the third commission, in charge of the composition, powers, and procedures of the security council. On 13 May 1945 Lester Pearson spoke briefly in support of differentiating between the importance of the "functional criteria of election" and geographical distribution.[24] On 16 May, in a vote of thirty-two in favour and four opposed, the committee approved the words of what became Article 23 of the UN Charter: "The General Assembly should elect six states to fill the non-permanent seats, due regard being specially paid in the first instance to the contribution of members of the Organization towards the maintenance of international peace and security and towards the other purposes of the Organization, and also to equitable geographical representation."[25] It was a partial victory.

Success was more complete on the question of the right of consent. Almost immediately after arriving in San Francisco, Mackenzie King warned

Lord Cranborne that Canada would not accept any "automatic obligation to contribute to enforcement action." He expected that his country's liability would be "precisely defined" in the charter. A security-council decision to commit Canadian troops to help resolve an international conflict would require prior consultation and might well necessitate the approval of the Canadian Parliament. Since King was preparing for a national election and his constituents were still fractious due to the conscription debate, this issue was particularly crucial.[26]

The Canadian delegation presented its amendments to restrict the military obligations of member states that were not on the security council in a committee discussion on 10 May. The proposal was met with resistance, as opponents alleged that taking the time to obtain the consent of non-members would slow down the council's ability to respond effectively to immediate security crises. Once again, the United States was most particularly unsympathetic.[27]

In response, Mackenzie King took matters into his own hands. Just before he returned to Ottawa to contest the election, he spoke to Chairman Stettinius personally and obtained what he believed was assurance that the rights of the smaller states would be protected. "My part has been done quietly, unobtrusively but effectively behind the scenes," he wrote confidently in his diary on 14 May.[28]

The prime minister had indeed been quiet and unobtrusive, but he had overestimated his effectiveness.[29] Not much later, one of Stettinius's assistants called on the Canadians at their hotel. According to a reputable American journalist, the official said "that he thought that Mr. Stettinius had given the Prime Minister too optimistic a picture of the problem, that Stettinius did not really understand the problem and that, therefore, he thought the Canadians should not count too much on the promise."[30]

The aide was clearly acting inappropriately, but he was also telling the truth. When the American delegation met the next day, only Jack Hickerson defended the Canadian prime minister's fears of the potential electoral consequences of the great-power proposals. Hickerson noted that the British also favoured King's position, but his words still had little immediate impact. Two American Congressional representatives rejected the argument outright. One even went so far as to say that "the Canadian problem was a political one at home." Nevertheless, after further discussion, the delegation elected to compromise. It would still oppose the Canadian amendments, but it would also "search for some formula to help Mackenzie King in facing the Canadian people." Two days later, it recommended that the problem be referred to a subcommittee.[31]

Under Leo Pasvolsky's firm guidance, the Americans gradually became more flexible. On their own, they approved a proposal to allow states with the military capacity to contribute to UN action to attend council meetings, one at a time, if – and only after – the UNSC had already decided that force would have to be used. "The new policy," Pasvolsky explained, "would meet the demand of Canada that its forces should not be used without the opportunity to vote in the Council on their use" and would ensure that the Canadian Parliament would accept the charter.[32]

Nevertheless, the situation was not settled until the end of May. The Canadian amendments had originally stipulated that nonmember states be invited to the security council not only when they were asked to provide military support for a United Nations operation, but also when their interests were being discussed more generally, including if and when their military facilities might be used. On 31 May the delegation reduced its demands to include only instances when the use of a nonmember's troops was in question. The other issues were less crucial to a state's independence, and the Canadian government did not wish to put in place a process that would delay the council's ability to act.[33]

In the end, the conference agreed to what became Article 44: "When a decision to use force has been taken by the Security Council, it shall, before calling upon any member not represented on it to provide armed forces in fulfillment of its obligations ... invite such member, if it so request, to send a representative to participate in the decisions of the Security Council concerning the employment of contingents of its armed forces."[34]

When Mackenzie King was told of the decision, he wrote in his diary: "I see that the Committee at San Francisco have agreed upon the proposals I made regarding the representation on the Security Council when matters affecting Canada's interests are concerned. The same to apply in the case of all countries not represented on the Security Council. This is fortunate indeed."[35] Looking back, the Canadian prime minister was taking far too much credit. Not only had King's remarks not been taken as seriously as he had thought, but the United Kingdom and even the United States had also in some ways already accepted the so-called Canadian position before the negotiations began. In Anthony Eden's 1943 "United Nations Plan for Organising Peace," Britain's foreign secretary had recommended that "smaller powers should always be summoned to sit on the Council when their special interests" were being considered.[36] The next year, a confidential American discussion had also contemplated a security council that would have a "practice of admitting other states to discuss matters on which they [had] a direct interest."[37] This explains why the difficulties in the United States delegation had come from its Congressional representatives. Leo Pasvolsky, who had been privy to the prior deliberations, was naturally at least somewhat more accommodating.

The Americans were less divided in their approach to economic and social issues. Generally, for the United States, they continued to be viewed as unimportant. In contrast, Canada's interest in the nonmilitary aspects of the future world organization was clear even before it put forth its amendments to ECOSOC. Lester Pearson articulated his delegation's case on a Canadian Broadcasting Corporation (CBC) radio program on 29 April: "The new organization," he said, must "come to think and act less and less in terms of force and more and more in terms of forces – the forces that create or destroy international unity and goodwill; the forces that create poverty or promote well-being. It is with such forces that the Economic and Social Council will be concerned, and it should be given enough power and prestige to make its concern effective."[38]

In the words of its chief economic adviser in San Francisco, Louis Rasminsky, what Canada therefore sought to do through its proposed amendments was "to arrange the Dumbarton Oaks material in what seem[ed] to be a more orderly sequence and to strengthen the position of the Economic and Social Council without in any way going beyond the recommendatory functions to governments and without impinging on the authority of the various agencies established by the intergovernmental agreement."[39]

During the plenary sessions, the delegation rearranged, redrafted, and augmented the bare-bones proposal that had emerged from the Washington talks. Its additions included a commitment to promoting higher standards of living worldwide, closer linkages between ECOSOC and related international economic and social organizations, and a specific reference to the need to "have due regard to the necessity of arranging for adequate representation of states of major importance" on the new body. The Canadian decision to hold back the proposal for a week until others had commented, to gather the recommendations together, and then to present them as a whole was praised privately by a member of the American planning staff as the best and most efficient way to speed up the conference and achieve the desired results.[40]

The economic and social proposals were discussed in detail at the committee level throughout May and into early June. On 11 May, at the first substantive meeting, the Canadian representative set the tone for the rest of the sessions by emphasizing the importance of economic and social cooperation and then explaining how the proposed reorganization would provide for greater clarity and coordination among the various new world bodies.[41]

The next day, the American delegates agreed privately to use the suggestions as the basis of future discussions.[42] Coincidentally, their Canadian counterparts resolved to increase the intensity of their lobby. "In view of the great possibilities of the Economic and Social Council for the advancement of human welfare," the Ottawa representatives concluded, "full support should be given to the efforts to avoid the present implication of Chapter

IV [of the Dumbarton Oaks proposals] that the Council is a 'subsidiary agency.'"[43] According to Maurice Pope, the economic and social aspects of the charter had become the delegation's most significant preoccupation.[44]

Louis Rasminsky reported this development to the Canadian public later that day through an interview with the CBC. "The provisions in the Charter for economic and social co-operation are ... not merely an appendage, something tacked on, but an important part of the whole security structure itself," he said. Canada had taken a leadership role in expanding and elaborating on the powers of ECOSOC. It hoped that the United Nations would accept them and thereby recognize the interconnections between military security and economic and social stability.[45]

According to the minutes of the next meeting, the Canadian proposal to extend the reach and powers of the council was well received. For what seems to have been the first time in the entire San Francisco negotiations, a drafting committee was formed, including Canada, to formally rewrite part of the old Dumbarton Oaks proposals in their entirety.[46]

Rasminsky remained active on the committee, which seemed to be making progress, until 28 May. That day, the Soviet Union formally objected to expanding the responsibilities of ECOSOC. After a difficult discussion, the Canadian delegation made some minor adjustments and returned on 4 June with a final proposal. Following a brief debate, the committee approved what became Chapters IX and X of the new charter.[47] When the results of the negotiations were released to the public, the *Winnipeg Free Press* reported: "The Economic and Social Council will be a powerful agency if the letter of the Charter is followed in the spirit of San Francisco." Canadians could take pride in their contribution to this new body.[48]

Along with these three major issues, the Canadian delegation was involved in a number of additional matters in a less significant capacity. Before and during San Francisco, it participated in the discussions to create an international court of justice.[49] Mackenzie King solved an early great-power logistical difficulty by applying his Parliament's rules of English-French translation to the San Francisco talks.[50] Canada had input into the decision to hold a meeting of the United Nations to revise the charter within ten years of its inception.[51] It took a leadership role in ensuring that the great powers did not manipulate the selection of the secretary and deputy secretary general of the new world body.[52] As M.J. Coldwell had hoped, thanks to Canada, among others, the United Nations also agreed to allow the public and the media open access to the meetings of the general assembly.[53] Finally, the delegation spoke against a provision for expulsion from the organization.[54]

Achievements on these issues, however, were relatively unimportant in comparison with the delegation's impact on the great-power veto. For Canada, the right of the great powers to make unilateral decisions at the security council had always been discomforting. It contradicted the spirit of the functional principle, which suggested that power should be adjusted based on a state's relative capacity. Nevertheless, Canadians were committed to a functioning, inclusive world organization, and it seemed unlikely that such a body could exist without allowing the Soviet Union, among others, a veto over international security issues.

The USSR's insecurity stemmed in part from a growing ideological conflict with the West that was evident to most, if not all, delegates at the conference from the time of their arrival.[55] The first significant public controversy arose when the Latin American states lobbied for Argentina's admission to the conference as a founding member. In the face of significant Soviet opposition, the United States succeeded in passing a resolution that granted full UN membership to a country that technically did not qualify. In what was evidently a sign of things to come, despite the objections from some members of its delegation (specifically M.J. Coldwell), Canada supported the Americans.[56]

As the tension between the East and the West increased, the Canadian delegation met privately to discuss its potential response to what would certainly be the next contentious issue: the great-power veto. There was no consensus. M.J. Coldwell – already upset about the decision on Argentina – argued that Canada had best forget about the opinions of both the Soviet Union and the United States and instead look out for its own interests at San Francisco. He received vocal support from Gordon Graydon and Maurice Pope, the latter of whom reflected: "I firmly believe that we are right in taking a back seat in this Conference, but I do not go so far as to believe that we should sit outside the hall and not in the Committee Room."[57] On the other side, in rare agreement, stood Norman Robertson, Hume Wrong, and Lester Pearson. Pearson took the lead, arguing that Canada had best not vote against the great powers, particularly not against less crucial Anglo-American proposals. The conference had to succeed, and Canada had to limit its opposition to "important questions of principle."[58]

The dispute was hardly a contest. With Robertson, Wrong, and thus also Mackenzie King on side, the others could only be thankful that the delegation remained so moderate. On 13 May, in a meeting that considered the power of the great states to veto resolutions at the security council, Pearson argued: "I think we should support any reasonable move to limit the veto strictly to the actual application of sanctions, but that we should not press this position to a vote in the face of strong Big Four opposition."[59]

When the Yalta formula came up for discussion on 18 May, in what must have been pleasantly surprising to some of his colleagues, Pearson suggested that "there should not only be no 'veto' under chapter VIII, section A (pacific settlement of disputes) for an interested party, as the Crimea formula provided, but also none for a permanent member who was not a party to a dispute." Temporarily, at least, Canada was willing to challenge the great

powers. The Soviets quickly spoke up in opposition, and the issue was referred to a subcommittee for further discussion.[60]

At this point, both the United Kingdom and the United States began to
fear that the conference might collapse. In a British-delegation meeting,
Alexander Cadogan expressed concern that the smaller states were preparing a dramatic protest that could alienate the Soviets. He immediately sought
advice from London.[61] The Americans found the situation equally difficult.
Their Soviet experts quietly supported the Canadian proposal, suggesting
that if the Yalta agreement were accepted, the new organization's ability to
prevent a future international conflict would be "but a pipe dream." At the
time, it appeared that a full four-fifths of the conference delegates desired
changes to the Crimea compromise. Nevertheless, Stettinius was obliged to
remind his officials at a delegation meeting that if the great powers abandoned their Yalta commitments, the Soviets would likely withdraw from
the conference altogether.[62]

Over the next week, members of both the British and the American delegations who insisted on a policy of extreme caution with the Soviets contemplated presenting the smaller states with a take-it-or-leave-it plan for
world organization. At the same time, other British representatives arranged
to meet with the dominion delegates more regularly, while their American
counterparts worked even harder to devise a diplomatic solution.[63]

The latter attempt was not immediately successful. On 1 June 1945 the
Soviet Union declared that it would no longer accept even the Yalta provisions. This pronouncement, which in the eyes of the Western powers was a
betrayal of the Crimea agreement, threatened to end the conference without
a charter. In response, the United States and Great Britain decided to approach Joseph Stalin directly.[64] President Roosevelt's former personal assistant, Harry Hopkins, quickly set up a series of meetings in Moscow. During
the sixth and final discussion on 6 June, Hopkins convinced the surprisingly
receptive Soviet leader to respect the Yalta pact. Gromyko made the decision
official the following day, and the conference resumed its deliberations.[65]

Consequently, the great powers assumed incorrectly that the problems
with the veto had ended. Many felt that since the Soviet concerns had been
satisfied, the small powers would simply fall into line.[66] On 10 June, Herbert
Evatt made it clear that they were wrong. Nearly three weeks earlier, the
secondary powers had presented the Big Four with a lengthy questionnaire
on the veto issue. It had never been answered satisfactorily, and Evatt was
furious. To him, according to a British report, "not one valid reason had been
given for the applicability of the veto to the pacific settlement of disputes.
The excuse put forward was that it might start a chain of events which
might end in the application of force." This, said Evatt, "was precisely the
reason why disputes should be settled at the earliest possible stage by conciliation unhampered by the veto."[67]

The fiery Australian leader spoke passionately, and the great-power re-
spondents were, according to Norman Robertson, "no match for [him] in
argument." By the end, while no action was taken, the Australian had condemned Britain's attitude as "contemptible" and "most dishonest." Only a
delicate intervention by Lester Pearson had saved the meeting from utter
disaster. "All told," concluded Robertson, "it was an extraordinary and deplorable exhibition of Commonwealth public manners."

It appears that it was this dispute that led Canada's undersecretary of
state for external affairs to conclude that it was time to draw back from the
veto issue. In one of his longest and most assertive memoranda of the Second World War period, he wrote to the acting undersecretary in Ottawa,
John Read:

> It seems clear to me that, in this year of grace, there cannot be a world
> organization established, with Russia as a member, unless it provides for
> voting rights in the Security Council substantially as set forth in the Great
> Power memorandum which you have seen. The effective choice appears,
> therefore, to be between such an Organization and an Organization from
> which the Soviet Union and those countries which feel their security most
> closely dependent on their relations with it are excluded. Our view is that it
> is better to take the Organization that we can get and, having come to that
> decision, to refrain from further efforts to pry apart the difficult unity which
> the Great Powers have attained. This means forgoing the luxury of making
> any more perfectionist speeches either on the voting procedure itself or on
> the general amendment procedure, which is very closely linked with it. We
> can continue to oppose the Soviet Union and other Great Powers on such
> essentially secondary questions as the method of election of the Secretary
> General, nomination of Deputy Secretaries or the omission of 'expulsion'
> from the Charter, but we should not insist on forcing decisions on such
> central questions as veto and amendment to a vote in which our associa-
> tion with the other middle and smaller Powers might well result in the
> rejection of the Dumbarton Oaks proposals.
>
> This general line of conduct carries, I think, the judgment of the mem-
> bers of our delegation. We may, however, be called on within the next day
> or two to translate this general attitude into votes on specific questions. I
> hope that, with the campaign now over, you may be able to have a word on
> these questions with the Prime Minister and let me know if he approves the
> sort of position I have tried to outline.[68]

With his prime minister's approval, Robertson convened the entire delegation the next morning to announce the Canadian position. It would not do
anything that would risk the withdrawal of the Soviet Union from the negotiations. Later that day, as Mackenzie King celebrated a third consecutive

majority government at home, Canada declared itself to the rest of the conference. Records of a committee meeting show that "the Canadian delegation would not oppose the adoption of the original Dumbarton Oaks draft [on the veto] and would abstain from voting on amendments to that text. In return, [the Canadian delegate, Lester Pearson] hoped that sponsoring governments and France could still find a suitably and reasonably flexible procedure for change so that the public asked to accept under special circumstances proposals difficult to justify, would not be asked to accept them in perpetuity."[69]

Pearson's comments received front-page coverage in the *New York Times*, which ran the headline: "Canada Switches to Back Big 5 Veto." The next day, the *Times* noted that five additional small- and medium-sized countries had followed the Canadian lead.[70] Nevertheless, despite what some members of the US delegation might have felt, the debate was not over. On 14 June the prime minister of New Zealand, Peter Fraser, described the veto as "an evil thing," and the Australians reasserted their objections to great-power dominance.[71]

The issue was finally resolved two days later when the committee voted on an Australian amendment that would have restricted the veto power provided for in the Dumbarton Oaks proposals. During the debate, Lester Pearson spoke for Canada. After reiterating his disapproval of the veto in principle, he asked the US delegation specifically whether it would sign the charter without it. The Americans consulted among themselves and announced that they would not. In response, Pearson declared that while Canada would not oppose the Australian amendment, it would also not support it. The delegation from Ottawa would abstain. The abstention decided the vote, denying the Australians the backing that they needed to carry the meeting. When it was over, a reflective and still somewhat idealistic Pearson asked himself: "I wonder if we should have beaten them [the great powers] on this."[72]

But Pearson did not control the political decisions of the Canadian delegation, and idealism did not govern Canada's negotiating strategy. Rather, Ottawa considered its own long-term interests and concluded that a stable, economically and socially integrated world order was more valuable than international recognition as the leader of the so-called middle powers. Herbert Evatt's intentions were certainly morally commendable, and his actions did earn Australia attention abroad entirely disproportionate to its actual importance, but the risks inherent in alienating the great powers were real.[73] At San Francisco the Canadian delegation showed a degree of maturity by choosing prudence over popularity. It sacrificed any chance of a position of middle power greatness to maintain international stability.

The Canadian people would remember this situation rather differently.

11
Shaping History
(June–October 1945)

With the debate over the veto finally resolved, the United Nations delegates quickly dealt with some remaining details and prepared to head home. The conference, which was supposed to last only three to four weeks, had spanned almost nine. Despite the delays, the disputes, and a California heat wave, most officials considered San Francisco a success: representatives of fifty countries had reached an agreement on the United Nations Charter and had thereby assured a reasonable basis for a new world order. Nevertheless, with the triumph came disappointment. The conflict between the West and the Soviet Union had expanded, and relations between the two sides continued to deteriorate.

Feelings in Canada were, on the whole, positive. Members of the Canadian delegation certainly recognized the challenges that the international community would face in the postwar period, but the national media were sending the general public highly optimistic messages about the future. Already proud of the role that they had played in the shaping of the peace, Canadians saw themselves as a growing force in world affairs. Journalists and academics wrote confidently of Canada's increasing respectability as an international mediator, and few knew enough to contest their analyses. The end of the conference marked the beginning of the memorialization of a new Canadian identity in world affairs. History was not just being made in San Francisco; it was also being shaped.

On 18 June 1945 Lord Halifax chaired a final meeting of the Commonwealth's San Francisco delegates. Still shaken by the embarrassing conflict with Australia less than one week earlier, Britain's ambassador to the United States spoke rather hesitantly. He was pleased that the dominions had found the opportunity to express their own points of view at San Francisco but was at the same time concerned that their performance could have suggested to the world that the British Commonwealth was not as united as it once had been. A still angry Herbert Evatt continued to blame London for any and all difficulties, but Norman Robertson was more positive. "From the point of view of official to official," he said, "co-operation had been perfect as between the United Kingdom and the Canadian delegations." Hume Wrong agreed, attributing most of the Anglo-dominion conflicts during the conference to the "unique" dynamic at San Francisco that allowed the Big Five to limit what discussion reached even the committee level.[1]

Fortunately, the delegates had persevered, and fresh off his election victory, Mackenzie King was set to fly back to San Francisco for the closing ceremonies. Himself almost completely absorbed by domestic affairs and therefore hardly aware of the increasing tension among the great powers, the Canadian prime minister was openly optimistic. Edward Stettinius and Harry Truman had both personally urged him to return to California to help close the conference, and he was flattered by their attention. "I have made no attempt myself," he wrote in his diary, "nor have I had special desire to be at the conclusion of the Conference to figure in its proceedings, least of all to participate by an open word at this final stage. But these things have come in spite of myself as they were foreordained or a matter of destiny."[2] Later, while drafting his closing comments, King reflected once again on his book *Industry and Humanity*. It contained, he believed, "the fundamental principles on which the whole work of the United Nations [was] based." Preparing this speech was "really the consummation of a heart's desire and life effort to bring about peace between nations to the extent that it might be possible."[3]

The media were also in high spirits, and only in part because peace had been restored in Europe. On 24 June the *New York Times* described in detail how, in less than forty-eight hours, approximately 200 delegates, representing fifty countries, would enter the auditorium of the Veterans Building for one final meeting. Each representative would sign two leather-bound books that would then be locked in a safe and eventually transported to the permanent home of the new world organization. The *Times* optimistically predicted that the event would last eight hours.[4]

On 26 June, after a few organizational difficulties (the ceremony was delayed close to two hours and then Canada was mistakenly called to sign after Chile and Costa Rica even though the nongreat states were supposed to be listed alphabetically),[5] Mackenzie King addressed the conference for the last time: "Today, we hope, may witness the dawn of a new era in the history of the world. Humanity is crying aloud for peace – a peace based on co-operation and brotherhood among men and nations. The hope of the future lies in a recognition of the profound truths that the interests of mankind are one, and that the claims of Humanity are supreme."[6] His words were well received.

King left San Francisco at 11 p.m. that evening and returned home at 2 p.m. the next day. He was received positively by the great majority of the national press corps. The *Winnipeg Free Press* had been touting Canada as "the chief" among the middle powers since the beginning of May. As the prime minister of "a nation which [had] won the admiration and respect of all by its achievements in the two world wars," Mackenzie King was now "in a position of great influence."[7] Because of him, "the voice of Canada [had become] the voice of the middle powers."[8] *Saturday Night* praised the delegation's ability to work cooperatively. It was proud of the soft-spoken and respectable approach to the negotiations. Canada, it said, did "not have to make a lot of noise to command attention for its views."[9] In Quebec, *La Presse* was perhaps the most enthusiastic. It reported on "l'augmentation de prestige et d'influence que la conférence de sécurité a value au Canada" and gave full credit to Mackenzie King and his temporary replacement as delegation leader, Louis St. Laurent, for this achievement.[10] Canada, it claimed not much later, "peut donc être justement fier de sa contribution à lédification de l'ordre nouveau."[11]

Radio reports were similar. "Canada in a quiet way has achieved very considerable prestige as a mediator at this conference," said the chair of the United Nations Information Organization, the Canadian-born Theodore Newton, "firmly proposing those things which it believes in, if no one else has put them forward, and with a minimum of talk." "It has already achieved a reputation for sagacity and friendliness as one of the leaders of the middle powers."[12]

Naturally, not every commentator was quite so optimistic. Back in May, Blair Fraser had emphasized the uncertainties that lay ahead. "This conference," he observed in the *Financial Post*, "has shown that the nations of the world can get together on paper, they can agree on verbal formulae. But there is nothing yet to show that they will be able to agree on important questions of action, and there are several things to show how empty an agreement in words might prove to be, at worst."[13] Just before the meetings ended, he reiterated his warning in *Maclean's*: "San Francisco demonstrated to everybody what some had already known – that the Russians are very, very difficult people with whom to deal. This is just a fact to which we might as well make up our minds."[14]

The *Globe and Mail*, which had never given up on the development of a single Commonwealth foreign policy, shared Fraser's caution. "The charter openly recognizes," it maintained, "as nations should do, the inescapable fact that power in the present world rests with those nations which can combine large populations with the efficient development of great industrial resources. The small nations, therefore, are at the mercy of the large unless they can combine their strength and in collaboration become large Powers."[15]

This advice generally went unheeded. A Canadian Institute of Public Opinion (CIPO) poll on 20 June found that national confidence in the ability of the new world organization to keep the peace had increased throughout the conference.[16] Canadians felt particularly proud of the diplomats who would be guiding their country's more activist foreign policy in the postwar period. As I. Norman Smith reported in the *Ottawa Journal*, "The feeling among San Francisco diplomats was that our East Block had turned out a band of unusually competent men, and they were doubly effective in that they were able to operate as a band, or a team." According to Smith, it had come to be known throughout San Francisco "that when Mr. Robertson or Mr. Wrong or Mr. Pearson put forth a suggestion, it was likely to be a good one, was certain not to be an old one and was unlikely to be a selfish one." The majority of Canada's academic analysts agreed.[17]

As for the members of the Department of External Affairs themselves, most preferred to stay in the background. One exception was Lester Pearson. On 1 July he spoke on Canadian Broadcasting Corporation (CBC) radio using language that was remarkably similar to that of the recent newspaper commentaries. "Canada," he said, "is now a leader among that group of middle powers, which is playing an increasingly important part on the international scene ... it is not I hope, because of any delusions of grandeur, or of overwhelming ambition. It is because she has acquired an intelligent understanding of her own enlightened self-interest."[18]

Whether this outpouring of national pride and self-importance was justified and whether Canada's role at San Francisco might have been exaggerated are both worth considering. The earliest official evaluation of the group from Ottawa seems to have come from the United States' Office of European Affairs. On 2 June 1945 a memorandum for President Truman concluded that the Canadian delegation had played "a cooperative and constructive part in the Conference." It was "a conspicuously able group."[19] Edward Stettinius even recommended that Norman Robertson be made the first UN secretary general.[20] And Anne O'Hare McCormick of the *New York Times* noted that Canada's potential as a middle power was "sure to grow."[21]

The United Kingdom officials also found the Canadian delegation to have been "helpful and cooperative throughout."[22] On 23 June a preliminary report to the Foreign Office concluded: "The Canadians have been one of the strongest and ablest teams at the Conference. They have displayed a real solicitude for the welfare of the organisation."[23]

Neither great power, however, was impartial. Since the Canadian approach at San Francisco had been designed with the interests of the United States and Great Britain in mind, it is no wonder that Canada was looked upon more fondly than Australia or New Zealand. Moreover, platitudes aside, even the great-power representatives would not go so far as to label Canada the leader of the middle powers. This title was clearly Australia's. On 30 June 1945 the American journalist Drew Pearson published a long story on how, just before the conference ended, the Peruvian foreign minister, Manuel Gallagher, proposed that the steering committee pay tribute to Herbert Evatt as the "great champion of the smaller nations." Evatt, reports Pearson, received a standing ovation. "Thanks to that hard-hitting lawyer from a little town in New South Wales," the article concluded, "Australia has become the spokesman for small nations everywhere."[24]

A month later, having had time to reflect on the impact of San Francisco, Jack Hickerson of the Office of European Affairs provided perhaps the most balanced account of the Canadian contribution. In a letter to the US ambassador in Ottawa, Ray Atherton, he wrote: "Canada sent a good Delegation which generally gave a good account of itself. I would not say that Canada's role at the Conference was spectacular or brilliant. It was simply good and solid."[25]

Similarly, a retrospective article in the September 1945 edition of the British periodical *The Round Table* concluded: "Canada's delegates went to San Francisco with four main objectives in the way of amendments to the Dumbarton Oaks draft. None was fully achieved. All were approached closely enough to let the Canadians return satisfied that they had got the essentials of their desire." Canada had clearly grown prouder and stronger that summer, and its influence was "by no means negligible," but it was not yet capable of competing with the great powers for influence on significant international issues.[26]

Malcolm MacDonald agreed. In November he wrote to London: "Canada's position in the world grows steadily in importance. No doubt there is a tendency in Canada itself to exaggerate it. The authority of any nation other than Russia, the United States of America and the United Kingdom in international affairs is small ... Nevertheless, Canada's significance is distinct and growing ... The variety, weight and generosity of its war effort establish it as 'a middlesized nation,' remarkable in both physique and spirit. It is not yet one of the Powers-that-be in world affairs, but perhaps it is one of the Powers-to-be."[27]

Considering the guarded nature of these observations, why then did Canadians still come to see themselves as middle power leaders? One significant reason was that, despite Herbert Evatt's brash and controversial tactics at San Francisco, the new world organization did not capture the interest of most Australians. A public opinion poll in the early summer of 1945 found that two-thirds of the women and half of the men in the country had not followed reports on the conference at all. Evatt's return from the United States did not change things. In August, when asked if Australia should agree to be bound by the United Nations Charter, 54 percent of those polled had no opinion. The foreign minister's impact at home was evidently far less significant than it was abroad. With the Australians uninterested in middle power leadership, there was room for another state to step in.[28]

Canada could also thank the United States. In the middle of the conference, with Evatt as rowdy as ever, an article in the US magazine *Newsweek* suggested that "for smooth, efficient performance, the Canadian Delegation probably ranked first." This observation was deliberately included in response to a request by a member of the official American press section. According to Jack Hickerson, it was "felt that a nice compliment of this sort coming at a particular time would do no harm," particularly when the representatives from Ottawa were working so much more cooperatively than the Australians. Members of the Canadian media, who collectively interpreted the comment as evidence of their country's superior performance, were never made aware of what had actually happened.[29]

The other reasons involve Lester Pearson. According to his biographer, John English, his "direct influence on Canadian policy and on Canada's work at the San Francisco Conference was not great."[30] And indeed, in terms of actual policy formulation, Pearson was a secondary player. Decisions were made by Mackenzie King on the basis of recommendations from Norman Robertson or Hume Wrong. On the long-term domestic impact of Canada's contribution to the United Nations, however, Pearson was much more important.

As the historian Patrick Brennan has explained in his book on Canada's wartime journalists, the most influential writers of the period "all shared an affection and respect bordering on hero worship for Lester Pearson."[31] It should therefore come as no surprise that the widely read reports of Grant Dexter and others from San Francisco generally echoed his optimism, his nationalism, and his necessarily exaggerated sense of Canada's contribution. Pearson, after all, was the functional principle's chief "salesman," and as a promoter, there was none better.[32]

At San Francisco his abilities were on display beyond just the Canadian-media circles. Thanks to a poorly organized conference secretariat, the international press rarely received legitimate updates on the delegates' progress, nor did the host Americans go to great lengths to explain the purposes and goals of the meetings. In response, Canada coordinated its own daily briefings. Unlike their British and American allies, who kept such forums exclusive, the Canadians chose to make their sessions public and, in fact, actively encouraged foreign writers to attend. These reporters, many of whom came from delegations that lacked the staff and resources to host their own briefings, were generally appreciative. The Wartime Information Board (WIB) noted that several "said the Canadian meetings provided the best facility for helping them understand and report the Conference." The sessions also allowed the Ottawa representatives to promote their proposals to a necessarily captive and sympathetic audience. "By hearing expositions of Mr. Pearson and other delegation members," the WIB concluded, "correspondents developed an increasing respect for the abilities and effectiveness of the Canadian delegation and for its general approach to Conference problems."[33]

With the Australian public uninterested, and the great powers unsympathetic to the tactics and manners of Herbert Evatt, it was not difficult for Canada – a country that had indeed made a significant contribution to the war both economically and militarily – to emerge from San Francisco with a reputation as a leader of the small, or middle, powers. The United States and Great Britain clearly appreciated the tact exhibited by the Canadian delegation in advancing its case. Lester Pearson, satisfied with his role on his country's diplomatic team and having acquired a reputation as "a man who knew what was going on,"[34] worked brilliantly as a communicator with the national press, passing on his enthusiasm to the Canadian public. His positive outlook was compounded by reports in the international media, most of which were influenced at least as much by the courtesy of the Ottawa group and the appeal of its leading public face as by the actual achievements of the delegates in the meeting rooms.

All of this together made the road to ratification in Canada what one US observer called "easy sledding" for Mackenzie King.[35] Still, taking no chances, the prime minister quickly dispatched the potentially controversial Escott Reid (along with Lester Pearson) to London to serve on the executive committee of the United Nations Preparatory Commission. The group was charged with putting the results of San Francisco into practice. With that, Canada's best draftsperson and smoothest negotiator were kept busy at a task they enjoyed, and any chance of a new dispute within the Department of External Affairs over Canadian foreign policy was effectively eliminated.[36]

There were other clashes to replace it. Over the summer and into the fall, the international situation worsened. A meeting of the Big Three at Potsdam in July concluded without agreement, and while explosions in Hiroshima and Nagasaki in August formally ended the Second World War, they also launched the atomic era, leaving the entire international community on edge. These events, along with the discovery of Soviet spy rings in Canada, caused Mackenzie King to wonder whether the new world organization had been worth the effort. "Mere promises in writing mean nothing unless there is means for all nations to keep fretful nations in order," he wrote in his diary. Gradually reverting to his prewar position on Canadian internationalism, he thought that it was "a great mistake to develop organizations or agreements which help to relieve the anxieties and consciences of large numbers of people but which in reality are first a delusion and a snare in that they give a positive advantage to a country that does not care a rap about the sanctity of contracts."[37]

The Canadian government tabled the Charter of the United Nations near the beginning of the first session of the twentieth Parliament on 10

September 1945. Members had five weeks to review their individual copies. On 16 October, Louis St. Laurent moved: "That it is expedient that the houses of parliament do approve the agreement establishing the united nations and constituting the charter of the united nations and the statute of the international court of justice signed at San Francisco on June 26, 1945, and that this house do approve the same."

In his speech defending the resolution, the minister of justice was quick to concede that the charter before him was a product of "compromises and adjustments." Clearly, it was not "an ideal document." Still, it was a significant improvement over Dumbarton Oaks, and Canada's contribution to the changes had been noteworthy. St. Laurent justified the delegation's decision to abstain on the vote on the great-power veto, reminding his colleagues that it had been influenced by great-power assurances that they would use their veto sparingly and responsibly. He took pride in having secured the right of consent and in the Canadian contribution to the Economic and Social Council. After warning the House that no organization could succeed without the will of its members, he concluded: "The charter of the united nations is a first step in the direction of that co-operation between nations which appears to be essential to the survival of civilization."[38]

Thanks to the multiparty nature of the Canadian delegation, the immediate opposition response to St. Laurent was supportive. Gordon Graydon paid tribute to the "outstanding service rendered by the permanent officials and the entire staff of the Department of External Affairs" and went on to describe the Canadian approach to San Francisco as one of "helpful co-operation." There was no "attempt to be spectacular at San Francisco," he said. "At San Francisco I found that Canada was the enemy of none and the friend of all." Like St. Laurent, Graydon stressed his country's leading role in creating a powerful economic and social council. Then, he too concluded cautiously: "I would say, let us look on San Francisco not as a cure-all, but as a great and important advance and a great adventure in international understanding."[39]

When M.J. Coldwell rose to speak two days later, he was similarly reserved. The charter, he told the House, was not "all that Canada hoped for, or probably that any one of the delegates from any of the nations would have wished." Nonetheless, it did represent the best result possible under the circumstances. Since the world had entered the atomic age, accepting the new world organization had become "a necessity." It was no longer safe for any nation to "continue to retain its own independent unlimited authority and jurisdiction in external affairs."[40]

Subsequent speeches, generally by members who had not attended the conference and who had therefore obtained the majority of their information from the press, were less realistic. A Liberal member of Parliament from

Quebec, Louis Beaudoin, referred to Canada as "one of the most important middle powers" at San Francisco. Its record in the war had been "unsurpassed by the other nations of the world."[41] According to Donald Fleming, a Conservative from Toronto, Canada was now "enjoying the expanding role of interpreter among the nations of the world." It had "a special opportunity to help to bring about understanding between the so-called major nations of the world, or the great powers, and those in lesser positions."[42] While others were less laudatory of the Canadian role, there was a clear discrepancy between the thoughts of those who had been at San Francisco and those who had heard about it second-hand.[43]

These differences did not affect the vote. The House of Commons passed the charter unanimously. It was officially ratified by the Canadian government on 9 November and was deposited in the United States less than three weeks later. Both in Canada and in the world at large, a new era had begun.

For Canada, this era was defined by a series of paradoxes. Its UN policy was still determined by Mackenzie King, who was at once fearful of international commitments and also a leading progressive force in the development of world order. His ideas were shaped and articulated by a diplomatic service made famous by its alleged cohesiveness but in fact internally divided thanks to some officers' utopianism. Political decisions were translated into a language that the general public could comprehend by journalists and academics who were themselves largely attracted to the aggressive internationalism of Lester Pearson and Escott Reid yet at the same time committed to the more prudent policies of Norman Robertson and Hume Wrong.

As a result, when it came to the United Nations, the Canadian people could choose what they wanted to believe. They could have looked at the new world structure as a disappointment; after all, the veto ensured that the great powers would control all of the significant decisions, and it was already becoming clear that they could not cooperate. But they could also view the UN as a beacon of hope – a triumph for those states that believed that security meant more than just military strength and for those individuals who had played a leading role in making this possible.

Given the choice, most Canadians rejected the "middle" course of finding a balance between the two and embraced the latter. To them, San Francisco saw Canada cement its role as a leading middle power, a state characterized by its decency, its thoughtfulness, and its ability to get along with other countries. Shamed by the failure of the League of Nations, Canadians came to view themselves as ambassadors of internationalism and leading mediators within the new world structure.

None of this was entirely untrue, but it was also a view of history shaped by only some of those who were there. Generally speaking, Canada's policy toward the United Nations reflected Norman Robertson's and Hume

Wrong's embrace of Mackenzie King's cautionary pragmatism and dismissed the assertive middle power rhetoric of Escott Reid (and Lester Pearson) as utopian. In the end, however, it was Pearson's vision of Canada and the new world order that was largely accepted, and then remembered, by the Canadian people.

Epilogue: Cherishing Illusions

In January 1946 one of the most vocal proponents of the middle power idea, Lionel Gelber, published an article on Canada's growing international stature in the American periodical *Foreign Affairs*. "The evidence of Canada's new position in the world is unmistakable," he proclaimed. "Her relatively small population and lack of colonial possessions prevent her from being a major Super Power. But her natural wealth, the capacity of her people, the strength she has exerted and the potentialities she has displayed show that she is not a minor one. Henceforth in world politics she must figure as a Middle Power." Thanks in large part to its role in founding the United Nations, Canada had created for itself a new role in world affairs that few other states were able, or willing, to play.[1]

Three months later, another historian, Arthur Lower, wrote a more cynical paper for the Canadian Institute of International Affairs' *International Journal*. He argued that Canada was a political and military subordinate in the Second World War; it never had the principal role that others had claimed for it. Certainly, most Canadians believed "that their country [had] risen considerably above the status of a small power," but in reality, it was still learning its place on the world stage and was not yet sufficiently internationally aware to play the role that some had anticipated. To Lower, Canada's reputation for activism and innovation exceeded its much more practical and limited achievements.[2]

In reflecting on Canada's contribution to the founding of the United Nations, one can find some truth in both interpretations. The Canadian idealism and influence that Gelber remembered were indeed present during the Second World War; however, while most would suggest that they were best personified by the words and actions of the Department of External Affairs' young and enthusiastic public servants, where they were truly evident, and indeed effective, was in the old curmudgeon William Lyon Mackenzie King. It was King, not Lester Pearson (or even Escott Reid), who first argued that world order could be maintained only by replacing the international

community's traditional dependence on power with faith in "the application of principles."[3] And it was King's articulation of the functional principle, not Hume Wrong's, that suggested that Canada's real capacity for
influence lay in the economic and social arenas. At San Francisco, while the
Pearson-led campaign to establish a formal category of middle powers failed,
Canada was successful in defining and increasing the responsibilities of the
institution closer to its prime minister's heart: the Economic and Social
Council (ECOSOC).

Lower's contention that Canadian foreign policy during this period was
generally far less ambitious – or even significant – than Gelber claims is
also, in its own way, convincing. After O.D. Skelton's death, it did not take
long for Norman Robertson and Hume Wrong to realize that Canada was
not going to be able to play a major role in the shaping of a new international security organization. Rather than bemoaning their country's lack of
influence, they strove instead to make what contribution they could from
the margins. In 1943 and 1944 they refused to allow their newly consti-
tuted committees on post-hostilities problems to waste time and resources
developing draft charter proposals, preferring to respond to the detailed
material coming to them from London. It was the right thing to do in view
of the relative inexperience of the Canadian planners and their limited numbers. When Canada had the opportunity to become a genuine leader among
the middle powers in the period leading up to and during the San Francisco
Conference, the Department of External Affairs again declined. Although
the general public would have liked to see its country as a guiding force in
world affairs, given the importance of great-power harmony to future Canadian prosperity, such a position simply was not in the national interest.

When the San Francisco Conference ended, many Canadians refused to
accept their country's small-power status. Thanks to the media and a series
of overly enthusiastic speeches by politicians and select civil servants, per-
ceptions of the national role in world affairs became clouded by unduly
optimistic, if not misguided, rhetoric. Canadians were correct in believing
that their country had changed dramatically during the war, but they misinterpreted their government's new interest and activity in foreign relations
(and flattering articles about it in the international press) as evidence of
increasing global influence.

Collectively, Canadian politicians, the national media, and citizens at large
failed to realize that their country was not the only one to have changed.
The war, and the United Nations, had made the United States and the Soviet Union, neither of which had been members of the League of Nations in
1939, infinitely more powerful. The security-council veto caused the discrepancy in power between the Big Five and the rest of the international
community, including Canada, to grow larger. The differential was not as
great on economic and social issues, but Canadian spokespeople never

defeats *him from LBP's*
other role

focused on ECOSOC. Rather, by trumpeting the noble, yet relatively unsuc-cessful, functional principle and the failed middle power idea, they adopted a vision of their country in the world that was more perceived than real.

What happened was understandable. The national embrace of what would later be termed Pearsonian internationalism meant that, in the words of John English, "Mike's concerns had become Canada's."[4] And since Pearson, "above all, wanted to be helpful and to be liked,"[5] Canadians came to see their contribution to the formation of the United Nations as evidence that their country had become the international community's helpful fixer. For many, this inflated sense of self-importance persists and is reflected in a yearning to return to the ways of the past.[6] For others, it has created a cyni-cism toward previous achievements that has obscured the credit that Canada does deserve for its leadership and innovation in broadening the meaning of international security to include factors other than military strength at a crucial turning point in world history.[7]

In retrospect, the problem is in large part historiographical. The writing of the history of Canadian external relations has been dominated by the civil servants, most particularly those who are sympathetic to Lester Pearson and Escott Reid (including themselves).[8] Their memoirs, diaries, and his-torical accounts have for years served as the basis of scholarly analyses of Canada's role in the world. National histories and commentaries written by accomplished academics have also focused on Canada's "wise men," once more assigning too much importance to the diplomats and not enough to the policy makers. In 1945 Mackenzie King, and Mackenzie King alone, controlled Canadian foreign policy. It was King who defined the Canadian approach to the UN negotiations and King who set the delegation's priori-ties; moreover, the officials in the East Block who tended to have the most significant impact on policy decisions were Robertson and Wrong, the two civil servants who were the most willing to respect and follow their prime minister's cautious approach to external affairs.

Canadians entered the Second World War sharing their leader's general aversion to international commitments. Over time, they grew bolder and began to envision a new place for themselves on the world stage. Their behaviour was not so much a product of an inherent commitment to world order as it was a rejection of British imperialism. Inasmuch as Canada came to rely on Great Britain in the postwar planning process, a growing con-stituency came to resent that dependence. Mackenzie King responded by accepting Hume Wrong's functional principle, albeit on his own terms, and even by standing up to the British and the other great powers when he felt it absolutely necessary. As prime minister, he would have preferred that Canada extend its global obligations incrementally, but there was no stopping the internationalist momentum that was building throughout the country.

As two political scientists have pointed out, the Canadian international personality is quite similar to that of Lester Pearson. Canadians also "like to be liked."[9] In the 1940s Mackenzie King chose not to interfere with their growing belief that Canada had become the world's helpful fixer. Indeed, in his talks with Churchill and Roosevelt, he often felt the same way. At the San Francisco Conference, the Canadian prime minister remained grounded; however, his general public – likely influenced by the need to justify the tremendous losses and sacrifices of the previous six years – was content to deceive itself into embracing the largely unsubstantiated belief that Canada's contribution to the new world order had been extensive.

When Canadians look back on the origins of the United Nations, they should feel tremendous pride. The "conservative and steady people, hardly daring to believe in [their] own capacity in the more complex affairs of statecraft," to which Bruce Hutchison had referred in 1940, were no more. To be Canadian in 1945 meant to be engaged in world affairs and actively concerned about the socio-economic state of less fortunate communities. Canadians wanted to help, to make a difference. But they also wanted these feelings to be noticed. Like many peoples caught up in a new nationalist impulse, they needed external affirmation that they were unique and exceptional.

One might suggest that this desire for approval was just as Pearsonian as the idealism that accompanied it. In this case, however, despite the talk, the passion, and the national enthusiasm, the Canada that helped to create the United Nations was not Lester Pearson's. It belonged to Mackenzie King.

Notes

Chapter 1: Introduction

1 Bruce Hutchison, "The Canadian Personality," CBC Broadcast, September 1940, in University of Calgary Library, Special Collections, Calgary, Alberta, Canada, Bruce Hutchison Fonds, MsC. 22, Box 10, File 5.

2 The only source devoted entirely to this topic is an unpublished German PhD thesis by Boris Stipernitz. His study is well researched, particularly regarding Canada's role, and comprehensive. There are, however, significant differences in interpretation between it and this study, many of which are based on this author's access to a wider variety of British archival sources along with the Records of the Foreign Service Posts of the US Department of State; see Boris Stipernitz, "Kanada und die Gründung der Vereinten Nationen, 1939-1945" (PhD dissertation, Universität zu Köln, 2001).

3 John Holmes, "Canadian Foreign Policy: Draft Project," August 1972, in University of Toronto, Trinity College Archives, Toronto, Ontario, Canada (hereafter UTTC), John Holmes Papers, Box 60, D/I/1/a.

4 Cecil C. Lingard and Reginald G. Trotter, *Canada in World Affairs: September 1941 to May 1944* (Toronto: Oxford University Press, 1950), 237-38.

5 J.L. Granatstein, *A Man of Influence: Norman A. Robertson and Canadian Statecraft, 1929-1968* (Toronto: Deneau Publishers, 1981), 139.

6 Inis Claude, *Swords into Ploughshares: The Problems and Progress of International Organization*, 4th ed. (1956; reprint, New York: Random House, 1984), 76.

7 Bernadotte E. Schmitt, *The United Nations Conference on International Organization*, vol. 5 (Department of State, 1950), in National Archives and Records Administration at College Park, Maryland, USA (hereafter NARA), RG59, Records of the Department of State, Records of Harley Notter, 1939-45 (hereafter Notter File), Records of the Advisory Committee on Post-War Foreign Policy, 1942-45, Entry 498, 250/46/22/06, Lot 60D-224, Box 106, PIO 729, vol. 5.

8 Maureen Appel Molot, "Where Do We, Should We, or Can We Sit? A Review of Canadian Foreign Policy Literature," *International Journal of Canadian Studies* 1, 2 (Spring-Fall 1990): 77.

9 John Holmes, for example, dedicates over 600 pages to Canada's role in shaping the postwar world order in a two-volume book that begins in "the formative year" of 1943; see *The Shaping of Peace: Canada and the Search for World Order, 1943-1957*, vol. 1 (Toronto: University of Toronto Press, 1979), 47.

10 The East Block is another name for the Department of External Affairs.

11 Douglas Owram, *The Government Generation: Canadian Intellectuals and the State, 1900-1945* (Toronto: University of Toronto Press, 1986), 331.

12 C.P. Stacey, "The Junior Partner, 1935-48," in *Mackenzie King and the Atlantic Triangle, 46-68* (Toronto: Macmillan, 1976), 66.

13 Carl Berger, *The Sense of Power: Studies in the Ideas of Canadian Imperialism, 1867-1914* (Toronto and Buffalo: University of Toronto Press, 1970), 265.
14 Angelika Sauer, "The Respectable Course: Canada's Department of External Affairs, the Great Powers, and the German Problem, 1943-1947" (PhD dissertation, University of Waterloo, 1994), 50.

Chapter 2: Two Steps Behind
1 William Lyon Mackenzie King, *Industry and Humanity* (1918; reprint, Toronto: University of Toronto Press, 1973), 335.
2 Ibid., 140.
3 "Biographical Sketch," n.d., in Robarts Library, Toronto, Ontario, Canada, Records of the Department of State, Microfilm Publication M1244, Records of the Office of European Affairs (Matthews-Hickerson File), 1934-47 (hereafter MHF), Roll 9, H. Freeman Matthews Correspondence and Memorandums.
4 Owram, *The Government Generation*, 260. The brain trust included the academic elite, members of the civil service, and members of the national media.
5 J.L. Granatstein, *Canada's War: The Politics of the Mackenzie King Government, 1939-1945* (1975; reprint, Toronto: University of Toronto Press, 1990), 325.
6 Memo, October 1955, n.d., in Library and Archives Canada, Ottawa, Ontario, Canada (hereafter LAC), Canadian Citizenship Council Papers, MG28 I85, vol. 54, Memorandum re: Its History and Activities, 1941-55.
7 C.P. Stacey, *Canada and the Age of Conflict*, vol. 2, *The Mackenzie King Era* (Toronto: University of Toronto Press, 1981), 269. See also J.L. Granatstein, *The Ottawa Men: The Civil Service Mandarins, 1935-1957* (1982; reprint, Toronto: University of Toronto Press, 1998), 28-44. Terry Crowley's suggestion that Skelton "envisioned a more active role" for Canada in world affairs after the war might well be true, but there is no evidence that he ever attempted to translate his vision into any sort of political action; see *Marriage of Minds: Isabel and Oscar Skelton Reinventing Canada* (Toronto: University of Toronto Press, 2003), 254.
8 Charles Ritchie, *The Siren Years: A Canadian Diplomat Abroad, 1937-1945* (Toronto: Macmillan, 1974), 9.
9 Lester B. Pearson, *Mike: The Memoirs of the Rt. Honourable Lester B. Pearson*, vol. 1, *1897-1948* (Toronto: University of Toronto Press, 1972), 192.
10 John Hilliker, *Canada's Department of External Affairs*, vol. 1, *The Early Years* (Montreal and Kingston: McGill-Queen's University Press, 1990), 239-40.
11 George Ignatieff, "Hume Wrong: A Study of Canadian Diplomatic Pioneering," n.d., in UTTC, George Ignatieff Papers, 989-0039, Box 18, File 8.
12 James A. Gibson, interview with author, Toronto, 25 September 2002.
13 Untitled transcript of dinner given by Mrs. Arthur J.R. Smith for Pearson, W.A. Mackintosh, Graham Towers, C.J. Mackenzie, John J. Deutsch, R.B. Bryce, and Louis Rasminsky, 20 November 1970, in Bank of Canada Archives (hereafter BCA), Louis Rasminsky Papers, Folder LR76-976. See also William Lyon Mackenzie King, diary entry, 6 August 1936, in Robarts Library, The Mackenzie King Diaries, 1893-1950 (hereafter King Diary), microfilm.
14 June Rogers, interview with author, Toronto, 24 September 2002.
15 Maurice A. Pope, *Soldiers and Politicians: The Memoirs of Lt.-Gen. Maurice A. Pope* (Toronto: University of Toronto Press, 1962), 150.
16 C.J. Mackenzie, interview with Robert Bothwell, 29 March 1976, in University of Toronto Archives, Toronto, Ontario, Canada (hereafter UT), Robert Selkirk Bothwell Papers (hereafter Bothwell Papers), B79-0055/002, File 2, Bothwell: Interviews re: Book on C.D. Howe, 1975-76. Pearson's biographer, John English, was probably the fairest when he wrote of Pearson's early education that "Lester excelled but he was no bookworm"; see *Shadow of Heaven: The Life of Lester Pearson*, vol. 1, *1897-1948* (Toronto: Lester and Orpen Dennys, 1989), 16. On Pearson's later studies, English added, "Academic pursuits did not really interest Mike" (57).
17 J.W. Pickersgill, interview with Robert Bothwell, 5 September 1975, in UT, Bothwell Papers, B79-0055/002, File 3, Bothwell: Interviews re: Book on C.D. Howe, 1975-76.
18 Walter Gordon, *A Political Memoir* (Toronto: McClelland and Stewart, 1977), 41.

19 Hilliker, *Canada's Department of External Affairs*, 240. On King's demand for obedience, see H.S. Ferns, *Reading from Left to Right: One Man's Political History* (Toronto: University of Toronto Press, 1983), 143.

20 Brooke Claxton, memoirs, in LAC, Brooke Claxton Papers, MG32 B5, vol. 253, 513-23.

21 Judith Robertson, interview with author, Toronto, 19 July 2002.

22 Granatstein, *A Man of Influence*, xii.

23 June Rogers, interview with author, Toronto, 24 September 2002.

24 Robertson to King, quoted in Granatstein, *A Man of Influence*, 113.

25 Pearson, quoted in Gordon, *A Political Memoir*, 42. Pearson makes a similar claim in *Mike: The Memoirs*, 194.

26 Pearson, diary entry, 29 March 1941, in LAC, L.B. Pearson Papers (hereafter Pearson Papers), MG26 N8, vol. 1, File 3, Diaries and Personal Papers, 1936-41, Part 3. See also Pearson, diary entry, 27 February 1941, in LAC, ibid.

27 Pearson to Massey, 27 May 1941, in LAC, Pearson Papers, MG26 N1, vol. 10, Massey, 1939-42.

28 Gordon Robertson, quoted in "Norman Robertson Round Table Transcript," 18 February 1978, in Personal Collections, Judith Robertson Papers.

29 Charles Ritchie, quoted in "Norman Robertson Round Table Transcript," 18 February 1978, in (Personal Collections, Judith Robertson Papers.)

30 For Pearson's explanation of the reason for the switch, see *Mike: The Memoirs*, 201.

31 World Citizens Association, *The World's Destiny and the United States: A Conference of Experts in International Relations* (Chicago: R.R. Donnelly and Sons, 1941), 276, 278-84.

32 League of Nations Society in Canada, *Annual Report of the National Executive Committee*, 1941-42, in LAC, Robert Boyer Inch Papers, MG30 C187, vol. 1, File 9.

33 Claxton to Robertson, 15 May 1941, in LAC, Department of External Affairs Papers (hereafter DEA Papers), RG25, Series G-2, vol. 3227, File 5475-40; Claxton to Robertson, 4 June 1941, in LAC, ibid.

34 C.G. Vickers to H.D. Henderson, 22 May 1939, in Bodleian Library, Oxford University, Oxford, UK (hereafter BL), Lionel Curtis Papers, MSS Curtis, vol. 110.

35 Minutes: World Order Preparatory Group, 17 July 1939, in BL, ibid.

36 Lothian to Churchill, 11 March 1940, in Churchill Archives Centre, Churchill College, Cambridge University, Cambridge, UK (hereafter CAC), Winston Churchill Papers (hereafter Churchill Papers), CHAR 20/15.

37 Harley Notter, *Postwar Foreign Policy Preparation, 1939-1945* (Washington, DC: Department of State, 1949), 453.

38 For a sense of public opinion at the time, see Raoul de Roussy de Sales, diary entries, 4 and 6 September 1939 and 14 October 1939, in *The Making of Yesterday: The Diaries of Raoul de Roussy de Sales* (New York: Reynal and Hitchcock, 1947), 60, 63, 73. On Roosevelt's commitment to postwar thinking from the beginning of the war onward, see Warren F. Kimball, *The Juggler: Franklin Roosevelt as Wartime Statesman* (Princeton: Princeton University Press, 1991), 61.

39 Hull, Memorandum of Conversation [with King], 17 April 1941, in Library of Congress, Manuscript Division, Washington, DC, USA (hereafter LC), Cordell Hull Papers, Reel 28, Conversations: Canada.

40 Address by President Franklin Roosevelt to the Congress on the Four Freedoms, 6 January 1941, in Published Documents, *The Dynamics of World Power: A Documentary History of United States Foreign Policy 1945-1973*, vol. 5, *The United Nations*, ed. Richard Hottelet (New York: Chelsea House Publishers, 1973), 9.

41 Halifax to Eden, 4 February 1941, in CAC, Edward Frederick Lindley Wood, Earl of Halifax, Papers (hereafter Halifax Papers), HLFX Reel II.

42 AIPO, 4 March 1941, in *Public Opinion Quarterly* (hereafter *POQ*) 5, 2 (June 1941): 319-20.

43 Anthony Eden [Earl of Avon], *The Eden Memoirs: The Reckoning* (London: Cassell and Company, 1965), 513.

44 Roosevelt to Grew, 21 January 1941, in Franklin Delano Roosevelt Library, Hyde Park, New York, USA (hereafter FDRL), Franklin Delano Roosevelt Papers (hereafter FDR Papers),

President's Secretary's Files (hereafter PSF), Confidential Files, Box 9, State Department: 1941-42.

45 Ruth B. Russell's suggestion that American planning slowed down during this period seems to be an exaggeration; see *A History of the United Nations Charter: The Role of the United States, 1940-1945* (Washington, DC: The Brookings Institution, 1958), 22.

46 Roosevelt, quoted in Theodore A. Wilson, *The First Summit: Roosevelt and Churchill at Placentia Bay, 1941* (1969; rev. ed., Lawrence, KS: University of Kansas Press, 1991), 15.

47 Memorandum to Sir George Crystal, 24 March 1941, in National Archives of England, Wales and the United Kingdom, Kew, UK (hereafter NAUK), Cabinet Office Papers (hereafter CAB) 117/245.

48 Machtig to Crystal, 13 June 1941, in NAUK, CAB 117/246. Lingard and Trotter are more positive, suggesting that the meeting "foreshadowed briefly the principles of the Atlantic Charter"; see *Canada in World Affairs*, 35. They wishfully imply, and without any real evidence, that the Commonwealth meeting had an impact on subsequent British foreign-policy activity.

49 Cadogan to Lady Theo, 11 August 1941, in CAC, Sir Alexander George Montagu Cadogan Papers, ACAD 3/13.

50 Welles, Memo of Conversation, 11 August 1941, in Published Documents, *Foreign Relations of the United States* (hereafter *FRUS*), *1941*, vol. 1, *General, the Soviet Union* (Washington, DC: Government Printing Office, 1958), 363.

51 Churchill, quoted in Clark M. Eichelberger, *Organizing for Peace: A Personal History of the Founding of the United Nations* (New York: Harper and Row, 1977), 181.

52 Churchill to Lord Privy Seal, 11 August 1941, in NAUK, CAB 21/405. See also Waldo Heinrichs, *Threshold of War: Franklin D. Roosevelt and American Entry into World War II* (New York and Oxford: Oxford University Press, 1988), 27; and Warren F. Kimball, ed., *Churchill and Roosevelt: The Complete Correspondence*, vol. 1, *Alliance Emerging, October 1933-November 1942* (Princeton: Princeton University Press, 1984), 227-28.

53 "The Atlantic Charter," in Douglas Brinkley and David R. Facey-Crowther, eds., *The Atlantic Charter* (New York: St. Martin's Press, 1994), xvii.

54 See King, diary entries, 6-12 August 1941, in Robarts Library, King Diary.

55 Robertson to King, 14 August 1941, in Published Documents, *Documents on Canadian External Relations* (hereafter *DCER*), vol. 7, *1939-1941*, part 1, ed. David R. Murray (Ottawa: Department of External Affairs, 1974), 239.

56 Foreign Research and Press Service, Note on the Atlantic Declaration, RR I/59/iii, 3 September 1941, in NAUK, CAB 117/58.

57 Notter, "Comment on the Joint Declaration of the Atlantic Joint Declaration of President Roosevelt and Prime Minister Churchill, August 14, 1941," 11 September 1941, in NARA, RG59, Records of the Department of State, Notter File, Miscellaneous Subject Files, Entry 496, 250/46/22/03, Lot 60D-224, Box 13, Atlantic Charter. See also *The White House Papers of Harry L. Hopkins*, vol. 1, ed. Robert E. Sherwood (London: Eyre and Spottiswoode, 1948), 363.

58 David Reynolds, *The Creation of the Anglo-American Alliance, 1937-1941: A Study in Diplomatic Competitive Co-operation* (Chapel Hill: University of North Carolina Press, 1982), 195.

59 MacDonald to Cranborne, 15 August 1941, in Durham University Library, Archives and Special Collections, Durham, UK (hereafter DUL), Malcolm MacDonald Papers, 14/5.

60 Lingard and Trotter, *Canada in World Affairs*, 42.

61 Minutes of the Executive Committee [of the CIIA], 6 October 1941, in LAC, Canadian Institute of International Affairs Papers, MG28 I250, Reel M-4619, vol. 5, Minutes of Meetings, 1941-42.

62 Minutes of the 14th Annual Meeting of the National [CIIA] Council, 1 November 1941, in LAC, ibid.

63 F.H. Soward, "Inside a Canadian Triangle: The University, the CIIA, and the Department of External Affairs, a Personal Record," *International Journal* 33, 1 (Winter 1977-78): 66-87; H.L. Keenleyside, "Canada's Department of External Affairs," *International Journal* 1, 3 (July 1945): 189-214.

64 Carlton Savage to Hull, 19 December 1941, in *FRUS, 1942*, vol. 1, *General, the British Commonwealth, the Far East* (Washington, DC: Government Printing Office, 1960), 1; and Hull to Roosevelt, 19 December 1941, in FDRL, FDR Papers, PSF, Safe Files, Box 5, State Department.
65 Reid to Robertson, 23 December 1941, in LAC, Escott Reid Papers, MG31 E46, vol. 6, File 1 [10].
66 Cordell Hull, *The Memoirs of Cordell Hull*, vol. 2 (New York: Macmillan, 1948), 1121.
67 Robertson to King, 29 December 1941, in Published Documents, *DCER*, vol. 9, *1942-43*, ed. John F. Hilliker (Ottawa: Minister of Supply and Services Canada, 1980), 100.
68 Memorandum [by Berle], 31 December 1941, in *FRUS, 1942*, vol. 1, 25.
69 Paul Martin, *A Very Public Life*, vol. 1, *Far From Home* (Ottawa: Debeau Publishers, 1983), 274.
70 Address of the Right Honourable Winston Churchill to Members of the Senate and the House of Commons, 30 December 1941, in Canada, House of Commons, *Debates*, 2nd Session, 19th Parliament, 7 November 1940 to 21 January 1942, vol. 228, 4479.
71 Moffat to Secretary of State (hereafter SS), 28 October 1941, in NARA, RG59, Records of the Department of State, 250, State Department Decimal Files, 1940-44, Box 5015, from 842.00/600 to 842.00/699.

Chapter 3: Private Failure

1 Douglas Anglin, "Canadian Policy Towards International Institutions, 1939-1950" (PhD dissertation, Oxford University, 1956), 260-61.
2 Robertson to King, 17 January 1942, in LAC, DEA Papers, RG25, vol. 2964, File 3265-A-40C, Part 1.
3 Wrong to Robertson, 20 January 1942, in LAC, DEA Papers, RG25, vol. 2963, File 3265-A-40C, Part 1.
4 David Mitrany, *The Functional Theory of International Politics* (London: Martin Robertson, 1975), specifically, "A War-time Submission (1941): Territorial, Ideological and Functional International Organization," 19, and the introduction by Paul Taylor. On the links between functionalism and American politics, see Holmes, *The Shaping of Peace*, 72.
5 Wrong to Robertson, 20 January 1942, in LAC, DEA Papers, RG25, vol. 2963, File 3265-A-40C, Part 1.
6 Wrong to Robertson, 27 January 1942, in LAC, ibid.
7 Wrong, Minute, 28 January 1942, in LAC, ibid.
8 Wrong to Pearson, 3 February 1942, in LAC, ibid.
9 Minutes of the Cabinet War Committee, 4 February 1942, in LAC, Privy Council Office Papers (hereafter PCO Papers), RG2, 7c, vol. 8, Minutes and Documents of the Cabinet War Committee, January-March 1942.
10 James Eayrs, *In Defence of Canada*, vol. 3, *Peacemaking and Deterrence* (Toronto: University of Toronto Press, 1972), 182.
11 Maisky, quoted in Winant to Hull, 22 January 1942, in *FRUS, 1942*, vol. 1, 89-90.
12 Roosevelt to Welles, 7 March 1942, in FDRL, FDR Papers, PSF, Departmental Files, Box 77, State: Welles, Sumner: January-April 1942.
13 Moffat, Memorandum of Conversation with Robertson, 16 September 1941, in NARA, RG59, Records of the Department of State, Records of the Office of Assistant Secretary and Under-Secretary of State Dean Acheson, 1941-49, 1950, Records Relating to Wartime Relief, Post-War Rehabilitation and International Monetary Stabilization, 1941-45 (hereafter Acheson Papers), Entry 671, 250/46/35/05, Box 5, File 2.
14 Claxton, Memoirs, in LAC, Brooke Claxton Papers, MG32 B5, vol. 253, 586-610.
15 Pasvolsky to Acheson, 19 March 1942, in NARA, RG59, Records of the Department of State, Acheson Papers, Entry 671, 250/46/35/05, Box 5, File 2. C.P. Stacey's two-page analysis of the UNRRA begins with events dating from 30 July 1942. In limiting his account to such a late stage of the negotiations, Stacey misses the changes in both British and American attitudes toward the executive committee of the council; see *Canada and the Age of Conflict*, vol. 2, *The Mackenzie King Era* (Toronto: University of Toronto Press, 1981), 331-32. Lester Pearson has the same problem; see *Mike: The Memoirs*, 250. The accounts of John Hilliker

and John Holmes are also misleading in suggesting that the United States first advocated a four-power executive. Holmes also minimizes Pearson's role in the negotiations; see Hilliker, *Canada's Department of External Affairs*, 298; and Holmes, *The Shaping of Peace*, 34.

16 Minutes of the Cabinet War Committee, 4 June 1942, in LAC, PCO Papers, RG2, 7c, vol. 9, Minutes of the Cabinet War Committee, 1 April-26 June 1942; Minutes of Cabinet War Committee, 12 June 1942, in LAC, ibid.

17 Leith-Ross to High Commissioner, 30 June 1942, in NAUK, Treasury Office Papers, Frederick William Leith-Ross Papers (hereafter Leith-Ross Papers), T 188/252.

18 Dexter to Ferguson, 12 February 1942, in Queen's University Archives, Kingston, Ontario, Canada (hereafter QUA), Grant Dexter Papers, Collection 2142, Series 1: Correspondence, Box 3, Folder 21, General, 1942, January-February.

19 Memorandum of Conversation re: United Nations Relief Organization, Second Meeting, 3 July 1942, in NAUK, Leith-Ross Papers, T 188/255; Memorandum of Conversation re: United Nations Relief Organization, Third Meeting, 7 July 1942, in NAUK, ibid.; and Acheson, Memorandum to UK, US, China, 11 July 1942, in NAUK, ibid.

20 Hickerson, Memo of Conversation with Robertson, 28 May 1942, in Robarts Library, Records of the Department of State, Microfilm Publication M1244, MHF, Roll 2, John D. Hickerson Memorandums, 1942-45.

21 Pearson, "Canada and the Combined Boards," 23 July 1942, in LAC, DEA Papers, RG25, vol. 2964, File 3265-A-40C, Part 1.

22 Moffat, Memorandum of Conversation with Pearson, 28 July 1942, in NARA, RG84, Records of the Foreign Service Posts of the Department of State, Entry 2195a, 350/51/09/03, Canada, Ottawa Embassy, Security, Segregated General Records 1939-49, Box 87, 1942, 800. On the Leith-Ross meeting, see Leith-Ross, Minute, [27 July 1942], in NAUK, Treasury Office Papers, Leith-Ross Papers, T 188/252.

23 Minutes of the Cabinet War Committee, 29 July 1942, in LAC, PCO Papers, RG2, 7c, vol. 10, Minutes of the Cabinet War Committee, 1 July-30 September 1942.

24 Angus to Robertson, 17 August 1942, in LAC, DEA Papers, RG25, vol. 2964, File 3265-A-40C, Part 1.

25 Clark to Robertson, 25 August 1942, in LAC, ibid.

26 Minutes of the Cabinet War Committee, 2 September 1942, in LAC, PCO Papers, RG2, 7c, vol. 10, Minutes of the Cabinet War Committee, 1 July-30 September 1942.

27 MacDonald to Attlee, 31 July 1942, in NAUK, Treasury Office Papers, Leith-Ross Papers, T 188/252.

28 War Cabinet: Official Committee on Post-War Commodity Policy and Relief: Report on Proposals for a United Nations Relief and Rehabilitation Administration, 12 October 1942, in NAUK, Treasury Office Papers, Leith-Ross Papers, T 188/256; Ronald, Minute, 13 October 1942, in NAUK, ibid.

29 Massey to Secretary of State for External Affairs (hereafter SSEA), 24 October 1942, in LAC, PCO Papers, RG2, Series B-2, vol. 44, File W-22-1, 1942-43.

30 British Embassy to Department of State, 27 November 1942, in *FRUS, 1942*, vol. 1, 150. Leith-Ross followed up with Acheson personally on 4 December; see Leith-Ross to Acheson, 4 December 1942, in NAUK, Treasury Office Papers, Leith-Ross Papers, T 188/255.

31 Maisky to Eden, 16 December 1942, in NAUK, ibid., T 188/256; Leith-Ross to Ronald, 28 December 1942, in NAUK, ibid.

32 DO to Canada, 23 December 1942, in NAUK, ibid.

33 Acheson, memorandum of conversation with Reinhardt and Litvinov, 30 December 1942, in NARA, RG59, Records of the Department of State, Acheson Papers, Entry 671, 250/46/35/05, Box 5, File 2; Acheson to Hull, 6 January 1943, in NARA, ibid., File 3. On the American desire to maintain positive relations with the Soviet Union, see John Lewis Gaddis, *The United States and the Origins of the Cold War, 1941-1947* (New York and London: Columbia University Press, 1972), 6.

34 FO to Halifax, 9 January 1943, in NAUK, Treasury Office Papers, Leith-Ross Papers, T 188/256.

35 Halifax to FO, 12 January 1943, in NAUK, ibid.

36 FO to Washington, 15, 20, and 22 January 1943, in NAUK, ibid.; Washington to FO, 21 January 1943, in NAUK, ibid.
37 Minutes of the Cabinet War Committee, 21 January 1943, in LAC, PCO Papers, RG2, 7c, vol. 12, Minutes of the Cabinet War Committee, 6 January-14 May 1943. On the new national confidence, see Claxton to Armstrong, 27 November 1942, in LAC, Brooke Claxton Papers, MG32 B5, vol. 21, Armstrong-Elizabeth, 1941-53.
38 Pearson, diary entry, 26 January 1943, in LAC, Pearson Papers, MG26 N8, vol. 1, File 4, Diaries and Personal Papers, 1943-45. See also Pearson, diary entry, 23 January 1943, in LAC, ibid., and Pearson, *Mike: The Memoirs*, 252.
39 Acheson, Memorandum of Conversation, 26 January 1943, in *FRUS, 1943*, vol. 1, *General* (Washington, DC: Government Printing Office, 1963), 865.
40 Washington to FO, 31 January 1943, in NAUK, Treasury Office Papers, Leith-Ross Papers, T 188/256.
41 Leith-Ross to [President], 2 February 1943, in NAUK, ibid.
42 Pearson, diary entry, 5 February 1943, in LAC, Pearson Papers, MG26 N8, vol. 1, File 4, Diaries and Personal Papers, 1943-45.
43 Canadian Legation to Department of State, 9 February 1943, in *FRUS, 1943*, vol. 1, 866-67.
44 Welles, Memorandum of Conversation with Pearson, 10 February 1943, in FDRL, Sumner Welles Papers, Box 161, Folder 05, Europe Files, 1933-43, Canada, 1933-43; Pearson to King, 10 February 1943, in LAC, PCO Papers, RG2, Series B-2, vol. 44, File W-22-1, 1942-43.
45 Memorandum of Discussion in Mr. Acheson's Office: Department of State, 17 February 1943, in NARA, RG59, Records of the Department of State, Acheson Papers, Entry 671, 250/46/35/05, Box 5, File 3.
46 Minutes of Cabinet War Committee, 24 February 1943, in LAC, PCO Papers, RG2, 7c, vol. 12, Minutes of Cabinet War Committee, 6 January-14 May 1943.
47 Pearson, diary entries, 26 and 27 February 1943, in LAC, Pearson Papers, MG26 N8, vol. 1, File 4, Diaries and Personal Papers, 1943-45. The response opposed the compromise; see Wrong to McCarthy, 1 March 1943, in LAC, DEA Papers, RG25, Series A-3-b, vol. 22-D(s), Part 1.
48 Washington to FO, 27 February 1943, in NAUK, Treasury Office Papers, Leith-Ross Papers, T 188/256.
49 Clark to Robertson, 3 March 1943, in LAC, PCO Papers, RG2, Series B-2, vol. 44, File W-22-a, 1942-43; Minutes of the Cabinet War Committee, 3 March 1943, in LAC, PCO Papers, RG2, 7c, vol. 12, Minutes of the Cabinet War Committee, 6 January-14 May 1943.
50 Pearson, diary entry, 4 March 1943, in LAC, Pearson Papers, MG26 N8, vol. 1, File 4, Diaries and Personal Papers, 1943-45. John Holmes is clearly unaware of what Pearson did; see *The Shaping of Peace*, 39.
51 Acheson, Memorandum of Conversation with Pearson, 4 March 1943, in NARA, RG59, Records of the Department of State, Acheson Papers, Entry 671, 250/46/35/05, Box 5, File 3; Wrong to King, 22 March 1943, in LAC, DEA Papers, RG25, Series A-3-b, vol. 22-D(s), Part 1.
52 MacDonald to DO, 7 March 1943, in NAUK, Treasury Office Papers, Leith-Ross Papers, T 188/256; MacDonald to Halifax, 13 March 1943, in DUL, Malcolm MacDonald Papers, 14/8.
53 Robertson to King, 17 March 1943, in LAC, DEA Papers, RG25, Series A-3-b, vol. 22-D(s), Part 1. See also Pearson to Robertson, 17 March 1943, in LAC, ibid.
54 Pearson, diary entry, week of 22-27 March 1943, in LAC, Pearson Papers, MG26 N8, vol. 1, File 4, Diaries and Personal Papers, 1943-45. Pearson's later comment, "I was, after all, a civil servant, not a policy maker," is hardly believable in this case; see *Mike: The Memoirs*, 197.
55 Pearson to Wrong, 25 March 1943, in LAC, PCO Papers, RG2, Series B-2, vol. 44, File W-22-1, 1942-43.
56 Pearson, diary entry, week of 26 March-1 April 1943, in LAC, Pearson Papers, MG26 N8, vol. 1, File 4, Diaries and Personal Papers, 1943-45.

57   Washington to FO, 29 March 1943, in NAUK, Treasury Office Papers, Leith-Ross Papers, T 188/256; MacDonald to FO [for Eden], 30 March 1943, in NAUK, ibid. See also Jebb, Minute, 26 March 1943, in NAUK, ibid.
58   Minutes of the Cabinet War Committee, 31 March 1943, in LAC, PCO Papers, RG2, 7c, vol. 12, Minutes of the Cabinet War Committee, 6 January-14 May 1943.
59   Leith-Ross, Minute, 1 April 1943, in NAUK, Treasury Office Papers, Leith-Ross Papers, T 188/256.
60   Robertson to King, 2 April 1943, in LAC, PCO Papers, RG2, Series B-2, vol. 44, File W-22-1, 1942-43. The proposal had been suggested informally by Gladwyn Jebb the month before; see Granatstein, *Canada's War*, 305.
61   King, diary entry, 7 April 1943, in Robarts Library, King Diary; Minutes of the Cabinet War Committee, 7 April 1943, in LAC, PCO Papers, RG2, 7c, vol. 12, Minutes of the Cabinet War Committee, 6 January-14 May 1943.
62   Pearson, diary entry, 8 April 1943, in LAC, Pearson Papers, MG26 N8, vol. 1, File 4, Diaries and Personal Papers, 1943-45.
63   Massey to King, in UT, Vincent Massey Papers, B-87-0082, Box 415, File 13, Miscellaneous: General.
64   Massey diary entry, 2 May 1943, in UT, Vincent Massey Papers, B-87-0082, Box 311, Massey Diaries, 1941-43, Diary 50, February-June 1943.
65   John Foster Dulles, Relief and Rehabilitation Administration, 27 July 1943, in Seeley G. Mudd Manuscript Library, Princeton, New Jersey, USA (hereafter SML), John Foster Dulles Papers, Box 22, Duplicate Correspondence, File: Federal Council of the Churches of Christ in America: Commission to Study the Bases of a Just and Durable Peace, 1943. See also Stipernitz, "Kanada und die Gründung der Vereinten Nationen, 1939-1945," ch. 4.

Chapter 4: Public Success

1   Canadian Institute of Public Opinion (CIPO), 10 January 1942, in *POQ* 6, 2 (Summer 1942): 313.
2   Patrick H. Brennan, *Reporting the Nation's Business: Press-Government Relations During the Liberal Years, 1935-1957* (Toronto: University of Toronto Press, 1994), 18; Ramsay Cook, *The Politics of John W. Dafoe and the Free Press* (Toronto: University of Toronto Press, 1963), 281.
3   Grant Dexter [autobiographical sketch], n.d., in QUA, Grant Dexter Papers, Collection 2142, Series 1: Correspondence, Box 1, Folder 7, General.
4   James H. Gray, *Troublemaker! A Personal History* (Toronto: Macmillan of Canada, 1978), 135.
5   R.O. MacFarlane, "Canada Tomorrow: Canada and the Post-War World," *Behind the Headlines* 2, 3 (January 1942); "Blueprints for a New World: Canada and the Post-War World, Part 2," *Behind the Headlines* 2, 4 (1 February 1942); and "Beginning at the End: Canada and the Post-War World, Part 3," *Behind the Headlines* 2, 5 (15 February 1942).
6   Reid to Glazebrook, 16 March 1942, in LAC, Escott Reid Papers, MG31 E46, vol. 6, File 1 [10].
7   See "Reviving the Ideal," *Winnipeg Free Press* (hereafter *WFP*), 2 May 1942, 15; and "Canada and Collective Security," *WFP*, 5 May 1942, 9.
8   Hanson, 25 March 1942, in Canada, House of Commons, *Debates*, 3rd Session, 19th Parliament, 5 March 1942 to 5 May 1942, vol. 230, 1635.
9   Escott Reid, *On Duty: A Canadian at the Making of the United Nations, 1945-1946* (Toronto: McClelland and Stewart, 1983), 7.
10   Reid, "The United States and Canada: Domination, Co-operation, Absorption," 12 January 1942, in LAC, Escott Reid Papers, MG31 E46, vol. 30, United States and Canada, 1942-45. See also Escott Reid, *Radical Mandarin: The Memoirs of Escott Reid* (Toronto: University of Toronto Press, 1989), 158-59.
11   Charles Vining, "Canadian Publicity in the United States: A Report to the Prime Minister," 10 July 1942, in LAC, W.L.M. King Papers, Memoranda and Notes, MG26 J4, vol. 326, File 3427, Public Opinion. Public opinion polls taken in June supported his claims; see Fortune, June 1942, in *POQ* 6, 3 (Fall 1942): 491.

12 King's decision to include Brais was particularly important since over 60 percent of Quebecers favoured improving relations with the United States and over 65 percent of French Canadians favoured active engagement in a postwar international organization similar to the League of Nations; see Marcel Cadieux, Saul F. Rae, and Paul Tremblay, "Quebec and the Present War: A Study of Public Opinion" (Ottawa: July 1942), in LAC, DEA Papers, RG25, vol. 2877, File 1889-1940.

13 WIB Survey 2, 16 January 1943, in LAC, W.L.M. King Papers, MG26 J2, vol. 379, File W-319-2, War: W.I.B. Surveys, 1943. See also William Robert Young, "Making the Truth Graphic: The Canadian Government's Home Front Information Structures and Programmes During World War II" (PhD dissertation, University of British Columbia, 1978), 284.

14 L.S.B. Shapiro, "Is Canada Really a Nation?" *Saturday Night*, 7 February 1942, 11; "Backstage at Ottawa," *Maclean's*, 15 March 1942, 14; Roger Duhamel, "M. Bennett se bat pour l'empire!" *Le Devoir*, 3 November 1942, 1, and "Plus ça va, plus ça 'empire,'" *Le Devoir*, 18 November 1942, 1.

15 Manley O. Hudson to Hickerson, 11 September 1942, in Robarts Library, RG59, Records of the Department of State, Microfilm Publication M1244, MHF, Roll 5, John D. Hickerson Correspondence H-N 1934-47.

16 Coldwell to Tarr, 18 January 1943, in LAC, CIIA Papers, MG28 I250, vol. 3, Edgar J. Tarr: IPR: Mont Tremblant Conference, re: Canadian Group, 1942-43. See also Paul Hasluck, *Diplomatic Witness: Australian Foreign Affairs, 1941-1947* (Melbourne: Melbourne University Press, 1980), 68.

17 Coldwell, 27 January 1943, in Canada, House of Commons, *Debates*, 3rd Session, 19th Parliament, 17 July 1942 to 27 January 1943, vol. 233, 5191.

18 Policy of the Progressive Conservative Party: Adopted at the National Convention, Held at Winnipeg, 9, 10, 11 December 1942, in QUA, T.A. Crerar Papers, Collection 2117, Series 2, Box 88, Correspondence, 1931-54, Folder 1942-43.

19 Blackmore, 27 January 1943, in Canada, House of Commons, *Debates*, 3rd Session, 19th Parliament, 17 July 1942 to 27 January 1943, vol. 233, 5191.

20 W.E. Harris, 29 January 1943, in Canada, House of Commons, *Debates*, 4th Session, 19th Parliament, 28 January 1943 to 5 March 1943, vol. 234, 15.

21 Cardin, 9 February 1943, in Canada, ibid., 286. For the CCF response, see Coldwell, 1 February 1943, in Canada, ibid., 60.

22 Green, 17 February 1943, in Canada, ibid., 501. See also Lingard and Trotter, *Canada in World Affairs*, 247.

23 CBC Press Release for [19 February] 1943, in LAC, DEA Papers, RG25, Series G-2, vol. 2870, File 1843-Q-40; "Of Things to Come," *WFP*, 15 June 1943, 11. A corresponding series in French was also planned, but there is no record as to whether it ever took place.

24 King, 19 March 1943, in Canada, House of Commons, *Debates*, 4th Session, 19th Parliament, 8 March to 9 April 1943, vol. 235, 1396-98. For criticism of King's answer, see [illegible] to Bracken, 22 March 1943, in LAC, Gordon Graydon Papers, MG27 III C15, vol. 5, File D-130.

25 Hansell, 25 March 1943, in Canada, House of Commons, *Debates*, 4th Session, 19th Parliament, 8 March to 9 April 1943, vol. 235, 1571-72.

26 Léopold Richer, "La vraie politique étrangère du Canada," *Le Devoir*, 22 March 1943, 1; WIB Survey 7, 27 March 1943, in LAC, W.L.M. King Papers, MG26 J2, vol. 379, File W-319-2, War: W.I.B. Surveys, 1943.

27 See, for example, "Le voyage de M. Eden," *La Presse*, 15 March 1943, 6; "Our Anomalous Position," *Globe and Mail* (hereafter *G&M*), 19 March 1943, 6.

28 Kimball, *The Juggler*, 13.

29 Hull to Roosevelt, 22 December 1941, in *FRUS, 1941*, vol. 1, 594.

30 P Minutes 4: 28 March 1942, in NARA, RG59, Records of the Department of State, Notter File, Records of the Advisory Committee on Post-War Foreign Policy, 1942-45, Entry 498, 250/46/22/06, Lot 60D-224, Box 54, P Documents.

31 Gladwyn Jebb, *The Memoirs of Lord Gladwyn* (London: Weidenfield and Nicolson, 1972), 114-15. See also Jebb, interview, in Dag Hammarskjöld Library, United Nations, New York,

USA (hereafter DHL), Oral History Collection, (02), J44, Lord Gladwyn Jebb, 21 June 1983; and Sir Llewellyn Woodward, *British Foreign Policy in the Second World War*, vol. 5 (London: Her Majesty's Stationary Office, 1976), 3-9.

32 Ibid., 11-13. For his own recollection, see Eden, *The Eden Memoirs*, 366. On Churchill's lack of support, see Churchill to Eden, 18 October 1942, in University of Birmingham Library, Special Collections, Birmingham, UK (hereafter UBSC), Lord Avon [Anthony Eden] Papers (hereafter Avon Papers), AP 20/9; and Churchill to Eden, 21 October 1942, quoted in Winston S. Churchill, *The Second World War,* vol. 4, *The Hinge of Fate* (Boston: Houghton Mifflin, 1950), 562.

33 "The United Nations Plan," in *The Historian as Diplomat: Charles Kingsley Webster and the United Nations, 1939-1946,* ed. P.A. Reynolds and R.J. Hughes, (London: Martin Robertson, 1976), 121-25. Provisions were included for France to reassert itself as a fifth great power later on.

34 Churchill to Attlee, 1 February 1943, in NAUK, Foreign Office Papers (hereafter FO), Anthony Eden Papers, FO 954/22; Halifax to Roosevelt, 2 February 1943, in *FRUS: The Conferences at Washington and Quebec, 1943* (Washington, DC: Government Printing Office, 1970), 704. Since this letter was found in the Eden Papers, it appears that the foreign secretary, who was much more abreast of postwar planning than was the prime minister, likely wrote the original draft.

35 Eden to Churchill, 10 February 1943, in NAUK, FO, Private Secretaries Papers, FO 800/404; Churchill to Roosevelt, 11 February 1943, in *FRUS, 1943*, vol. 3, *The British Commonwealth, Eastern Europe, the Far East* (Washington, DC: Government Printing Office, 1963), 2.

36 Eden to Churchill, 28 March 1943, in NAUK, FO, Private Secretaries Papers, FO 800/404. On the origins of the "four policemen" idea, see Russell, *A History of the United Nations Charter,* 43; and Kimball, *The Juggler,* 85.

37 Memorandum by Hopkins, 27 March 1943, in *FRUS, 1943*, vol. 3, 39.

38 King diary entry, 5 December 1942, in Robarts Library, King Diary. See also Minutes of the Cabinet War Committee, 9 December 1942, in LAC, PCO Papers, RG2, 7c, vol. 11, Minutes of the Cabinet War Committee, 7 October-30 December 1942.

39 MacDonald to DO, 2 April 1943, in NAUK, Treasury Office Papers, Leith-Ross Papers, T 188/256.

40 Minutes of the Cabinet War Committee, 31 March 1943, in LAC, PCO Papers, RG2, 7c, vol. 12, Minutes of the Cabinet War Committee, 6 January-14 May 1943.

41 Eden, 1 April 1943, in Canada, House of Commons, *Debates*, 4th Session, 19th Parliament, 8 March to 9 April 1943, vol. 235, 1748.

42 "Backstage at Ottawa," *Maclean's,* 1 May 1943, 57.

43 Crerar to Dafoe, 15 April 1943, in QUA, T.A. Crerar Papers, Collection 2117, Series 3, Box 104, Folder 15, Correspondence: Dafoe, J.W., September 1923, January 1924, February 1936-April 1943.

44 Mark A. Stoler, *Allies and Adversaries: The Joint Chiefs of Staff, the Grand Alliance, and U.S. Strategy in World War II* (Chapel Hill and London: University of North Carolina Press, 2000), 106-17.

45 SSDA to SSEA, 12 April 1943, in Published Documents, *DCER*, vol. 9, *1942-43*, ed. John F. Hilliker (Ottawa: Minister of Supply and Services Canada, 1980), 1016. See also King, diary entry, 12 April 1943, in Robarts Library, King Diary.

46 Conversation with Roosevelt and Churchill after Pacific War Meeting, in King, diary entry, 20 May 1943, in Robarts Library, King Diary. See also Memorandum Prepared by British Embassy, 22 May 1943, in *FRUS: The Conferences at Washington and Quebec, 1943*, 167-72; and Record of a Conversation at Luncheon at the British Embassy, Washington, 22 May 1943, in NAUK, FO, Anthony Eden Papers, FO 954/22.

47 Memorandum of Conversation, 19 May 1943, in NAUK, ibid.; Trident: Meeting with Dominions, Minutes of Meeting Held in the White House on Thursday, 20 May 1943, in NAUK, Dominions Office Papers (hereafter DO), DO 35/1638; Conversation with Roosevelt and Churchill after Pacific War Meeting, 20 May 1943, in Robarts Library, King Diary; Memorandum of Conversation between King and Sumner Welles, 21 May 1943, in Robarts Library, ibid.

48 Lloyd C. Gardner and Warren F. Kimball, "The United States: Democratic Diplomacy," in *Allies at War: The Soviet, American and British Experience, 1939-1945*, ed. David Reynolds et al., 387-416 (New York: St. Martin's Press, 1994), 396.

49 Eden to Churchill, 12 July 1943, in UBSC, Avon Papers, AP/20/10.

50 For the British side, see Eden to War Cabinet, "United Nations Plan for Organising Peace," 7 July 1943, in NAUK, DO 35/1841; and Woodward, *British Foreign Policy in the Second World War*, 50-51. For the American side, see H 1019, 19 July 1943, in NARA, RG59, Records of the Department of State, Notter File, Policy Summaries, 1943-44, Entry 500, 250/46/24/07, Lot 60D-224, Box 156, I.O. Pol. Sum. No. 3, Steps to Perm. Org.; and Notter to Pasvolsky, 14 August 1943, in NARA, RG59, Records of the Department of State, Notter File, Miscellaneous Subject Files, Entry 496, 250/46/22/03, Lot 60D-224, Box 8, Notter's Chronological File, 3 May-23 August 1943. The Americans eventually settled on Hull's advisory committee's draft, which gave more power to the general assembly than did the draft prepared by Welles's subcommittee; see Notter, *Postwar Foreign Policy Preparation*, 169-76, 534.

51 "Planning Postwar Canada," *Canadian Forum* 23, 267 (April 1943): 11, 14.

52 WIB Survey 10, 8 May 1943, in LAC, W.L.M. King Papers, MG26 J2, vol. 379, File W-319-2, War: W.I.B. Surveys, 1943; WIB: Information Brief: "The Why of Post-War Goals," no. 10, 14 June 1943, in LAC, Department of Finance Papers, RG19, Series E-5, vol. 4028, Files 129-W-1-3, 129-W-1-4, and 129-W-1-5.

53 W.L. Morton, *Canada and the World Tomorrow: Opportunity and Responsibility: Report of the Proceedings of the Ninth Annual Study Conference of the Canadian Institute of International Affairs, Hamilton, Ontario, 22-23 May 1943* (Toronto: CIIA, 1943), 34, 20.

54 Quoted in Adam Chapnick, "The Canadian Middle Power Myth," *International Journal* 55, 2 (Spring 2000): 192.

55 King, 1 July 1943, in Canada, House of Commons, *Debates*, 4th Session, 19th Parliament, 28 May 1943 to 1 July 1943, vol. 237, 4226; Blackmore, 1 July 1943, in Canada, ibid., 4227-28; MacInnis, 1 July 1943, in Canada, ibid., 4229.

56 King, 9 July 1943, in Canada, House of Commons, *Debates*, 4th Session, 19th Parliament, 2 July 1943 to 26 January 1944, vol. 238, 4558.

57 SFR to Wrong, 22 July 1943, in LAC, DEA Papers, RG25, Series G-2, vol. 3227, File 5475-40.

58 European Division, Memorandum, 12 August 1943, in Robarts Library, Records of the Department of State, Microfilm Publication M1244, MHF, Roll 12, Subject File: British Commonwealth. For the original report, see Hickerson to Atherton, [end of July 1943], in Robarts Library, ibid., Roll 8, John D. Hickerson Miscellaneous Files 1937-47.

59 Canada, House of Commons, *Debates*, 4th Session, 19th Parliament, 2 July 1943 to 26 January 1944, vol. 238, 4563-4654.

60 See, for example, "Canada Takes the Lead," *Montreal Gazette*, 10 July 1943, 8; G.C. Whittaker, "Mr. King Blueprints Canada's Status," *Saturday Night*, 17 July 1943, 8; "Canada's Foreign Policy," *WFP*, 19 July 1943, 11; Bruce Hutchison, "The Road Ahead," *Maclean's*, 15 August 1943, 1.

61 Joint Meeting of the War Cabinet of the United Kingdom and the Canadian War Cabinet, 11 August 1943, in LAC, PCO Papers, RG2, 7c, vol. 13, Minutes of the Cabinet War Committee, 19 May-18 September, 1943.

62 Recommendations on Post-Hostilities Planning Machinery by the Working Committee on Post-Hostilities Problems, 3 November 1943, in LAC, DEA Papers, RG25, Series B-11, vol. 2103, File AR 405/1/2, Part 1. On the development of the PHP committees, see Don Munton and Don Page, "Planning in the East Block: The Post-Hostilities Problems Committees in Canada, 1943-45," *International Journal* 32, 4 (Autumn 1977): 677-726.

63 John Holmes, Notes on Interview of Don Page with Mr. George Ignatieff on the Post-Hostilities Planning Working and Advisory Committee, Toronto, 23-24 September 1975, in UTTC, John Holmes Papers, Box 61, File D/I/6/d.

64 J.W. Pickersgill, *The Mackenzie King Record*, vol. 1, *1939-1944* (Toronto: University of Toronto Press, 1960), 528. See also Stacey, *Arms, Men and Governments*, 182-83; Conversation with Churchill, the Citadel, 10 August 1943, in Robarts Library, King Diary. For a critical view of King's actions, see Pearson, *Mike: The Memoirs*, 215.

65 Wrong, memorandum "Post-War International Organization," [7 August 1943], in LAC, DEA Papers, RG25, Series A-3-b, vol. 5707, File 7-V(s), Part 1.
66 Department of State Draft Protocol on a Proposed Four Power Security Agreement Pending Permanent Peace, [June 1943], in *FRUS: The Conferences at Washington and Quebec, 1943*, 683.
67 King, diary entry, 21 August 1943, in Robarts Library, King Diary. See also Eayrs, *In Defence of Canada*, vol. 3, 153.
68 Massey, diary entry, 24 August 1943, in UT, Vincent Massey Papers, B-87-0082, Box 311, Massey Diaries 1941-43, Diary 51, June-October 1943.
69 Minutes of the Cabinet War Committee, 31 August 1943, in LAC, PCO Papers, RG2 7c, vol. 13, Minutes of the Cabinet War Committee, 19 May-8 September 1943.
70 English, *Shadow of Heaven*, 241. See also Stoler, *Allies and Adversaries*, 113; and Kimball, *Churchill and Roosevelt*, vol. 1, 6, 10, 15.
71 Minutes of the Cabinet War Committee, 31 August 1943, in LAC, PCO Papers, RG2 7c, vol. 13, Minutes of the Cabinet War Committee, 19 May-8 September 1943.
72 SSDA to SSEA, 6 September 1943, in LAC, DEA Papers, RG25, Series A-3-b, vol. 5706, File 7-S(s); SSDA to SSEA, 13 September 1943, in LAC, DEA Papers, RG25, Series A-3-b, vol. 5707, File 7-V(s), Part 1.
73 Memorandum to Massey, re: Four Power Declaration, in UT, Vincent Massey Papers, B-87-0082, Miscellaneous, Box 359, File 19, Governor General: Telegrams; Massey, diary entry, 27 September 1943, in UT, Vincent Massey Papers, B-87-0082, Miscellaneous, Box 311, Massey Diaries 1941-43, Diary 51, June-October 1943; FO to Washington, 2 October 1943, in NAUK, FO, Private Secretaries Papers, FO 800/408.
74 Tuthill, Memorandum of Conversation with Saul Rae, 14 October 1943, in NARA, RG84, Records of the Foreign Service Posts of the Department of State, Entry 2195a, 350/51/09/ 03, Canada, Ottawa Embassy, Security, Segregated General Records 1939-49, Box 95, 1943, 710, Relations with Great Britain. See also Stacey, *Arms, Men, and Governments*, 155.
75 United States, Department of State, *Bulletin* (18 September 1943); and House Concurrent Resolution 25 on Aggression and Maintenance of Peace, 15-16 June 1943 [passed 21 September 1943], and Senate Resolution 192 on Peace and an International Authority to Preserve Peace, October 1943 [Connally Resolution], both in *The Dynamics of World Power*, ed. Richard Hottelet, 12-14.
76 Notter to Pasvolsky, Ross and Shaw, 9 October 1943, in NARA, RG59, Records of the Department of State, Notter File, Miscellaneous Subject Files, Entry 496, 250/46/22/03, Lot 60D-224, Box 11, Political Studies, Division of; Notter to Whittaker, 18 October 1943, in NARA, ibid., Box 8, Notter's Chronological File, 24 August-28 October 1943.
77 Wrong to Pearson, 18 October 1943, in LAC, DEA Papers, RG25, Series A-3-b, vol. 5706, File 7-S(s).
78 See, for example, "La conférence de Moscou et le communisme international," *Le Devoir*, 18 October 1943, 1; "The Moscow Conference," *G&M*, 20 October 1943, 6.
79 Andrei Gromyko, *Memories*, trans. Harold Sukman (London: Hutchinson, 1989), 104. See also Simon Sebag Montefiore, *Stalin: The Court of the Red Tsar* (London: Weidenfeld and Nicolson, 2003), 466-67.
80 Eden, *The Eden Memoirs*, 514.
81 Milovan Djilas, *Conversations with Stalin*, trans. Michael B. Petrovich (1962; reprint, Orlando, FL: Harcourt and Brace, 1990), 191.
82 Bohlen, Summary of the Proceedings of the First Session of the Moscow Tripartite Conference, 19 October 1943 at Spiridonovka, in *FRUS, 1943*, vol. 1, 580-81. The Soviet Union was neutral in the war against Japan and therefore was not allied with China, but Roosevelt insisted on including China as a great power.
83 Bohlen, Summary of the Proceedings of the Third Session of the Moscow Tripartite Conference, 21 October 1943, in *FRUS, 1943*, vol. 1, 598.
84 Wilgress to SSEA, 22 October 1943, in LAC, DEA Papers, RG25, Series A-3-b, vol. 5706, File 7-S(s); Wilgress to SSEA, 23 October 1943, in LAC, ibid.
85 SSDA to SSEA, 23 October 1943, in LAC, ibid.; Bohlen, Summary of the Proceedings of Eighth Session of the Tripartite Conference, 26 October 1943, in *FRUS, 1943*, vol. 1, 642.

86 Protocol, signed at Moscow, 1 November 1943, Annex 1: Declaration of Four Nations on General Security, in *FRUS, 1943*, vol. 1, 755-56.
87 Prime Minister's Office, Press Release, 1 November 1943, in QUA, Grant Dexter Papers, Collection 2142, Series 4: Subject Files, Box 12, Folder 62, Commonwealth, December 1943-April 1944, Continued.
88 Warwick Chipman [in Chile] to SSEA, 11 November 1943, in LAC, DEA Papers, RG25, Series A-3-b, vol. 5706, File 7-S(s).
89 Hull, *Memoirs*, 1479. For Hull's more candid account, see Private Memorandum, 30 November 1943 [137-39], in SML, Arthur Krock Papers, Box 1, Works: Memoranda, Book 1.

Chapter 5: Canada, the British Commonwealth, and the New World Order
1 Judith Robinson, "Canada's Split Personality," *Foreign Affairs* 22, 1 (October 1943): 72.
2 King, diary entry, 17 May 1943, in Robarts Library, King Diary.
3 War Cabinet, Memorandum by Malcolm MacDonald containing "some thoughts on the post-war position of the British Commonwealth of Nations," 22 March 1943 [drafted 23 February 1943], in NAUK, DO 35/1838; DO, "The Relation of the British Commonwealth to the Post-War International Political Organisation," June 1943, in NAUK, DO 35/1840.
4 Claxton to Curtis, 14 June 1943, in BL, Lionel Curtis Papers, MSS Curtis, 26.
5 Curtis to Claxton, [shortly after 14 June 1943], in BL, ibid.
6 Coldwell, in "Principles of Foreign Policy, Defence, and Communications, War and Post-war," 23 June 1943, in Contemporary Scholarship, Empire Parliamentary Association (hereafter EPA), *Report of the Proceedings of the Parliamentary Conference Held in the Houses of Parliament* (Ottawa: EPA, Dominion of Canada Branch, 1943), 25. On Claxton, see EPA, ibid., 15.
7 EPA, United Kingdom Branch, "Report of United Kingdom Delegates upon the Parliamentary Visit and Conference, Dominion of Canada, June-July 1943," in CAC, Phillip Noel-Baker Papers, NBKR 4/54; Percy Harris to Churchill, 20 July 1943, in CAC, Churchill Papers, CHAR 20/96B/141.
8 Green, 9 July 1943, in Canada, House of Commons, *Debates*, 4th Session, 19th Parliament, 2 July 1943 to 26 January 1944, vol. 238, 4564; Diefenbaker, 9 July 1943, in Canada, ibid., 4593.
9 Claxton, Memoirs, in LAC, Brooke Claxton Papers, MG32 B5, vol. 253, 576-85.
10 Claxton, 9 July 1943, in Canada, House of Commons, *Debates*, 4th Session, 19th Parliament, 2 July 1943 to 26 January 1944, vol. 238, 4598, 4603.
11 King, 12 July 1943, in Canada, ibid., 4685. On the position of the Department of External Affairs, see Kenneth Wilson, Memorandum to Mr. Napier Moore, 19 July 1943, in LAC, W. Arthur Irwin Papers, MG31 E97, vol. 16, File 16-9.
12 Curtin, "Extracts from Statement," 14 August 1943, in Published Documents, *Documents and Speeches on British Commonwealth Affairs, 1931-1952*, vol. 1, ed. Nicholas Mansergh (London: Oxford University Press, 1953), 562.
13 Curtin, "Statement on his Proposal for an Empire Council to the Press, Canberra," 6 September 1943, in Published Documents, *War and Peace Aims of the United Nations*, vol. 2, *From Casablanca to Tokio Bay, January 1, 1943-September 1, 1945*, ed. Louise W. Holborn (Boston: World Peace Foundation, 1948), 638-39. See also Lingard and Trotter, *Canada in World Affairs*, 283-84.
14 "The Commonwealth and the Settlement," *The Round Table* 132 (September 1943): 312. For Curtin's proposal, see John Holmes, Memorandum, "Comments on Telegram No. 18 of September 18th from the Prime Minister of Australia to the Prime Minister Concerning the Proposed Four Power Declaration," 22 September 1943, in LAC, DEA Papers, RG25, Series A-3-b, vol. 5707, File 7-V(s), Part 1.
15 Wrong, "Some Comments on Intra-Commonwealth Relations," 17 August 1943, in LAC, Hume Wrong Papers, MG30 E101, vol. 4, File 24, Miscellaneous 1943-46.
16 Keenleyside to Gwendolyn M. Carter, 6 October 1943, in LAC, DEA Papers, RG25, Series G-2, vol. 2870, File 1843-P-40.
17 "Smuts for Spadework," *G&M*, 7 October 1943, 6.
18 Hatch, quoted in Chester A. Bloom, "Concern about Canada," *WFP*, 1 November 1943, 15.

19   Cranborne, "Extract for a Speech ... in the House of Lords," 2 November 1943, in Published Documents, *Documents and Speeches on British Commonwealth Affairs*, 566, 568.
20   CIPO, 6 November 1943, in *POQ* 7, 4 (Winter 1943): 763. The numbers in Quebec were 41 percent in favour, 32 percent opposed, and 27 percent undecided.
21   Robertson to Riddell, 19 November 1943, in Published Documents, *DCER*, vol. 9, *1942-43*, 981.
22   Riddell to Robertson, 24 December 1943, in Published Documents, ibid., 987.
23   MacDonald, "The British Commonwealth and the Future," Speech at the Alumni Federation of the University of Toronto, 17 November 1943, in DUL, Malcolm MacDonald Papers, 95/8.
24   Smuts, "Extracts from a Speech ... to the Empire Parliamentary Association," 25 November 1943, in Published Documents, *Documents and Speeches on British Commonwealth Affairs*, 574. See also Lingard and Trotter, *Canada in World Affairs*, 287-90.
25   Hutchison, editorial, attached to *Daily Herald* (London), to Dexter, 4 December 1943, in QUA, Grant Dexter Papers, Collection 2142, Series 4: Subject Files, Box 12, Folder 61, Commonwealth, December 1943-April 1944.
26   "Smuts' 'Explosive' Ideas," *WFP*, 6 December 1943, 11; "Intolerance Attacks Smuts," *G&M*, 8 December 1943, 6.
27   Claxton to Tarr, 25 February 1943, in LAC, Brooke Claxton Papers, MG32 B5, vol. 67, Gen. T. Tarr, Edgar J. For a list of participants, see Montebello Conference: Who's Who, in LAC, CIIA Papers, MG28 I250, vol. 18, CIIA General: Montebello Conference 1943, File 1.
28   Tarr to Claxton, 28 September 1943, in LAC, Brooke Claxton Papers, MG32 B5, vol. 67, Gen. T. Tarr, Edgar J.; Grant Dexter, *Canada and the Building of Peace* (Toronto: Canadian Institute of International Affairs, 1944).
29   Wrong to MacLennan, 11 November 1943, in LAC, CIIA Papers, MG28 I250, vol. 18, CIIA General: Montebello Conference, File 1.
30   Rapporteur's Report on the Discussion on *The General Approach*, 4-5 December 1943, in LAC, ibid., File 2. For a more detailed analysis, see Stipernitz, "Kanada und die Gründung der Vereinten Nationen, 1939-1945," ch. 5.
31   Tarr to Robertson, 20 December 1943, in LAC, CIIA Papers, MG28 I250, vol. 2, Edgar J. Tarr: Conferences: British Commonwealth Relations Conference, 1943-45; Tarr to Claxton, Robertson, Wrong, Keenleyside, Heeney, Skelton, and Rasminsky, 30 December 1943, in LAC, CIIA Papers, MG28 I250, vol. 1. Edgar J. Tarr: C.I.I.A. World Affairs Correspondence, 1941-44.
32   Sifton to Tarr, 3 January 1944, in LAC, ibid.
33   Holmes, Note on the Agenda for British Commonwealth Relations Conference, 5 January 1944, in LAC, ibid.; Claxton to Sifton, 10 January 1944, in LAC, ibid.; Brady to Sifton, 4 January 1944, in LAC, ibid. See also JSM to Sifton, 5 January 1944, McLean to Sifton, 6 January 1944, N. Fry to Sifton, 6 January 1944, and W.A. Irwin to Sifton, 7 January 1944, all in LAC, ibid.
34   British Commonwealth Relations Conference 1944, The Agenda of the Conference, Drafted and Approved by the Committee on Arrangements and Agenda at Its Meeting in New York, 17-18 January 1944, in QUA, Grant Dexter Papers, Collection 2142, Series 4: Subject Files, Box 12, Folder 62, Commonwealth, December 1943-April 1944, Continued.
35   See, for example, "Mr. Curtin's Proposals," *G&M*, 15 December 1943, 6; "A Bourbon Attitude," *G&M*, 23 December 1943, 6; "Shadow for Substance," *WFP*, 28 December 1943, 10; and "More and Bigger Dominions," *WFP*, 30 December 1943, 11.
36   Claxton to Massey, 10 January 1943, in LAC, Brooke Claxton Papers, MG32 B5, vol. 56, Gen. M. Vincent Massey.
37   Massey, diary entry, 10 January 1944, in UT, Vincent Massey Papers, B-87-0082, Box 312, Massey Diaries, Diary 52, October 1943-February 1944.
38   "Welcome to Lord Halifax," *G&M*, 24 January 1944, 6. See also Lingard and Trotter, *Canada in World Affairs*, 290-98.
39   Winship to Atherton, 25 January 1944, in NARA, RG84, Records of the Foreign Service Posts of the Department of State, Entry 2197, 350/51/13/01, Canada, Ottawa Legations and Embassy, Confidential General Records 1936-45, Box 2, 1942-45, 800, 1944.

40 Halifax, "Extract from Speech ...," 24 January 1944, in Published Documents, *Documents and Speeches on British Commonwealth Affairs*, 575-79.
41 Halifax to Cranborne, 30 January 1944, in CAC, Halifax Papers, HLFX Reel 2; Massey, diary entry, 4 March 1944, in UT, Vincent Massey Papers, B-87-0082, Box 312, Massey Diaries, Diary 53, February-May 1944. According to Jack Pickersgill, Lester Pearson later told King that if Halifax had only consulted him, everything would have been all right; see Pickersgill, *King Record*, vol. 1, 641. This report is questionable given that Grant Dexter later noted: "Halifax sent a copy of his Toronto speech to Mike some days before delivery. Mike had been too busy to read it. He didn't read it until the day it was delivered"; see Dexter to Ferguson, 12 February 1944, in QUA, Grant Dexter Papers, Collection 2142, Series 1: Correspondence, Box 3, Folder 26, General, 1944.
42 Omer Hereux, "Le discours de lord Halifax," *Le Devoir*, 25 January 1944, 1.
43 "The Halifax Speech," *WFP*, 26 January 1944, 13. See also, "The Real Issue," *WFP*, 29 January 1944, 15.
44 "Halifax Raises a Vital Issue," *G&M*, 26 January 1944, 6.
45 "Lord Halifax Misunderstood," *Ottawa Journal*, 27 January 1944, in QUA, Grant Dexter Papers, Collection 2142, Series 4: Subject Files, Box 12, Folder 61, Commonwealth, December 1943-April 1944.
46 King, diary entry, 25 January 1945, in Robarts Library, King Diary. A good summary of King's thoughts before his official response can be found in Pickersgill, *King Record*, vol. 1, 637-39.
47 King, 31 January 1944, in Canada, House of Commons, *Debates*, 5th Session, 19th Parliament, 27 January to 29 February 1944, vol. 239, 40, 42.
48 See, for example, T.L. Church, 1 February 1944, in Canada, ibid., 103-5; R.B. Hanson, 2 February 1944, in Canada, ibid., 127-28; and Howard Green, 10 February 1944, in Canada, ibid., 352-53.
49 Halifax to MacDonald, 29 January 1944, in LAC, W.L.M. King Papers, MG26 J1, vol. 361.
50 Halifax to Cranborne, 30 January 1944, in CAC, Halifax Papers, HLFX Reel 2.
51 Cranborne to Halifax, 9 February 1944, in CAC, ibid. In a brief hand-written note, Winston Churchill also expressed support; see Churchill to Halifax, 27 January 1944, in CAC, ibid., Reel 1.
52 Massey, diary entry, 25 January 1944, in UT, Vincent Massey Papers, B-87-0082, Box 312, Massey Diaries, Diary 52, October 1943-February 1944.
53 Massey, diary entry, 26 January 1944, in UT, ibid.
54 Charles Ritchie, diary entry, 27 January 1944, in Memoirs and Diaries, Ritchie, *The Siren Years*, 163.
55 See, for example, "A Theme for Cool Reason," *G&M*, 2 February 1944, 6; "Canada Takes Its Stand," *WFP*, 2 February 1944, 11; J.H. Fieldhouse, "The 'Commonwealth' Issue Calls for Open Minds," *Saturday Night*, 12 February 1944, 6-7; Richer, "L'opinion de la 'Saturday Night' sur la politique extérieure," *Le Devoir*, 9 March 1944, 1, 10; "Mischievous Journalism," *G&M*, 31 March 1944, 6.
56 Citizens' Forum, "Canada within the British Empire," 22 February 1944, in Archives of Ontario, Toronto, Ontario, Canada (hereafter AO), Timothy Eaton Papers, F 229-163, Box 2, Canadian Association for Adult Education (Citizens' Forum), 3/8; Citizens' Forum, "Canada in the Anglo-American World," 29 February 1944, in AO, ibid.
57 CIPO, 25 March 1944, in *POQ* 8, 2 (Summer 1944): 303.
58 Massey, diary entry, 17 February 1944, in UT, Vincent Massey Papers, B-87-0082, Box 312, Massey Diaries, Diary 53, February-May 1944.
59 Halifax to Eden, 21 February 1944, in CAC, Halifax Papers, HLFX Reel 2; MacDonald to Cranborne, 11 March 1944, in NAUK, DO 35/1489. See also Granatstein, *Canada's War*, 318; and C.P. Stacey, *Canada and the Age of Conflict*, vol. 2, *The Mackenzie King Era, 1921-1948* (Toronto: University of Toronto Press, 1981), 364-65.
60 Memorandum of Conversation with Maurice Pope, 28 January 1944, in Robarts Library, Records of the Department of State, Microfilm Publication M1244, MHF, Roll 7, John D. Hickerson Miscellaneous Files 1942-47. For a summary of the limited reaction in the American press, see Chester A. Bloom, "Washington and Halifax," *WFP*, 1 February 1944, 13.

61 Winship to Atherton, 15 February 1944, in NARA, RG84, Records of the Foreign Service Posts of the Department of State, Entry 2197, 350/51/13/01, Canada, Ottawa Legation and Embassy, Confidential General Records 1936-45, Box 2, 1942-45, 800, 1944.

62 British Policy towards the Nations of Western Europe, H-147 Preliminary, 28 February 1944, in NARA, RG59, Records of the Department of State, Notter File, Policy Summaries, 1943-44, Entry 500, 250/46/24/07, Lot 60D-224, Box 154, H-Policy Summaries 126-49. The author's identity here is unclear, but the document was likely written by a mid-level civil servant reporting to Pasvolsky.

63 Claxton to Curtis, 14 June 1943, in BL, Lionel Curtis Papers, MSS Curtis, 26.

64 Thomas A. Hockin, "The Foreign Policy Review and Decision Making in Canada," in Lewis Hertzman, John W. Warnock, and Thomas A. Hockin, *Alliances and Illusions: Canada and the NATO-NORAD Question*, 93-136 (Edmonton: M.G. Hurtig, 1969), 98; Michael Tucker, *Canadian Foreign Policy: Contemporary Issues and Themes* (Toronto: McGraw Hill Ryerson Limited, 1980), 5; Costas Melakopides, *Pragmatic Idealism: Canadian Foreign Policy, 1945-1995* (Montreal and Kingston: McGill-Queen's University Press, 1998).

65 Peter C. Dobell, *Canada's Search for New Roles: Foreign Policy in the Trudeau Era* (London: Royal Institute of International Affairs, 1972), 146.

66 Jane Errington, *The Lion, the Eagle, and Upper Canada: A Developing Colonial Ideology* (Montreal and Kingston: McGill-Queen's University Press, 1987), 9.

Chapter 6: Forked Roads

1 King, quoted in Pickersgill, *King Record*, vol. 1, 589.

2 Léopold Richer, "Le Canada se dégage avec timidité des liens impériaux," *Le Devoir*, 15 November 1943, 1. See also "Un role important," *La Presse*, 17 November 1943, 6.

3 CIPO, 20 November 1943, in *POQ* 8, 1 (Spring 1944): 160. Eighty-five percent of those outside of Quebec said "yes." Across the country, 78 percent were in favour, 15 percent were opposed, and 7 percent were undecided.

4 CIPO, 27 November 1943, in ibid.

5 WIB: Information Brief: "Post-War Hopes in Canada," No. 22, 13 December 1943, in LAC, Department of Finance Papers, RG19, Series E-5, vol. 4028, Files 129-W-1-3, 129-W-1-4, and 129-W-1-5. See also WIB: Information Brief: "Canadian Concern with World Affairs," No. 24, 10 January 1944, in LAC, ibid.

6 Henry Somerville, "The Religious Demand for a New World Order," *Saturday Night*, 23 October 1943, 22.

7 The League of Nations and the Post War World: A Letter from the National Executive of the League of Nations Society in Canada to the Hon. W.L. Mackenzie King, M.J. Coldwell, M.P., J.H. Blackmore, M.P., the Hon. John Bracken, 11 November 1943, in LAC, Robert Boyer Inch Papers, MG30 C187, vol. 1, File 9.

8 Coldwell to Jones, 20 December 1943, in LAC, ibid.; King to Jones, 24 December 1943, in LAC, ibid.

9 Minutes of the 2nd Meeting (1944) of the Executive Committee, 18 February 1944; and Minutes of the 10th Meeting (1944) of the Executive Committee, 31 October 1944, both in LAC, CIIA Papers, MG28 I250, Reel M-4619, vol. 6, Minutes, 1943-44.

10 "The International Law of the Future," *Canadian Bar Review* 22, 4 (April 1944): 277-376. On functionalism, see proposal four, which discusses the composition of the executive council.

11 Claxton to Dafoe, 10 December 1943, in LAC, Brooke Claxton Papers, MG32 B5, vol. 27, Dafoe, John (2). For the DEA report, see Memorandum on the U.N.R.R.A. Conference, Atlantic City [November 1943], 8 December 1943, in LAC, DEA Papers, RG25, Series 3-A-b, vol. 5711, File 7-AD(s), Part 1.

12 "Foreign Policy Achievements," *WFP*, 3 April 1944, 13. See also Lingard and Trotter, *Canada in World Affairs*, 266-67.

13 Massey, Guildhall Speech, 15 December 1943, in UT, Vincent Massey Papers, B-87-0082, Box 348a, File 08, Addresses.

14 WIB, *Canada at War* 32 (January 1944): 8; WIB, *Canada at War* 33 (February 1944): 32.

15 [British] War Cabinet, Chiefs of Staff Committee, Association of Dominions with Work of Post-Hostilities Planning Sub-Committee, Memorandum by Dominions Office, 10 September 1943, in NAUK, CAB 122/417.

16 Ritchie to DEA, 1 October 1943, in LAC, DEA Papers, RG25, Series A-3-b, vol. 5722, File 7-CB(s), Part 1.2.

17 Minutes of the Cabinet War Committee, 24 November 1943, in LAC, PCO Papers, RG2 7c, vol. 14, Minutes of the Cabinet War Committee, 15 September-21 December 1943. For the poll, see CIPO, 20 November 1943, in *POQ* 8, 1 (Spring 1944): 160.

18 Wilgress to SSEA, 16 February 1944, in LAC, DEA Papers, RG25, Series A-3-b, vol. 5707, File 7-V(s), Part 1.

19 Memo to Prime Minister, 19 February 1944, in Published Documents, *DCER*, vol. 11, *1944-1945*, part 2, ed. John F. Hilliker (Ottawa: Minister of Supply and Services Canada, 1990), 323; Holmes, *The Shaping of Peace*, 106-8.

20 Ritchie to Jebb, 21 February 1944, in LAC, DEA Papers, RG25, Series B-11, vol. 2103, File AR 405/1/2, Part 1.

21 Wrong, Memorandum, 23 February 1944, in Published Documents, *DCER*, vol. 11, 1; Minutes of the Cabinet War Committee, 1 March 1944, in LAC, PCO Papers, RG2 7c, vol. 15, Minutes of the Cabinet War Committee, 5 January-28 June 1944.

22 Holmes, Memorandum on the Organization of Work on Post-Hostilities Planning, n.d., in LAC, DEA Papers, RG25, Series A-3-b, vol. 5712, File 7-AQ(s).

23 On the belief in collective security, see ibid.; and Ritchie to Wrong, 11 March 1944, in Published Documents, *DCER*, vol. 11, 335-36. On the PHP decision, see Wrong to Ritchie, 14 April 1944, in LAC, DEA Papers, RG25, Series B-11, vol. 2103, File AR 405/1/2, Part 1.

24 PHP, Draft 2, Canadian Defence Relationships with the United States, 18 May 1944, in LAC, PCO Papers, RG2, Series B-2, vol. 18, File W-22-8, Part 4; Eayrs, *In Defence of Canada*, vol. 3, 148-50.

25 Holmes, *The Shaping of Peace*, 233.

26 "Plus comme avant," *La Presse*, 28 January 1944, 22.

27 Pearson to Robertson, 1 February 1944, in LAC, DEA Papers, RG25, Series A-3-b, vol. 5707, File 7-V(s), Part 1.

28 S.H. Knowles, 18 April 1944, in Canada, House of Commons, *Debates*, 5th Session, 19th Parliament, 18 April to 23 May 1944, vol. 241, 2147.

29 Wrong, Notes on Some Relief Questions of International Organization which May Arise During the Meeting of the Relief Council at Atlantic City, 3 November 1943, in LAC, PCO Papers, RG2, Series B-2, vol. 44, File W-22-1, 1942-43.

30 Pope to Pearson, 17 April 1944, in LAC, DEA Papers, RG25, Series B-2, vol. 2459, File P-15, "Post-War Security."

31 King, 1 May 1944, in LAC, DEA Papers, RG25, Series C3, vol. 2283, File S/25/1, Meeting of Prime Ministers, May 1944. See also Lingard and Trotter, *Canada in World Affairs*, 299-303.

32 Eden to Churchill, 27 February 1944, in UBSC, Avon Papers, AP/20/11. See also P-252, "British War Aims," 16 February 1944, in NARA, RG59, Records of the Department of State, Notter File, Records of the Advisory Committee on Post-War Foreign Policy, 1942-45, Entry 498, 250/46/22/06, Lot 60D-224, Box 58, P-241-261.

33 Woodward, *British Foreign Policy in the Second World War*, 89-92; Eden to Churchill, 4 May 1944, in UBSC, Avon Papers, AP/20/11.

34 "A Startling Suggestion," *G&M*, 4 May 1944, 6. The information seems to have come from a combination of word of mouth and published Canadian statements.

35 Fraser to Arthur Irwin, 4 May 1944, in LAC, W. Arthur Irwin Papers, MG31 E97, vol. 37, File 37-1.

36 Dexter to *WFP*, 4 May 1944; Ministry of Information, Press Conference, 4 May 1944, Talk by Mr. John Curtin; and Dexter, Memorandum, 6 May 1944, all in QUA, Grant Dexter Papers, Collection 2142, Series 4: Subject Files, Box 28, Scrapbook 6. The Australian diplomat Paul Hasluck's contention that Curtin approached the Conference of Commonwealth Prime Ministers in an imperial state of mind is a misinterpretation; see *Diplomatic Witness*, 137.

37   Meeting of Prime Ministers: Future World Organization, 8 May 1944, in LAC, DEA Papers, RG25, Series C-3, vol. 2283, File S/25/1, Meeting of Prime Ministers, May 1944.

38   King to Commonwealth Prime Ministers, 11 May 1944, in LAC, DEA Papers, RG25, Series A-3-b, vol. 5707, File 7-V(s), Part 1.2; Stacey, *Canada and the Age of Conflict,* vol. 2, 366-67.

39   Churchill, BBC radio transcript, 11 May 1944, quoted in Massey to Smith [WIB], 17 May 1944, in LAC, DEA Papers, RG25, Series A-3-b, vol. 5757, File 62(s).

40   Dexter to *WFP,* 11 May 1944, in QUA, Grant Dexter Papers, Collection 2142, Series 4: Subject Files, Box 28, Scrapbook 6.

41   "Backstage at Ottawa," *Maclean's,* 15 June 1944, 14.

42   Lewis Clark to [US] Secretary of State, 12 May 1944, in NARA, RG59, Records of the Department of State, Records of the Office of United Nations Affairs, Official Commitments Numerical File, 1940-45, Entry 681, 250/47/01/04, Box 23, 710: Canada: British Empire; Massey, diary entry, 11 May 1944, in UT, Vincent Massey Papers, B-87-0082, Box 312, Massey Diaries, Diary 54, May-August 1944.

43   Meeting of Prime Ministers: Text of Declaration Signed by the Five Prime Ministers, 16 May 1944, in LAC, DEA Papers, RG25, Series A-3-b, vol. 5757, File 62(s).

44   Churchill, quoted in Massey to SSEA, 17 May 1944, in LAC, ibid. A British secretary called the meetings "an outstanding success." See Bridges to Heeney, 6 July 1944, in NAUK, CAB 21/4559.

45   Dexter to *WFP,* [16-17 May 1944], in QUA, Grant Dexter Papers, Collection 2142, Series 4: Subject Files, Box 28, Scrapbook 6.

46   Crerar to Dexter, 18 May 1944, in QUA, T.A. Crerar Papers, Collection 2117, Series 3, Box 105, Correspondence, Folder: Grant Dexter, July 1940, May 1944-June 1950.

47   "A Co-ordinated Commonwealth," *G&M,* 19 May 1944, 6; "A Common Policy Achieved," *G&M,* 27 May 1944, 6; "A Great Commonwealth Achievement: I," *G&M,* 2 June 1944, 6; "A Great Commonwealth Achievement: III," *G&M,* 4 June 1944, 6.

48   CIPO, 17 May 1944, in *POQ* 8, 2 (Summer 1944): 303.

49   King, 22 May 1944, in Canada, House of Commons, *Debates,* 5th Session, 19th Parliament, 18 April to 23 May 1944, vol. 241, 3100. See also Lingard and Trotter, *Canada in World Affairs,* 303-4.

50   Theodore F.M. Newton, "Gleam of the Beacon," Empire Day Address before the Canadian Society of New York, 24 May 1944, in LAC, Theodore F.M. Newton Papers, MG31 E74, vol. 1, File 1-15. At the time, Newton was the associate chair of the United Nations Information Board and an executive officer with the WIB.

51   FDR-Stalin Meeting, FDR's Quarters at Soviet Embassy, 29 November 1943, in *FRUS: The Conferences at Cairo and Teheran, 1943* (Washington, DC: Government Printing Office, 1961), 531; FDR-Stalin Meeting, 1 December 1943, in ibid., 596.

52   Robertson to Massey, 2 December 1943; and SSDA to King, 15 December 1943, both in LAC, DEA Papers, RG25, Series A-3-b, vol. 5711, File 7-AG(s); Massey, diary entries, 8 and 14 December, in UT, Vincent Massey Papers, B-87-0082, Box 312, Massey Diaries, Diary 52, October 1943-February 1944.

53   Memorandum to Hull, 4 December 1943, in Robarts Library, Records of the Department of State, Microfilm Publication M1244, MHF, Roll 2: John D. Hickerson Memorandums, 1942-45. In his own account, Lester Pearson exaggerates the extent of information that he was receiving; see *Mike: The Memoirs,* 209.

54   Wrong to Pearson, 12 January 1944, in LAC, DEA Papers, RG25, Series A-3-b, vol. 5710, File 7-AB(s), Part 1.1.

55   Pearson to Wrong, 14 January 1944, in LAC, ibid.

56   Ward [in Washington] to Jebb, 26 January 1944, in NAUK, FO 371/40736.

57   See, for example, Pearson to Wrong, 27 April 1944; and Wrong to Pearson, 11 May 1944, both in LAC, DEA Papers, RG25, Series A-3-b, vol. 5710, File 7-AB(s), Part 2.1.

58   Wrong to Pearson, 2 June 1944, in LAC, DEA Papers, RG25, Series A-3-b, vol. 5723, File 7-CH(s), Part 1.

59   Wrong to Pearson, 17 June 1944, in LAC, ibid. Wrong was not alone. Maurice Pope generally thought that, when it came to postwar thinking, Escott Reid was a fool. See Pope, diary

entry, 17 April 1944, in LAC, Maurice Pope Papers, MG27 IIIF4, vol. 1, Diary, 1944. For an understated explanation of the DEA divide, see Holmes, *The Shaping of Peace*, 233-35.

60 Wrong to Pearson, 23 May 1944, and 2 June 1944, both in LAC, DEA Papers, RG25, Series A-3-b, vol. 5723, File 7-CH(s), Part 1. In London, on the other hand, Charles Ritchie made a similar suggestion to Gladwyn Jebb. Clearly, Ritchie was trusted to be tactful, while Reid was not. See Ritchie to Jebb, 31 May 1944, in LAC, DEA Papers, RG25, Series A-3-b, vol. 5716, File 7-BY(s), Part 2.

61 MacDonald to Cranborne, 16 January 1945, in NAUK, FO 371/50365. Granatstein's explanation is slightly different; see *A Man of Influence*, 193.

62 Pearson to Robertson, 24 June 1944, in LAC, Pearson Papers, MG 26 N1, vol. 13, Robertson, 1942-46. For a copy of the report, see Holmes, "Draft Report on Prime Ministers Meetings, London, May 1944," 2 June 1944, in LAC, DEA Papers, RG25, Series A-3-b, vol. 5757, File 62(s).

63 Reid to Pearson, 26 June 1944, in LAC, DEA Papers, RG25, Series A-3-b, vol. 5710, File 7-AB(s), Part 2.3.

64 Hull to Roosevelt, 29 December 1943, in *FRUS, 1944*, vol. 1, *General* (Washington, DC: Government Printing Office, 1966), 614-15; Minutes: Department of State Policy Committee, 14 February 1944, in NARA, RG59, Records of the Department of State, Notter File, Records Relating to Miscellaneous Policy Committees, Entry 499, 250/46/22/07, Lot 60D-224, Box 138, Policy Committee: Minutes, 1-22.

65 Quincy Wright, "Representation and Voting in International Organizations," 25 February 1944, in LC, Benjamin Gerig Papers, Box 5, Folder 2, Subject File: Division of International Security and Organization, Office of Special Political Affairs: Reports, Memoranda, and Letters by Quincy Wright Regarding International Organization and/or Territories.

66 Pearson to SSEA, 11 July 1944, in LAC, DEA Papers, RG25, Series A-3-b, vol. 5723, File 7-CH(s), Part 1.

67 Robertson to Pearson, 15 July 1944, in LAC, ibid.

Chapter 7: Disappointment at Dumbarton Oaks

1 SSDA to SSEA, 19 April 1944, in LAC, DEA Papers, RG25, Series A-3-b, vol. 5707, File 7-V(s), Part 1.

2 Wrong, memorandum to Robertson, "Representation of Smaller Countries on World Security Council," 25 April 1944, in LAC, ibid.

3 British Foreign Office to British Embassy in the United States, 4 June 1944, in *FRUS, 1944*, vol. 1, 640; Hull to Harriman, 7 July 1944, in ibid., 644; and Soviet Embassy to Department of State, 20 July 1944, in ibid., 669.

4 The Conservatives would have preferred that Great Britain attend the meetings representing the entire empire, while Léopold Richer argued that Great Britain was going to represent Canada whether it was supposed to or not, proving that Canada was not truly independent; see Graydon, Question, 20 July 1944, in Canada, House of Commons, *Debates*, 5th Session, 19th Parliament, 28 June to 26 July 1944, vol. 243, 5116; and Richer, "Le Canada ne participera pas à la prochaine conférence des quatre grandes puissances à Washington," *Le Devoir*, 21 July 1944, 1, 10.

5 Wrong, "Notes on Paper P.M. (44) 4 of 8 May, 1944, 'Future World Organization,'" 19 June 1944, in LAC, DEA Papers, RG25, Series A-3-b, vol. 5707, File 7-V(s), Part 1.2.

6 Meeting of Prime Ministers, 8 May 1944, in LAC, ibid., Part 1.

7 Minutes of A.P.W. [Armistice and Postwar] Committee, 20 July 1944, in NAUK, CAB 123/235, A. Clement Attlee Papers.

8 Wilgress to SSEA, 30 June 1944, in LAC, DEA Papers, RG25, Series A-3-b, vol. 5710, File 7-AB(s), Part 2.1.

9 Holmes, "The Functions of a World Assembly," 13 July 1944, in LAC, ibid., vol. 5707, File 7-V(s), Part 1.2.

10 Ritchie to Robertson, 12 June 1944, in LAC, ibid.

11 Reid, "Summary of the United States Paper Dated July 18, 1944, on the Establishment of a General International Security Organization," 19 July 1944, in LAC, ibid.; Pearson to SSEA, 25 July 1944, in LAC, ibid., vol. 5708, File 7-V (s), Part 2.

12 PWC 62, ISO 3, Tentative Draft: An Executive Council, 13 March 1944, in NARA, RG59, Records of the Department of State, Notter File, Records of the Division of International Security and Organization (ISO), 1944 and 1945, Entry 501, 250/46/24/07, Lot 60D-224, Box 158, ISO Documents 1-16.

13 ISO 45, Section 3 Preliminary, 15 July 1944, in NARA, ibid., Box 160, ISO Document 45. On the internal criticism, see for example, US Supreme Court Justice Charles Hughes to Taylor, 6 May 1944, in NARA, RG59, Records of the Advisory Committee on Post-War Foreign Policy, 1942-45, Entry 498, 250/46/22/06, Lot 60D-224, Box 58, Myron C. Taylor, International Organization.

14 Malinin was almost certainly a pseudonym. The man most commonly suspected of having written the piece was Maxim Litvinov; see Minutes of the Twenty-Eighth Meeting of the Working Committee on Post-Hostilities Problems, 10 August 1944, in LAC, DEA Papers, RG25, Series A-3-b, vol. 5711, File 7-AD(s), Part 2.

15 Political Distribution from Moscow to Foreign Office, 27 July 1944, in LAC, ibid., vol. 5707, File 7-V(s), Part 1.2; Pearson to SSEA, 25 July 1944, in LAC, ibid., vol. 5708, File 7-V(s), Part 2.

16 Meeting of Prime Ministers, 8 May 1944, in LAC, ibid., vol. 5707, File 7-V(s), Part 1.

17 Robertson to King, 2 August 1944, in LAC, W.L.M. King Papers, Memoranda and Notes, MG26 J4, vol. 338, File 3667.

18 SSEA to SSDA, 2 August 1944, in LAC, DEA Papers, RG25, Series A-3-b, vol. 5708, Part 2. On King's caution, see also Stipernitz, "Kanada und die Gründung der Vereinten Nationen, 1939-1945," ch. 7.

19 King, 4 August 1944, in Canada, House of Commons, *Debates*, 5th Session, 19th Parliament, 27 July 1944 to 31 January 1945, vol. 244, 5909. See also Canada, ibid., 5910-18.

20 Green, 4 August 1944, in Canada, ibid., 5920, 5922. On the Canadian attitude toward an imperial council, see CIPO, 13 September 1944, in *POQ* 8, 4 (Winter 1944-45): 602.

21 Coldwell, 4 August 1944, in Canada, House of Commons, *Debates*, 5th Session, 19th Parliament, 27 July 1944 to 31 January 1945, vol. 244, 5926.

22 King, 14 August 1944, in Canada, ibid., 6426. For more on the debate, see F.H. Soward, *Canada in World Affairs: From Normandy to Paris, 1944-1946* (London: Oxford University Press, 1950), 126-28, 222-24.

23 Robertson [drafted by Ignatieff] to Wilgress, 5 August 1944, in LAC, DEA Papers, RG25, Series A-3-b, vol. 5710, File 7-AB(s), Part 2.2 (it was Wilgress who had the concern); Holmes to Soward, 2 September 1944, in LAC, ibid., vol. 5757, File 62(s); Pope, diary entry, 8-10 September 1944, in LAC, Maurice Pope Papers, MG27 III4, vol. 1, Diary 1944.

24 ISO 45, Section 11 Preliminary, 14 July 1944, in NARA, RG59, Records of the Department of State, Notter File, Records of the Division of International Security and Organization (ISO), 1944 and 1945, Entry 501, 250/46/24/07, Lot 60D-224, Box 160, ISO Document 45.

25 Machtig to Cadogan, 16 June 1944, in NAUK, DO 35/1856.

26 ISO 82, Confidential Information about the British Participants at Dumbarton Oaks, 19 August 1944, in NARA, RG59, Records of the Department of State, Notter File, Records of the Division of International Security and Organization (ISO), 1944 and 1945, Entry 501, 250/46/24/07, Box 161, ISO Documents 64-85. See also *The Historian as Diplomat*, ed. Reynolds and Hughes, 86.

27 Shannon to Ward, 16 August 1944, in NAUK, DO 35/1860. See also Woodward, *British Foreign Policy in the Second World War*, 135-36.

28 Pearson to Robertson, 19 August 1944, in LAC, DEA Papers, RG25, Series A-3-b, vol. 5708, Part 2.

29 SSDA to SSEA, 21 August 1944, in LAC, ibid. James Eayrs has exaggerated the British commitment to Canadian interests; see *In Defence of Canada*, vol. 3, 165.

30 Memorandum by Reid on Conversation with Pasvolsky on 17 August 1944, 18 August 1944, in LAC, DEA Papers, RG25, Series A-3-b, vol. 5708, Part 2. Lester Pearson, who later claimed that Canada made its views known effectively during Dumbarton Oaks, was, at best, exaggerating; see *Mike: The Memoirs*, 270. Similarly, for Escott Reid to call the preliminary talks with the Americans a "high point" is utterly misleading; see *Radical Mandarin*, 190.

31 James A. Gibson, interview with author, Toronto, 25 September 2002. See also Cadogan to Lady Theo, 16 August 1944, in CAC, Sir Alexander George Montagu Cadogan Papers, ACAD 3/14.

32 DHL, Oral History Collection (02), J44, Lord Gladwyn Jebb, 24 October 1985.

33 ISO 89, Confidential Information about the Soviet Participants at Dumbarton Oaks, 24 August 1944, in NARA, RG59, Records of the Department of State, Notter File, Records of the ISO, 1944 and 1945, Entry 501, 250/46/24/07, Lot 60D-224, Box 162, ISO Documents 86-97. See also DHL, Oral History Collection (02), S7, Harold Stassen, 29 April 1983.

34 Harriman to Hull, 21 August 1944, in *FRUS, 1944*, vol. 1, 712-13.

35 [Cadogan], Confidential Release for Publication at 10:30 a.m., E.W.T., Monday, 21 August 1944, in LAC, DEA Papers, RG25, Series A-3-b, vol. 5708, Part 2.

36 [Hull,] Confidential Release for Publication at 10:30 a.m., E.W.T., Monday, 21 August 1944, in LAC, ibid.

37 Gromyko, Speech Delivered at the Opening of the Conference on International Security, Dumbarton Oaks, 21 August 1944, in Published Documents, *War and Peace Aims of the United Nations*, vol. 2, 772.

38 Pearson to SSEA, 25 August 1944, in LAC, DEA Papers, RG25, Series A-3-b, vol. 5708, Part 2.

39 Stettinius to Hull, 3 September 1944, in *FRUS, 1944*, vol. 1, 765. See also Holmes, *The Shaping of Peace*, 108; and Robert C. Hildebrand, *Dumbarton Oaks: The Origins of the United Nations and the Search for Postwar Security* (Chapel Hill and London: University of North Carolina Press, 1990), 108.

40 Stettinius to Hull, 24 August 1944, in *FRUS, 1944*, vol. 1, 729.

41 Extract from Stettinius Diary, 24 August 1944, in ibid., 732; Stettinius to Hull, 25 August 1944, in ibid., 733; Stettinius to Hull, 2 September 1944, in ibid., 763.

42 Minutes of the Twenty-Ninth Meeting of the Working Committee on Post-Hostilities Problems, 25 August 1944, in LAC, DEA Papers, RG25, Series A-3-b, vol. 5711, File 7-AD(s), Part 2.

43 Holmes, Minute, 31 August 1944, in LAC, ibid.

44 Minutes of the Cabinet War Committee, 31 August 1944, in LAC, PCO Papers, RG2, 7c, vol. 16, Minutes of the Cabinet War Committee, 5 July-22 December 1944. John Holmes unjustly downplays the first priority; see *The Shaping of Peace*, 240.

45 Hickerson, Memorandum of Conversation with Pearson, 31 August 1944, in Robarts Library, Records of the Department of State, Microfilm Publication M1244, MHF, Roll 12, Subject File: British Commonwealth. On Pearson's instructions to the contrary, see Wrong to Pearson, 28 August 1944, in LAC, DEA Papers, RG25, Series A-3-b, vol. 5708, File 7V-(s), Part 2.

46 Pearson to SSEA, 1 September 1944, in LAC, ibid., Part 3.

47 Cadogan to Halifax, 6 September 1944, in NAUK, DO 35/1866. John Holmes's account suffers from a lack of access to British and American documents; see *The Shaping of Peace*, 162, 231.

48 FO to Cadogan, 7 September 1944, in NAUK, DO 35/1866; FO to Washington, 8 September 1944, in NAUK, ibid.

49 Informal Minutes of Meeting No. 12 of the Joint Steering Committee, 9 September 1944, in *FRUS, 1944*, vol. 1, 791-93.

50 Stettinius, diary entry, 13 September 1944, in ibid., 805; Stettinius, diary entry, 15 September 1944, in ibid., 814; Stettinius to Hull, 19 September 1944, in ibid., 825.

51 Informal Minutes of Meeting No. 6 of the Joint Steering Committee, 28 August 1944, in ibid., 741-42; Stettinius, diary entry, 29 August 1944, in ibid., 750. See also Jebb, *Memoirs*, 158-59.

52 Churchill to Roosevelt, 26 September 1944, in NAUK, FO, Anthony Eden Papers, FO 954/22; King to Churchill, 28 September 1944, in CAC, Churchill Papers, CHAR 20/172, 56-57, 28 September 1944.

53 King, diary entries, 12 August, 10 September, and 16 September 1944, in Robarts Library, King Diary; Minutes of the Cabinet War Committee, 20 September 1944, in LAC, PCO Papers, RG2, 7c, vol. 16, Minutes of the Cabinet War Committee, 5 July-22 December

1944; King to Churchill, 28 September 1944, in CAC, Churchill Papers, CHAR 20/172, 56-57, 28 September 1944.

54 *FRUS, 1944*, vol. 1, 859-84; Russell, *A History of the United Nations Charter*, 415-16. Hildebrand suggests that the meetings were slightly more meaningful; see *Dumbarton Oaks*, 229-44.

55 Stephen Holmes to Stephenson, 26 September 1944, in NAUK, DO 35/1871.

56 King to Churchill, 28 September 1944, in CAC, Churchill Papers, CHAR 20/172, 56-57, 28 September 1944.

57 Minutes of the Thirty-Second Meeting of the Working Committee on Post-Hostilities Problems, 5 October 1944, in LAC, DEA Papers, RG25, Series A-3-b, vol. 5711, File 7-AD(s), Part 2.

58 Wrong to Robertson, 28 September 1944, in LAC, ibid., vol. 5757, File 62-A(s), Part 1.

59 "Dumbarton Oaks Progress," *WFP*, 4 October 1944, 13. See also "At Dumbarton Oaks," *WFP*, 30 September 1944, 15.

60 Hutchison to Ferguson, 6 October 1944, in QUA, Grant Dexter Papers, Collection 2142, Series 1: Correspondence, Box 3, Folder 26, General, 1944.

61 Escott Reid, Tentative Draft of a Possible Statement by the Canadian Government Commenting on the Draft Charter of the United Nations, 22 September 1944, in LAC, DEA Papers, RG25, Series A-3-b, vol. 5708, File 7-V(s), Part 3.

62 Wrong, Draft Press Statement to Be Issued by Prime Minister for Publication in Morning Papers of October 10th, 7 October 1944, in LAC, ibid.

63 Wrong to Reid, 11 October 1944, in LAC, ibid., Part 4.

64 Stettinius to Atherton, 13 September 1944, in NARA, RG84, Records of the Foreign Service Posts of the Department of State, Entry 2195a, 350/51/09/03, Canada, Ottawa Embassy, Security, Segregated General Records 1939-49, Box 108, 127-710, 500: 1944: Dumbarton Oaks Conference.

65 Hickerson, Memorandum, 14 September 1944, in Robarts Library, Records of the Department of State, Microfilm Publication M1244, MHF, Roll 12, Subject File: British Commonwealth.

66 Hickerson to Parsons, Stewart and Achilles, 3 October 1944, in Robarts Library, ibid., Roll 2, John D. Hickerson Memorandums, 1942-45. Pearson's boast that both he and his American colleagues "pulled no punches in [their] official and confidential expression of viewpoints" is clearly questionable; see *Mike: The Memoirs*, 217.

67 Clark to Parsons, 842.00/10-1844, 18 October 1944, in NARA, RG59, Records of the Department of State, 250, State Department Decimal Files, 1940-44, Box 5016, from 842.00/701 to 842.00 P.R./189; Clark to Parsons, 842.00/1/1645, 16 January 1945, in NARA, ibid., 1945-49, Box 5995, from 841E.5151/1-145 to 842/00/12-3146.

68 Pearson to Robertson, 12 October 1944, in LAC, DEA Papers, RG25, Series A-3-b, vol. 5708, File 7-V(s), Part 4.

69 Memorandum of Conversation [Elizabeth Armstrong and James Frederick Green present for certain; author of the document unclear], 19 October 1944, in NARA, RG59, Records of the Department of State, Records of the Office of United Nations Affairs, Official Commitments Numerical File, 1940-45, Entry 681, 250/47/01/04, Box 30, International Organization, Interim Discussion and Reactions to Draft Proposal.

70 Robertson to Pearson, 24 October 1944, in LAC, Pearson Papers, MG26 N1, vol. 13, Robertson, N.A., 1942-46.

71 Pearson to Robertson, 30 October 1944, in LAC, ibid. Pearson is deceptively kind to McCarthy in *Mike: The Memoirs*, 207-8. James Eayrs sees Reid's contribution in a less flattering light; see *In Defence of Canada*, vol. 3, 157.

72 Hickerson to Matthews and Dunn, 31 October 1944, in Robarts Library, Records of the Department of State, Microfilm Publication M1244, MHF, Roll 12, Subject File: British Commonwealth.

73 Parsons, Memorandum, 30 October 1944, in NARA, ibid.

Chapter 8: Middle Power Politics

1 Lionel Gelber, "A Greater Canada among Nations," *Behind the Headlines* 4, 2 (1944): 10.

2 WIB, *Canada at War* 41 (October 1944): 29.
3 "Canada at San Francisco," *WFP*, 13 February 1945, 9. See also Radio Broadcast, "Of Things to Come," 26 October 1944, in LAC, DEA Papers, RG25, Series G-2, vol. 2870, File 1843-Q-40; Editorial, *MacLean's*, 15 January 1945, 1; "The Middle Powers," *WFP*, 28 March 1945, 15; and John P. Humphrey, "Dumbarton Oaks at San Francisco," *Canadian Forum* 25, 291 (April 1945): 6-10.
4 John W. Holmes, *Canada: A Middle-Aged Power* (Toronto: McClelland and Stewart, 1976), vi. For a summary of the critical literature, see Adam Chapnick, "The Canadian Middle Power Myth," *International Journal* 55, 2 (Spring 2000): 188-206.
5 Sauer, "The Respectable Course," 9.
6 Bohlen, Memorandum of Conversation with Atherton and Robertson re: Dumbarton Oaks, 5 November 1944, in NARA, RG84, Records of the Foreign Service Posts of the Department of State, Entry 2195a, 350/51/09/03, Canada, Ottawa Embassy, Security, Segregated General Records 1939-49, Box 108, 127-710, 500: 1944: Dumbarton Oaks Conference. For Wrong's report, see Wrong to Robertson, 30 October 1944, in LAC, DEA Papers, RG25, Series B-11, vol. 2103, File AR 405/1/4, Part 3. In the British view of the conversation, Canada is depicted as having a "small power complex"; see Garner to Stephenson, 2 November 1944, in NAUK, DO 35/1870.
7 Official Canadian Comments on Dumbarton Oaks, 9 February 1945, in NARA, RG59, Records of the Department of State, Alger Hiss Files, 1940-46, Subject Files of the Office of Special Political Affairs, 1940-46, Entry 684, 250/47/03/05, Lot File 61-D-146, Box 1, Canadian Consultations.
8 Adolf Berle, cited in B.T.R., "Canada as Conciliator," *WFP*, 20 November 1944, 11. John Holmes includes more detail than what follows but does not connect the results of the conference to Escott Reid's subsequent approach to world organization; see *The Shaping of Peace*, 60-71. For Reid's own account of the events surrounding the Chicago Conference, see *Radical Mandarin*, 170-89.
9 David Mackenzie, *Canada and International Civil Aviation, 1932-1948* (Toronto: University of Toronto Press, 1989), 199.
10 Robertson to King, 13 December 1944, in LAC, W.L.M. King Papers, Memoranda and Notes, MG26 J4, vol. 342, File 3679; Mackenzie, *Canada and International Civil Aviation*, 195; and "Is This 'Success'?" *WFP*, 21 December 1945, 13.
11 On the disappointment, see Wrong to King, 4 January 1945, in LAC, W.L.M. King Papers, Memoranda and Notes, MG26 J4, vol. 342, File 3679; and Massey to Cranborne, 24 January 1945, in LAC, DEA Papers, RG25, Series B-11, vol. 2103, File AR 405/1/4, Part 3. On Roosevelt, see Memorandum of Conversation [including Roosevelt, Stettinius, Dunn, Pasvolsky, and Bohlen], 8 January 1945, in LC, Leo Pasvolsky Papers, Box 4, Subject File: International Organizations: Memoranda of Conversations, 1945.
12 Reid to Robertson, 24 January 1945, in LAC, DEA Papers, RG25, Series A-3-b, vol. 5709, File 7-V(s), Part 5.2. Reid had gone so far as to rewrite the Dumbarton Oaks proposals, but the Canadian government refused to release his new UN Charter as a policy document. Instead, Reid was allowed to circulate his paper only anonymously; see Reid to Pearson, 1 November 1944, in LAC, DEA Papers, RG25, Series B-2, vol. 2157, File 7.
13 Canada, *Final Act of the International Civil Aviation Conference Held at Chicago from November 1 to December 7, 1944*, Treaty Series 1944, no. 36 (Ottawa: King's Printer, 1945), Appendix 1, 23-24.
14 Pearson to Robertson, 15 December 1944, in LAC, DEA Papers, RG25, Series A-3-b, vol. 5708, File 7-V(s), Part 4; on the *Times* crisis, see Wrong to Pearson, 28 November 1944, in LAC, ibid.
15 SSEA to Pearson, 20 December 1944, in LAC, ibid.
16 Pearson, "Dumbarton Oaks: From an Address Delivered to the Winnipeg Canadian Club on Dec. 28, 1944, by Mr. Lester B. Pearson, Canadian Ambassador to the United States," *WFP*, 29 December 1944, 15.
17 Holmes, *The Shaping of Peace*, 240.
18 Memorandum, Office of European Affairs, Division of British Commonwealth Affairs, 5 January 1945, in NARA, RG59, Records of the Department of State, Notter File, Records

Relating to the Dumbarton Oaks Conversations, 1944, Entry 502, 250/46/25/02, Lot 60D-224, Box 185, Views of the Dumbarton Oaks Proposals: Other Governments.

19 Hickerson to Hiss and Sandifer, 12 January 1945, in NARA, ibid.

20 Wrong, Draft Memorandum on Dumbarton Oaks for Communication to United States, United Kingdom, Soviet, Chinese, and French Governments, 30 December 1944, in LAC, DEA Papers, RG25, Series A-3-b, vol. 5708, File 7-V(s), Part 4.

21 Read to Robertson, 2 January 1945, in LAC, ibid., vol. 5709, File 7-V(s), Part 5.1. See also Holmes, *The Shaping of Peace*, 240-42.

22 Minutes of the Cabinet War Committee, 8 January 1945, in LAC, PCO Papers, RG2 7c, vol. 17, Minutes of the Cabinet War Committee, 8 January-16 May 1945; Cabinet Conclusions, 9 January 1945, in LAC, ibid., Series A5a, vol. 2636, 14 February 1945 to 5 September 1945. The document was delivered officially on 12 January 1945; see SSEA to Massey, 12 January 1945, in Published Documents, *DCER*, vol. 11, 683.

23 Department of State, Memorandum of Conversation [including Pearson, Reid, Sandifer, Green, Achilles, and Parsons], 11 January 1945, in NARA, RG59, Records of the Department of State, Alger Hiss Files, 1940-46, Subject Files of the Office of Special Political Affairs, 1940-46, Entry 684, 250/47/03/05, Lot File 61-D-146, Box 1, Canadian Consultations.

24 Ibid. John English covers this development but neglects to mention that the Pearson-Reid proposal had not been cleared with Ottawa; see *Shadow of Heaven*, 286-87.

25 Pearson to Robertson, 11 January 1945, in LAC, DEA Papers, RG25, Series A-3-b, vol. 5709, File 7-V(s), Part 5.1; Pearson to SSEA, 15 January 1945, in LAC, ibid.

26 Reid, Reception of Canadian Observations of 12 January 1945 on the Dumbarton Oaks Proposals, 23 January 1945, in LAC, ibid., vol. 2157, File 1; Minutes of the Cabinet War Committee, 24 January 1945, in LAC, PCO Papers, RG2 7c, vol. 17, Minutes of the Cabinet War Committee, 8 January-16 May 1945.

27 Memorandum of Conversation, 10 February 1945, in NARA, RG59, Records of the Department of State, Notter File, Records Relating to the Dumbarton Oaks Conversations, 1944, Entry 502, 250/46/25/02, Lot 60D-224, Box 185, Views of the Dumbarton Oaks Proposals: Other Governments.

28 Reid, Memorandum of Discussion at Blair House, Washington, 10 February 1945, in LAC, DEA Papers, RG25, Series A-3-b, vol. 5709, File 7-V(s), Part 6.1.

29 Reid, Memorandum of Discussion in Pasvolsky's Office, 12 February 1945, in LAC, ibid. Wrong hoped to exclude "those who had, by a certain date, refused to enter into special military agreements" and "those in default on their financial obligations."

30 Wrong to King, 15 February 1945, in LAC, Albert Edgar Ritchie Papers, MG31 E44, vol. 16, File 8.

31 United States, Department of State, *Report of the Delegation of the United States of America to the Inter-American Conference on Problems of War and Peace, Mexico City, Mexico, February 21-March 8, 1945* (Washington, DC: United States Government Printing Office, 1946), 2. For a Canadian interpretation, see B.T.R., "Act of Chapultepec," *WFP*, 31 March 1945, 15.

32 Bateman to Butler, 14 March 1945, in NAUK, FO 371/50690. See also Hadow to Jebb, 10 March 1945, in NAUK, FO 371/50683; Canada could thank the Venezuelan foreign minister, Parra Perez, for the lack of agreement.

33 Grew to Roosevelt, 8 March 1945, in FDRL, FDR Papers, PSF, Diplomatic Correspondence, Box 25, Canada: 1944-45.

34 Wrong to King, 5 March 1945, in LAC, Albert Edgar Ritchie Papers, MG31 E44, vol. 16, File 8.

35 Wrong to King, 7 March 1945, in Published Documents, *DCER*, vol. 11, 702.

36 Pearson, quoted in Jebb [through Halifax] to FO, 21 March 1945, in NAUK, CAB 122/604.

37 Minutes of the Sixth Meeting of the United States Delegation, 10 April 1945, in *FRUS, 1945*, vol. 1, 228-29; Minutes of the Seventh Meeting of the United States Delegation, 11 April 1945, in ibid., 249-50; Minutes of the Ninth Meeting of the United States Delegation, 12 April 1945, in ibid., 273; Minutes of the Fourteenth Meeting of the United States Delegation, 24 April 1945, in ibid., 378.

38 Minutes of the Ninth Meeting of the United States Delegation, 12 April 1945, in ibid., 274. See also Reid, "Dumbarton Oaks Proposals, Comments by Mr. Pasvolsky," 17 April 1945, in LAC, DEA Papers, RG25, Series A-3-b, vol. 5709, File 7-V(s), Part 7.2.
39 Stephenson to Machtig, 15 December 1945, in NAUK, DO 35/1870.
40 Holmes, Memorandum, 25 January 1945, in LAC, DEA Papers, RG25, Series A-3-b, vol. 5709, File 7-V(s), Part 5.2.
41 Minutes of War Cabinet and Postwar Committee: World Organisation Views of Dominions Governments, Memorandum by Minister of State, 25 February 1945, in NAUK, CAB 122/604. On Cranborne, see SSDA to War Cabinet, 24 January 1945, in NAUK, DO 35/1877; and Woodward, *British Foreign Policy in the Second World War*, 180.
42 Wrong to Pearson, 28 February 1945, in LAC, DEA Papers, RG25, Series A-3-b, vol. 5709, File 7-V(s), Part 6.1.
43 No data (no name given) to Stephenson, 1 March 1945, in NAUK, DO 35/1881.
44 War Cabinet: Armistice and Post-War Committee, Note by Minister of State, 9 March 1945, in NAUK, CAB 122/604.
45 War Cabinet: Armistice and Post-War Committee: San Francisco Conference: Election of Non-Permanent Members of Security Council with Particular Reference to Position of Dominions: Memorandum by Minister of State, 22 March 1945, in NAUK, CAB 122/605; Eden, Memorandum to War Cabinet: Armistice and Post-War Committee, 23 March 1945, in NAUK, FO 371/50688.
46 Dunn to Stettinius, 10 November 1944, in *FRUS: The Conferences at Malta and Yalta* (Washington, DC: Government Printing House, 1955), 47-8; Cadogan to War Cabinet, 22 November 1944, in NAUK, DO 35/1872. For the Soviet view, see Stalin, "Address on War and Policy at the Meeting of the Moscow Soviet of Deputies of the Working People, Together with Representatives of the Party, Public and Red Army Organizations, in Honor of the 27th Anniversary of the Socialist Revolution, Moscow," 6 November 1944, in Published Documents, *War and Peace Aims of the United Nations*, vol. 2, 777.
47 Third Plenary Meeting, 6 February 1945, in *FRUS: The Conferences at Malta and Yalta*, 664.
48 Byelorussia was also known as White Russia.
49 Fourth Plenary Meeting, 7 February 1945, in *FRUS: The Conferences at Malta and Yalta*, 714. See also William D. Leahy, *I Was There* (New York: Wittlesey House, 1950), 306.
50 Copy of Letter(s) from President Roosevelt to Prime Minister, Marshal Stalin, 10 February 1945, in CAC, Churchill Papers, CHAR 23/14.
51 Wilgress to SSEA, 22 March 1945, in Published Documents, *DCER*, vol. 11, 720; Atherton, Memorandum of Conversation [with Robertson], 26 March 1945, in NARA, RG84, Records of the Foreign Service Posts of the Department of State, Entry 2196, 350/51/13/01, Canada, Ottawa Legation and Assembly, Secret General Records 1943-49, Box 1, Secret: 1945.
52 Pearson to SSEA, 2 April 1945, in LAC, DEA Papers, RG25, vol. 3680, File 5475-40C, Part 3. It was difficult for Washington to do much else given that the *New York Herald Tribune* had published details of the deal; see Robert A. Divine, *Second Chance: The Triumph of Internationalism in America during World War II* (New York: Antheum, 1967), 274.
53 Halifax to FO, 2 April 1945, in NAUK, CAB 122/605.
54 Pearson to Robertson, 5 April 1945, in LAC, DEA Papers, RG25, Series G-2, vol. 3744, File 6834-40, Part 3.
55 Extracts from President Roosevelt's Press and Radio Conference at the Little White House, Warm Springs, Georgia, 5 April 1945, in *FRUS, 1945*, vol. 1, *General: The United Nations* (Washington, DC: Government Printing Office, 1967), 198. On US popular opinion, see Halifax to FO, 31 March 1945, in NAUK, CAB 122/605.
56 Wilgress to SSEA, 13 March 1945, in LAC, DEA Papers, RG25, Series A-3-b, vol. 5709, File 7-V(s), Part 6.2.
57 Riddell to Robertson, 7 November 1944, in LAC, ibid., vol. 5757, File 62-A(s), Part 1. On the *Telegraph* articles, see A.J. Pick to SSEA, 8 November 1944, in LAC, ibid., Series G-2, vol. 3281, File 6834-40, Part 2. Pick quoted from a *Telegraph* article written on 6 November.
58 Robertson to King, 27 December 1944, in LAC, W.L.M. King Papers, Memoranda and Notes, MG26 J4, vol. 342, File 3679.

59 Wrong to David Wilson, 13 January 1945, in LAC, DEA Papers, RG25, Series A-3-b, vol. 5709, File 7-V(s), Part 5.1.

60 On South Africa, see Wrong to King, 13 January 1945, in LAC, W.L.M. King Papers, Memoranda and Notes, MG26 J4, vol. 338, File 3668; and Wrong to King, 29 January 1945, in LAC, ibid., File 3679. On Australia, see High Commissioner for Canada in Australia to SSEA, 12 February 1945, in LAC, DEA Papers, RG25, Series A-3-b, vol. 5709, File 7-V(s), Part 6.1. On New Zealand, see Walter Riddell to SSEA, 8 and 12 March 1945, in LAC, ibid., Part 6.2.

61 SSEA to Massey, 13 January 1945, in LAC, ibid., Part 5.1.

62 Holmes to Wrong, 24 January 1945, in LAC, ibid., Part 5.2; No data (no name given) to SSEA, 10 March 1945, in LAC, ibid., Part 6.2; and Vanier to SSEA, 20 March 1945, in LAC, ibid., Part 7.1.

63 Turgeon to SSEA, 14 February 1945, in LAC, ibid., Part 6.1; Ritchie, Memorandum, 5 March 1945, in LAC, ibid., Part 6.2; Turgeon to SSEA, 21 March 1945, in LAC, ibid., Series B-2, vol. 2157, File 4.

64 Ambassador to Chile to SSEA, 18 February 1945, in LAC, ibid., Series A-3-b, vol. 5709, File 7-V(s), Part 6.1.

65 Record of Informal Meeting with Diplomatic Representatives of Certain American Republics, 5 February 1945, in FRUS, 1945, vol. 1, 50.

66 Atherton, Memorandum of Conversation with Robertson, 26 March 1945, in NARA, RG59, Records of the Department of State, Alger Hiss Files, 1940-46, UNCIO Subject Files of Alger Hiss, 1945, Entry 686, 250/47/03/05, Lot File 61-D-146, Box 8, Memos of Conversation. On the Mexican proposal, see C.H. Bateman to Eden, 17 February 1945, in LAC, DEA Papers, RG25, Series A-3-b, vol. 5709, File 7-V(s), Part 6.1; Keenleyside to SSEA, 22 and 26 February 1945, in LAC, ibid.; and Keenleyside to SSEA, 3 April 1945, in LAC, ibid., Part 7.1. On Brazil, see D. Gainer to Eden, 24 March 1945, in LAC, ibid., Part 6.1. On Cuba, see Sir G. Ogilvie Forbes to Hadow, 28 February 1945, in NAUK, FO 371/50683.

67 Bidault, Statements on the Organization of Security Made in Two Press Interviews, Paris, January 1945, in Published Documents, War and Peace Aims of the United Nations, vol. 2, 884.

68 Holman to Harvey, 16 February 1945, in NAUK, FO 371/50679. On the East Block's awareness, see for example, SSEA to Vanier, 9 March 1945, in LAC, DEA Papers, RG25, Series A-3-b, vol. 5709, File 7-V(s), Part 6.2.

69 SSDA to Dominions, 22 February 1945, in NAUK, CAB 21/1610. The meeting was originally scheduled for 15 March but was moved to 4 April to accommodate concerns raised by New Zealand and South Africa.

70 King to SSDA, 26 February 1945, in LAC, DEA Papers, RG25, Series A-3-b, vol. 5709, File 7-V(s), Part 6.1; SSEA to SSDA, 27 February 1945, in LAC, ibid.

71 "A Commonwealth Preliminary," G&M, 1 March 1945, 6. On the Canadian delegation's instructions, see Clark to Parsons, 21 March 1945, 842.00/3-2145, in NARA, RG59, Records of the Department of State, 250, State Department Decimal Files, 1945-49, Box 5995, from 841E.5151/1-145 to 842/00/12-3146.

72 Minutes of Minister of State's Committee on World Organization, 28 March 1945, in NAUK, FO 371/50691; Cockram to Jebb, 23 March 1945, in NAUK, FO 371/50689; U.S. Department of State, Memorandum, 28 March 1945, in NAUK, FO 115/4192.

73 World Organisation: Minutes of Ninth Meeting of the A.P.W. Committee, 29 March 1945, in NAUK, FO 371/50692.

74 Minutes of the War Cabinet, 3 April 1945, in NAUK, CAB 123/237. For Cranborne's memorandum, see SSDA to War Cabinet, 31 March 1945, in NAUK, ibid.

75 Minutes of 1st Meeting [of the Commonwealth Conference], 4 April 1945, in LAC, DEA Papers, RG25, Series C-3, vol. 2283, File s/26/1, British Commonwealth Meeting, April 1945. The Canadians went so far as to refuse to accept an offer to join other members of the Commonwealth on a British ship to travel to San Francisco; see FO to Washington, 16 March 1945, in NAUK, FO 371/50682.

76 Evatt and Smuts, in Minutes of 1st Meeting, 4 April 1945, in LAC, DEA Papers, RG25, Series C-3, vol. 2283, File s/26/1, British Commonwealth Meeting, April 1945; Massey, diary

entry, 4 April 1945, in UT, Vincent Massey Papers, B-87-0082, Box 312, Massey Diaries, Diary 57, February-May 1945.

77 Minutes of a Meeting Held in Conference Room "B," Offices of the War Cabinet, S.W.1., 6 April 1945, in LAC, DEA Papers, RG25, Series A-3-b, vol. 5708, File 7-V(s), Part 3fp. On the Canadian comments, see British Commonwealth Meeting: Dumbarton Oaks Proposals, 5 April 1945, in LAC, ibid.

78 British Commonwealth Meeting: Minutes of a Meeting Held in Conference Room "B," Offices of the War Cabinet, 9 April 1945, in LAC, ibid.

79 British Commonwealth Meeting: Election of Non-Permanent Members of the Security Council, Draft Report of Committee of Experts, 10 April 1945, in LAC, ibid.

80 Minutes of 7th Meeting, 19 April 1945, in LAC, ibid., Series C-3, vol. 2283, File s/26/1, British Commonwealth Meeting, April 1945.

81 Paul Sauriol, "Le principe de souveraineté," *Le Devoir*, 9 April 1945, 1.

82 E.E. Bridges to Heeney, 13 April 1945, in LAC, Arnold Danford Patrick Heeney Papers, MG30 E144, vol. 1, Clerk of the Privy Council 1941-46, Correspondence, Memoranda.

83 Massey to SSEA, 23 April 1945, in Published Documents, *DCER*, vol. 11, 743.

Chapter 9: The Public Road to San Francisco

1 CIPO, 6 January 1945, in *POQ* 9, 1 (Spring 1945): 107. By comparison, in January 1945 polls suggested that over 25 percent of Americans still preferred that their country stay out of any world organization. See National Opinion Research Center, 28 January 1945, in ibid., 101.

2 Dexter to Ferguson, 9 January 1945, in QUA, Grant Dexter Papers, Collection 2142, Series 1: Correspondence, Box 4, Folder 27, General 1945.

3 Massey, diary entry, 25 November 1944, in UT, Vincent Massey Papers, B-87-0082, Box 312, Massey Diaries, Diary 56, October 1944-February 1945.

4 King, diary entry, 23 February 1945, in Robarts Library, King Diary; J.W. Pickersgill and D.F. Forster, *The Mackenzie King Record*, vol. 2, *1944-1945* (Toronto: University of Toronto Press, 1968), 153.

5 King, diary entry, 10 March 1945, in Robarts Library, King Diary.

6 Minutes of the 17th Annual Meeting of the [CIIA] National Council, 16 December 1944, in LAC, CIIA Papers, MG28 I250, Reel M-4619, vol. 6, Minutes, 1943-44. On individual members' contributions, see for example, R.G. Trotter, "Commonwealth: Pattern for Peace?" *Behind the Headlines* 4, 5 (1944); Brooke Claxton, "The Place of Canada in Post-War Organization," *Canadian Journal of Economics and Political Science* 10, 4 (November 1944): 409-21 (Claxton's article was also drawn from a public speech); and Canadian Council for Education in Citizenship, Secretary's Report to Fourth Annual Council Meeting, October 1945, in LAC, Canadian Citizenship Council Papers, MG28 I85, vol. 45, 1944-50.

7 Citizens' Forum [flyer], "*This Is the Way to Help Build a Better Canada*," [1945], in LAC, DEA Papers, RG25, Series G-2, vol. 2870, File 1843-Q-40; Citizens' Forum, "National Report Broadcast," 27 February 1945, in LAC, ibid.

8 Canada, Dominion Bureau of Statistics, Department of Trade and Commerce, *The Canada Year Book 1945* (Ottawa: Edmond Cloutier, 1945), xliii. See also "The World in Action: Now the Peace," in LAC, Academy of Motion Picture Arts and Sciences Fonds, United Artists Presents: "The World in Action: Now the Peace," Film, [VI 7901-0013]. On the US interest, see Robertson to King, 26 January 1945, in LAC, DEA Papers, RG25, Series G-2, vol. 3228, File 5475-40, Part 2. Grierson was quickly released to the United States so that the project could benefit from American sponsorship, and within days, a representative from the NFB had begun plans for the film; see Reid to Robertson, 5 February 1945, in LAC, ibid., vol. 3281, File 6834-40, Part 2.

9 Mallory to Armstrong, 7 December 1944, in SML, Hamilton Fish Armstrong Papers, Box 69, Organizations and Committees, File CFR: General Correspondence 1941-44. See also Gaddis, *The United States and the Origins of the Cold War*, 86, 175.

10 Uncle Joe, the name that Churchill and Roosevelt used to refer to Stalin.

11 Churchill to Roosevelt, 18 March 1945, in CAC, Churchill Papers, CHAR 20/199/76-77.

12 Churchill to Roosevelt, 27 March 1945, in CAC, Churchill Papers, CHAR 20/213A.

13   Berle, diary entry, 5 April 1945, in FDRL, Adolf Berle Papers, Box 216, Diary, April-July 1945.
14   Broadcast to the United States by the Lord President of the Council [Attlee], 6 April 1945, in BL, Clement Attlee Papers, MSS Attlee, Dep. 17; "San Francisco Issues Are Now Foreshadowed: Observers Question Whether the Public Realizes the Difficulties to Be Met," *New York Times*, 8 April 1945, E7.
15   Confidential Annex, Minutes of 4th Meeting [of the Commonwealth Conference], 6 April 1945, in LAC, DEA Papers, RG25, Series C-3, vol. 2283, File s/26/1, British Commonwealth Meeting, April 1945.
16   "Turning Point," *WFP*, 8 February 1945, 13.
17   "Canada at San Francisco," *WFP*, 13 February 1945, 9.
18   "The Conference at Yalta," *G&M*, 14 February 1945, 6.
19   "Amitié plus solide que jamais," *La Presse*, 14 March 1945, 8.
20   Tarr to Dr. Hu Shih, 26 January 1945, in LAC, CIIA Papers, MG28 I250, vol. 3, Edgar J. Tarr: IPR Conferences: Hot Springs, 1944-45.
21   Pearson to SSEA, 20 February 1945, in LAC, DEA Papers, RG25, Series G-2, vol. 3228, File 5475-40, Part 2.
22   Wrong to Wilgress, 10 March 1945, in LAC, ibid., vol. 5709, File 7-V(s), Part 6.2.
23   Department of State: Memorandum of Conversation [Pearson, Reid, Sandifer, Green, Achilles, and Parsons], 11 January 1945, in NARA, RG59, Records of the Department of State, Alger Hiss Files, 1940-46, Subject Files of the Office of Special Political Affairs, 1940-46, Entry 684, 250/47/03/05, Lot File 61-D-146, Box 1, Canadian Consultations. Pearson found the Economic and Social Council sufficiently unimportant at this time that, while the Americans noted the discussion in their report of the January meeting, he did not mention it in his; see Pearson to Robertson, 11 January 1945, in LAC, DEA Papers, RG25, Series A-3-b, vol. 5709, File 7-V(s), Part 5.1. On Wrong's beliefs and actions, see Wrong to Heeney, 17 January 1945, in LAC, ibid., Part 5.2; and Wrong to Heeney, 18 January 1945, in LAC, ibid., Part 5.1.
24   Wrong, Memorandum, 2 February 1945, in LAC, ibid., Part 5.2; Wrong to King, 15 February 1945, in LAC, ibid., Part 6.1; Wrong, Memorandum, 2 March 1945, in LAC, ibid., Part 6.2.
25   Pearson, diary entry, 20 March 1945, in LAC, Pearson Papers, MG26 N8, vol. 1, File 4, Diaries and Personal Papers, 1943-45; Halifax to Eden, 21 March 1945, in NAUK, FO 115/4192. On the FO, see Falla, Minute, "Suggestions for Discussion at Minister of State's Committee Meeting of 14th March," 12 March 1945, in NAUK, FO 371/50682. On Baruch, see Stettinius, diary entry, 12 March 1945, in *The Diaries of Edward R. Stettinius Jr.*, ed. Thomas M. Campbell and George C. Herring (New York: New Viewpoints, 1975), 298. Baruch was a strange choice given that his financial advice had cost Churchill dearly in 1929. On Pearson, see Pearson to SSEA, 15 March 1945, in LAC, DEA Papers, RG25, vol. 3680, File 5475-40C, Part 3.
26   Holmes, *The Shaping of Peace*, 47. See also Hilliker, *Canada's Department of External Affairs*, 272.
27   King, diary entry, 22 February 1945, in Robarts Library, King Diary. On the lack of public knowledge, see for example, "Canada at San Francisco," *WFP*, 23 February 1945, 11; "Get All Behind the Peace Plan," *Financial Post*, 3 March 1945, 6; and "M. King sera chef de la délégation," *La Presse*, 13 March 1945, 6. King was equally evasive when asked about this issue by other dominions; see Robertson to Australian High Commissioner, 23 February 1945, in LAC, DEA Papers, RG25, Series A-3-b, vol. 5709, File 7-V(s), Part 6.1; and King to No data (name unclear) New Zealand, 16 March 1945, in LAC, ibid., Part 7.1. He even left his Cabinet guessing; see Crerar to Dexter, 7 March 1945, in QUA, T.A. Crerar Papers, Collection 2117, Series 3, Box 105, Correspondence, Folder: Grant Dexter, July 1940, May 1940-June 1950.
28   SSEA to Atherton, 5 March 1945, in Published Documents, *DCER*, vol. 11, 748-49. On 27 February, King had warned his Cabinet that he would accept the invitation when it came, but there had not been any discussion; see Pickersgill and Forster, *King Record*, vol. 2, 315. On the Cabinet decision, see Cabinet Conclusions, 16 March 1945, in LAC, PCO Papers, RG2, Series 5a, vol. 2636, 14 February-5 September 1945.

29 Soward, *Canada in World Affairs,* 131.
30 King, 19 March 1945, in Canada, House of Commons, *Debates,* 6th Session, 19th Parliament, 19 March 1945 to 16 April 1945, vol. 245, 11.
31 King, diary entry, 10 March 1945, in Robarts Library, King Diary.
32 King, 20 March 1945, in Canada, House of Commons, *Debates,* 6th Session, 19th Parliament, 19 March 1945 to 16 April 1945, vol. 245, 22-9. Soward suggests that the speech foreshadows Canada's approach to San Francisco. He is correct, but his reasoning is mistaken. His contention that it demonstrated Canada's commitment to middle power advocacy is disputed below. Moreover, he does not pay sufficient attention to the Economic and Social Council; see *Canada in World Affairs,* 134.
33 Coldwell, 20 March 1945, in Canada, House of Commons, *Debates,* 6th Session, 19th Parliament, 19 March 1945 to 16 April 1945, vol. 245, 37-8.
34 Martin, 20 March 1945, in Canada, ibid., 41-5. For his own interpretation, see Martin, *A Very Public Life,* 359-61.
35 Roebuck, 22 March 1945, in Canada, House of Commons, *Debates,* 6th Session, 19th Parliament, 19 March 1945 to 16 April 1945, vol. 245, 112.
36 McCann, 22 March 1945, in Canada, ibid., 132.
37 G.E. Wood, 22 March, 1945, in Canada, ibid., 176.
38 Claxton, 27 March 1945, in Canada, ibid., 255. The only English-speaking Liberal member of Parliament to counsel caution was an obscure Nova Scotian, J.J. Kinley; see Kinley, 26 March 1945, in Canada, ibid., 225.
39 Graydon, 21 March 1945, in Canada, ibid., 68-69.
40 Green, 22 March 1945, in Canada, ibid., 116-18. For the Conservative view, see for example, Diefenbaker, 22 March 1945, in Canada, ibid., 164. For Liberal opinion, see for example, Crerar, 26 March 1945, in Canada, ibid., 202-5.
41 Formerly the Communist Party of Canada.
42 Rose, 21 March 1945, in Canada, ibid., 97.
43 Blackmore, 22 March 1945, in Canada, ibid., 152. Blackmore's hand-written comments on the Dumbarton Oaks proposals suggest that his greatest concerns centred on the responsibilities of the Economic and Social Council, but his marginal notations are too vague to be conclusive; see United Nations [annotated information] 1945, in Glenbow Museum Archives, Calgary, Alberta, Canada, John Horn Blackmore Papers, Series 8, M100/215. For the clearest explanation of Blackmore's comments, see Francis Flaherty, "Debate on Security Conference Showed Reassuring Agreement," *Saturday Night,* 7 April 1945, 8; and Soward, *Canada in World Affairs,* 132.
44 Casselman, 20 March 1945, in Canada, House of Commons, *Debates,* 6th Session, 19th Parliament, 19 March 1945 to 16 April 1945, vol. 245, 46.
45 Pouliot, 21 March 1945, in Canada, ibid., 91-4. For the French Canadian view generally, see Maurice Lalonde, 22 March 1945, in Canada, ibid., 186; and René Jutras, 22 March 1945, in Canada, ibid.
46 Lacombe, 20 March 1945, in Canada, ibid., 59-60; Dorion, 22 March 1945, in Canada, ibid., 125-27. The legal claim was ably refuted by Maurice Lalonde two days later; see Lalonde, 22 March 1945, in Canada, ibid., 186.
47 Lacroix, 21 March 1945, in Canada, ibid., 101. See also Roy, 27 March 1945, in Canada, ibid., 280; d'Anjou, 22 March 1945, in Canada, ibid., 146.
48 King, 28 March 1945, in Canada, ibid., 298-308.
49 "L'attitude canadienne à San Francisco," *La Presse,* 21 March 1945, 6.
50 "Our Country and Our People," *WFP,* 26 March 1945, 13.
51 Francis Flaherty, "Debate on Security Conference Showed Reassuring Agreement," *Saturday Night,* 7 April 1945, 8.
52 "Words without Action," *G&M,* 22 March 1945, 6; "A Sovereign Alternative," *G&M,* 23 March 1945, 6; "Isolationists Do Not Learn," *G&M,* 26 March 1945, 6.
53 Vigeant, "Le débat sur la politique étrangère," *Le Devoir,* 26 March 1945, 1; Vigeant, "M. Maxime Raymond estime que le Canada doit être représenté à San-Francisco," *Le Devoir,* 28 March 1945, 2; and Omer Hereux, "De Québec et de Téhéran à San-Francisco," *Le Devoir,* 28 March 1945, 1.

54 Parsons to Office of Special Political Affairs, 28 March 1945, in NARA, RG59, Records of the Department of State, Alger Hiss Files, 1940-46, Pre-UNCIO Subject Files of John C. Ross, 1945, Entry 687, 250/47/03/05, Lot File 61-D-146, Box 11, Canada.
55 Regardless of her gender, Casselman was a legitimate choice. She had been active both in the League of Nations Society and at meetings of the CIIA. Nevertheless, it was probably more important to King that a CIPO poll showed that 64 percent of Canadians (although only 38 percent of Quebecers) believed that women should be taking part in the postwar planning conferences; see CIPO, 18 April 1945, in *POQ* 9, 2 (Summer 1945): 257.
56 Department of External Affairs, "Commentary on the Dumbarton Oaks Proposals for the Establishment of a General International Organization," 14 April 1945, in LAC, DEA Papers, RG25, A4, vol. 3456, File 6-1-1945/6. While there is no author listed on the document, its language and tone reflect previous work by Hume Wrong. For a complete listing of the Canadian delegation, see Canada, DEA, *Report on the United Nations Conference on International Organization Held at San Francisco, 25th April-26th June 1945* (1 September 1945), 9-14.
57 Memorandum of Conversation by Stettinius, 17 April 1945, in *FRUS, 1945*, vol. 1, 324-25. On the framework, see Department of State to the British Embassy, 3 April 1945, in ibid., 181-82.
58 King, diary entry, 12 April 1945, in Robarts Library, King Diary.
59 Harriman to Stettinius, 13 April 1945, in *FRUS, 1945*, vol. 1, 289. On the American decision, see United States, Department of State, *Bulletin* (22 April 1945). On the British attitude, see Jebb, in DHL, Oral History Collection (02), J44, Lord Gladwyn Jebb, 24 October 1945; and Eden to Churchill, 21 and 23 April 1945, in NAUK, FO, Anthony Eden Papers, FO 954/2.
60 King to Patteson, 22 April 1945, in Robarts Library, King Diary.

Chapter 10: Growing Up
1 "San Francisco," *Canadian Forum* 25, 294 (July 1945): 81. See also Webster, diary entry, 20 June 1945, in *The Historian as Diplomat*, ed. Reynolds and Hughes, 69.
2 LAC, W.L.M. King Papers, Memoranda and Notes, MG26 J4, vol. 339, File 3672.
3 Pope, diary entry, 25 April 1945, in LAC, Maurice Pope Papers, MG27, IIIF4, vol. 2, Diary 1945.
4 Pearson to Robertson, 3 March 1945, in LAC, DEA Papers, RG25, Series A-3-b, vol. 5709, File 7-V(s), Part 6.2; Pearson to Massey, 20 April 1945, in LAC, Pearson Papers, MG26 N1, vol. 10, Massey, 1943-52.
5 Pearson, diary entry, 20-24 April 1945, in LAC, Pearson Papers, MG26 N8, vol. 1, File 4, Diaries and Personal Papers, 1943-45.
6 Minutes of Meeting of Canadian Delegation, [24 April 1945], 27 April 1945, in Published Documents, *DCER*, vol. 11, 751. The Canadian delegation was medium-sized. In all, 282 delegates, along with 1,444 assistants, advisers, consultants, technical experts, and other staff members, attended the conference, as did representatives of a number of nongovernmental organizations; see Herbert Vere Evatt, *The United Nations* (Cambridge, MA: Harvard University Press, 1948), 15. A more complete list of statistics can be found in Clyde Eagleton, "The United Nations: Peace and Security," *American Political Science Review* 39, 5 (October 1945): 935.
7 Pope, diary entry, 25 April 1945, in LAC, Maurice Pope Papers, MG27 IIIF4, vol. 2, Diary 1945.
8 Reid, letter to wife, 25 April 1945, in *On Duty*, 29.
9 E.G. Smith to J.H. Campbell and S. Friefeld [all members of the WIB], 25 April 1945, in LAC, DEA Papers, RG25, Series G-2, vol. 3744, File 6834-40, Part 3.
10 United States, Department of State, *Report to the President on the Results of the San Francisco Conference by the Chairman of the United States Delegation, the Secretary of State, June 26, 1945* (Washington, DC: Department of State, 1945), 30.
11 Over the first ten days, Mackenzie King caught a bad cold, as did Norman Robertson and a number of others. Warwick Chipman also took ill, and Charles Ritchie seems to have either contracted the measles or experienced a serious allergic reaction.

12 Pearson, diary entry, 27 April 1945, in LAC, Pearson Papers, MG26 N8, vol. 1, File 4, Diaries and Personal Papers, 1943-45.
13 King, Second Plenary Session, 27 April 1945, in Published Documents, *Documents of the United Nations Conference on International Organization, San Francisco, 1945* (hereafter *UNCIO*), vol. 1, *General* (London and New York: United Nations Information Organizations, 1945), 193-94. See also King, *Industry and Humanity*, 28; and Holmes, *The Shaping of Peace*, 230.
14 King, diary entry, 28 April 1945, in Robarts Library, King Diary; Cockram to Machtig, 28 April 1945, in NAUK, DO 35/1884; Eden to Churchill, 30 April 1945, in CAC, Churchill Papers, CHAR 20/216.
15 King, diary entry, 2 May 1945, in Robarts Library, King Diary.
16 Francis Flaherty, "Canadian Delegation Is Following Policy of Watching and Waiting," *Saturday Night*, 5 May 1945, 8.
17 Reid, personal entries, 1 and 4 May 1945, in *On Duty*, 31-2. On 23 May, in what was perhaps his most brilliant decision of the conference, Norman Robertson found a way to silence Reid by giving him a job that he liked as an adviser on the coordination committee. For the next five weeks, Reid worked diligently, going over every word of the texts proposed by the technical committees and making recommendations as to how the language might be improved; see Reid, personal entry, 23 May 1945, in *On Duty*, 49; and English, *Shadow of Heaven*, 289.
18 Proposed Amendments to Dumbarton Oaks Proposals, 4 May 1945, in Published Documents, *DCER*, vol. 11, 756-60.
19 Reid, personal entries, 6 and 10 May 1945, in *On Duty*, 33-4, 37.
20 "End of the 'Single-Voice' Idea," *WFP*, 1 May 1945, 11. The official Canadian report on the conference, drafted by Escott Reid, profoundly exaggerates the Canadian contribution to this issue; see Canada, DEA, *Report on the United Nations Conference on International Organization*, 29-30.
21 Minutes of the First Four-Power Consultative Meeting on Charter Proposals, 2 May 1945, in *FRUS, 1945*, vol. 1, 558.
22 Minutes of the Twenty-Eighth Meeting of the United States Delegation, 2 May 1945, in ibid., 576-77.
23 Minutes of the Third Four-Power Consultative Meeting on Charter Proposals, 3 May 1945, in ibid., 584-85. Russell appears to have misinterpreted the results of this meeting. She alleges that the British insisted on the geographical-representation clause; see *A History of the United Nations Charter*, 649.
24 Pearson, "Commission III, Committee 1: The Security Council: Composition, Powers and Procedures," 13 May 1945, in LAC, DEA Papers, RG25, Series A-4, vol. 3456, File 6-1-1945/3.
25 Summary of Report of 8th Meeting of Committee III/1, 16 May 1945, in *UNCIO*, vol. 11, *Commission III, Security Council* (London and New York: United Nations Information Organizations, 1945), 298-99.
26 W.A.W. Clark to Cadogan, 25 April 1945, in NAUK, DO 35/1213.
27 Summary of Report of 4th Meeting of Committee III/3, 10 May 1945, in *UNCIO*, vol. 12, *Commission III, Security Council* (London and New York: United Nations Information Organizations, 1945), 303; Minutes of the Thirty-Eighth Meeting of the United States Delegation, 14 May 1945, in *FRUS, 1945*, vol. 1, 711-12.
28 King, diary entry, 14 May 1945, in Robarts Library, King Diary.
29 The editors of the *King Record*, and also C.P. Stacey, are in error here; see Pickersgill and Forster, *King Record*, vol. 2, 386; and Stacey, *Canada and the Age of Conflict*, vol. 2, 384. James Eayrs – who relies almost exclusively on the King diary in this case – is similarly mistaken; see *In Defence of Canada*, vol. 3, 159-61. So too is F.H. Soward; see *Canada in World Affairs*, 136-39.
30 Illegible to Krock, [June 1945], in SML, Arthur Krock Papers, Box 1, Works: Memoranda, Book 1, 164-66.
31 Minutes of the Thirty-Ninth Meeting of the United States Delegation, 15 May 1945, in *FRUS, 1945*, vol. 1, 728-29; Minutes of the Forty-Third Meeting of the United States Delegation, 17 May 1945, in ibid., 772.

32 Minutes of the Forty-Seventh Meeting of the United States Delegation, 19 May 1945, in ibid., 806-8.
33 Summary Report of the 17th Meeting of Committee III/3, 2 June 1945, in *UNCIO*, vol. 12, 417-19. The meeting on 31 May was a joint subcommittee meeting of commission III, committee 1, subcommittee B and III/3/A. See also Record of the United Kingdom Delegation Meeting, 1 June 1945, in NAUK, CAB 21/1611.
34 Verbatim Minutes of the First Meeting of Commission III, 12 June 1945, in *UNCIO*, vol. 11, 15.
35 King, diary entry, 1 June 1945, in Robarts Library, King Diary.
36 Eden to War Cabinet, "United Nations Plan for Organising Peace," 7 July 1943, in NAUK, DO 35/1841.
37 Quincy Wright, "Representation and Voting in International Organizations," 25 February 1944, in LC, Benjamin Gerig Papers, Box 5, Folder 2, Subject File: Division of International Security and Organization, Office of Special Political Affairs: Reports, Memoranda, and Letters by Quincy Wright Regarding International Organization and/or Territories.
38 Pearson, Broadcast over CBC Network, 29 April 1945, in LAC, W.L.M. King Papers, Memoranda and Notes, MG26 J4, vol. 340, File 3674. On the early interest, see for example, "Address Delivered by M. Craig McGeachy over CBC to Inaugurate the Canadian Program of Broadcasts on the San Francisco Conference," 11 March 1945, in LAC, DEA Papers, RG25, Series G-2, vol. 3281, File 6834-40, Part 2. John Holmes underestimates the Canadian commitment to ECOSOC in *The Shaping of Peace*, 272, as does C.P. Stacey in *Canada and the Age of Conflict*, vol. 2, 384.
39 Rasminsky, "Comparison of Canadian Redraft of Chapter IX and Chapter X of Dumbarton Oaks Proposals," 9 May 1945, in BCA, Louis Rasminsky Papers, Folder LR76-57, File FR76-57-6-5. On Rasminsky and ECOSOC, see Bruce Muirhead, *Against the Odds: The Public Life and Times of Louis Rasminsky* (Toronto: University of Toronto Press, 1999), 115-17.
40 Proposed Amendments to Dumbarton Oaks Proposals, 4 May 1945, in Published Documents, *DCER*, vol. 11, 758. On the positive response from the US, see Cox to Stettinius, 9 May 1945, in FDRL, Oscar Cox Papers, Box 151, Diary: March-April-May 1945.
41 Summary Report of the Fourth Meeting of Committee II/3, 11 May 1945, in *UNCIO*, vol. 10, *Commission II, General Assembly* (London and New York: United Nations Information Organizations, 1945), 21. Divine's suggestion that economic and social issues "received little emphasis at San Francisco" is an unfair, American-centric view of the negotiations; see *Second Chance*, 289.
42 Minutes of the Thirty-Seventh Meeting of the United States Delegation, 12 May 1945, in *FRUS, 1945*, vol. 1, 689. Russell understates the Canadian role in the negotiations; see *A History of the United Nations Charter*, 777-807.
43 L.W., "Questions of Policy Relative to Membership and Principal Organs of the Organization, Amendment and Revision of the Charter," 13 May 1945, in LAC, DEA Papers, RG25, Series A4, vol. 3456, File 6-1-1945/3.
44 Robert English, Conversation with Maurice Pope, 14 May 1945, in NARA, RG84, Records of the Foreign Service Posts of the Department of State, Entry 2195a, 350/51/09/03, Canada, Ottawa Embassy, Security, Segregated General Records 1939-49, Box 116, 1945, 020-701.1, 020-500.
45 Rasminsky, CBC Broadcast, 13 May 1945, in BCA, Louis Rasminsky Papers, Folder LR76-51, File LR76-51-7-1.
46 Summary Report of the Fifth Meeting of Committee II/3, 14 May 1945, in *UNCIO*, vol. 10, 27.
47 Summary Report of the Thirteenth Meeting of Committee II/3, 28 May 1945, in Published Documents, ibid., 121; Commission II, Committee 3: Economic and Social Co-operation: Suggested Rearrangement of Chapter IX, 4 June 1945, in Published Documents, ibid., 205-8.
48 B.T.R., "The Economic Council," *WFP*, 20 June 1945, 11. On the success of the changes to ECOSOC, see Charles K. Webster, "The Making of the United Nations," *History* 32 (March-September 1947): 16-38; and William Hardy McNeil, *America, Britain and Russia: Their Co-operation and Conflict, 1941-1946* (London: Oxford University Press, 1953), 598.

49 Holmes, *The Shaping of Peace*, 257-59.
50 Speeches in French or English in the plenary session would not be translated, but translations would appear in the official conference journal. Speeches in committees would be translated into both English and French; see UK Delegation to FO, 27 April 1945, in NAUK, CAB 21/2307.
51 L.W., "Questions of Policy Relative to Membership and Principal Organs of the Organization, Amendment and Revision of the Charter," 13 May 1945, in LAC, DEA Papers, RG25, Series A-4, vol. 3456, File 6-1-1945/3.
52 Summary Report of the Fifth Meeting of Committee II/1, 14 May 1945, in *UNCIO*, vol. 8, *Commission II, General Assembly* (London and New York: United Nations Information Organizations, 1945), 332-33; Minutes of the Forty-First Meeting of the United States Delegation, 16 May 1945, in *FRUS, 1945*, vol. 1, 755-57; Working Paper for Committee II/1/A (Drafting Subcommittee), 19 May 1945, in *UNCIO*, vol. 8, 532-33.
53 Summary Report of the Fourteenth Meeting of Committee II/1, 8 June 1945, in Published Documents, ibid., 475.
54 Summary Report of the Twenty-First Meeting of Committee I/2, 12 June 1945, in *UNCIO*, vol. 7, *Commission I: General Provisions* (London and New York: United Nations Information Organization, 1945), 195-96.
55 See for example, Reid, *On Duty*, 24; Gromyko, *Memories*, 118-19; Fraser to Jean Fraser, 29 April 1945, in LAC, Blair Fraser Papers, MG31 D84, vol. 4, "Canada and the Postwar World, Part B"; Alan Watt, *Australian Diplomat: Memoirs of Sir Alan Watt* (Sydney: Angus and Robertson Publishers, 1972), 67.
56 Coldwell opposed the inclusion of Argentina until it agreed to "remove the police censorship of news, restore the freedom of universities and schools, and empty the concentration camps where democrats are incarcerated"; see UK monthly Political and Economic Report [on Canada], mid-April to mid-May 1945, 21 June 1945, in NAUK, FO 371/50365.
57 Pope, diary entry, 10 May 1945, in LAC, Maurice Pope Papers, MG27 III4, vol. 2, Diary 1945.
58 Pearson, diary entry, 10 May 1945, in LAC, Pearson Papers, MG26 N8, vol. 1, File 4, Diaries and Personal Papers, 1943-45.
59 Pearson, "Commission III, Committee 1: The Security Council: Composition, Powers and Procedures," 13 May 1945, in LAC, DEA Papers, RG25, Series A-4, vol. 3456, File 6-1-1945/3.
60 Summary Report of the 10th Meeting of Committee III/1, 18 May 1945, in *UNCIO*, vol. 11, 332.
61 Record of the United Kingdom Delegation Meeting, 19 May 1945, in NAUK, CAB 21/1611.
62 Memorandum by Harriman and Bohlen, 19 May 1945, in Joseph Grew, *Turbulent Era: A Diplomatic Record of Forty Years, 1904-1945*, vol. 2, ed. Walter Johnson (Cambridge, MA: The Riverside Press, 1952), 1446; Minutes of the Forty-Eighth Meeting of the United States Delegation (Executive Session), 20 May 1945, in *FRUS, 1945*, vol. 1, 821-22.
63 Cadogan, diary entry, 26 May 1945, *The Diaries of Sir Alexander Cadogan, O.M., 1938-1945*, ed. David Dilks (New York: G.P. Putnam's Sons, 1972), 746; Minutes of the Fifty-Eighth Meeting of the United States Delegation, 30 May 1945, in *FRUS, 1945*, vol. 1, 992-93; Cockram to Stephenson, 2 June 1945, in NAUK, DO 35/1884.
64 Minutes of the Sixty-Second Meeting (Executive Session) of the United States Delegation, 2 June 1945, in *FRUS, 1945*, vol. 1, 1089-92; Grew to Harriman, 2 June 1945, in ibid., 1118; UK Delegation to FO, 2 June 1945, in NAUK, CAB 121/162.
65 *The White House Papers of Harry L. Hopkins*, vol. 1, 901; Minutes of the Seventeenth Five-Power Informal Consultative Meeting on the Proposed Amendments, 7 June 1945, in *FRUS, 1945*, vol. 1, 1190. It appears that Stalin had not fully understood the Anglo-American proposal.
66 See for example, Vandenberg, diary entry, 7 June 1945, in *The Private Papers of Senator Vandenberg*, ed. Arthur H. Vandenberg, Jr. (Boston: Riverside Press, 1952), 208; UK Delegation to FO, 7 June 1945, in NAUK, CAB 121/162; and Minutes of the Sixty-Sixth Meeting of the United States Delegation, 8 June 1945, in *FRUS, 1945*, vol. 1, 1201-11.

67 UK Delegation to FO, 10 June 1945, in NAUK, CAB 121/162. See also John David Edward Plant, "The Origins and Development of Australia's Policy and Posture at the United Nations Conference on International Organization, San Francisco, 1945" (PhD dissertation, Australian National University, 1967), 385-86.

68 Robertson to Read, 10 June 1945, attached to Read, Note for Prime Minister, 11 June 1945, in LAC, W.L.M. King Papers, Memoranda and Notes, MG26 J4, vol. 340, File 3676. The "amendment procedure" referred to whether the great powers would have the right to veto amendments to the UN Charter. With such power, the Big Five could guarantee that they would never lose their UNSC veto.

69 Summary of Report of the Seventeenth Meeting of Committee III/1, 11 June 1945, in *UNCIO*, vol. 11, 459; Riddell, Memorandum, 11 June 1945, in UTTC, John Holmes Papers, Box 61, File D/I/6/b.

70 John H. Crider, "Canada Switches to Back Big 5 Veto," *New York Times*, 12 June 1945, 1, 13; Crider, "More Nations Back Yalta Voting Plan," *New York Times*, 13 June 1945, 16.

71 UK Delegation to FO, 14 June 1945, in NAUK, CAB 121/162. On the views of the US delegation, see Minutes of the Seventieth Meeting of the United States Delegation, 13 June 1945, in *FRUS, 1945*, vol. 1, 1274.

72 Pearson, diary entry, 16 June 1945, in LAC, Pearson Papers, MG26 N8, vol. 1, File 4, Diaries and Personal Papers, 1943-45.

73 John Holmes makes a similar suggestion in *The Shaping of Peace*, 192. See also Granatstein, *Canada's War*, 327; and John English, "A Fine Romance," in *Canada and the Early Cold War*, ed. Greg Donaghy, 73-89 (Ottawa: Canadian Government Publishing, Department of Foreign Affairs and International Trade, 1998), 80-2.

Chapter 11: Shaping History

1 Cockram to Stephenson, 23 June 1945, in NAUK, DO 35/1884.
2 King, diary entry, 23 June 1945, in Robarts Library, King Diary. See also his entries for 13 and 15 June 1945.
3 King, diary entry, 26 June 1945, in Robarts Library, ibid.
4 "Charter for Peace," *New York Times*, 24 June 1945, E1.
5 Paul Sauriol, "Les dernières heures de la conférence mondiale," *Le Devoir*, 27 June 1945, 1.
6 Statement by King, San Francisco Conference, 26 June 1945, in LAC, W.L.M. King Papers, Memoranda and Notes, MG26 J4, vol. 340, File 3676.
7 Grant Dexter, "Mr. King's Useful Role," *WFP*, 11 May 1945, 13. For an earlier article, see "End of the 'Single-Voice' Idea," *WFP*, 1 May 1945, 11.
8 "Let Us Be Proud of Canada," *WFP*, 8 June 1945, 11.
9 Francis Flaherty, "Canadian Delegation Is Following Policy of Watching and Waiting," *Saturday Night*, 5 May 1945, 8.
10 "Le Canada tenu en haute estime," *La Presse*, 21 May 1945, 6.
11 "Un beau succès pour le Canada," *La Presse*, 30 May 1945, 6.
12 "Sideflights from San Francisco," a Broadcast by T.F. Newton for the Canadian Association of Broadcasters, 22 May 1945, in LAC, DEA Papers, RG25, Series G-2, vol. 3744, File 6834-30, Part 3. The majority of Canada's nongovernmental organizations felt the same way. For an example, see "Minutes of the New National Executive [UN Society of Canada]," 19 May 1945, in LAC, Robert Boyer Inch Papers, MG30 C187, vol. 1, File 15.
13 Blair Fraser, "Expect Nations to Okay Revised Peace Charter," *Financial Post*, 12 May 1945, 1.
14 Fraser, "Backstage at San Francisco," *Maclean's*, 15 June 1945, 48.
15 "Means to an End," *G&M*, 26 June 1945, 6.
16 CIPO, 20 June 1945, in *POQ* 9, 2 (Summer 1945): 257.
17 I. Norman Smith, "That Competent Team from the East Block," *Ottawa Journal*, 28 June 1945, 8. For corroboration, see for example, R.G. Trotter, "Canada and World Organization," *Canadian Historical Review* 26, 2 (June 1945): 128-47. For a contrary view, see J.E. Hodgetts, "The San Francisco Conference: Old Worlds for New?" *University of Toronto Quarterly* 14, 4 (July 1945): 431-40.

18 Pearson, Broadcast over CBC, 1 July 1945, in LAC, Pearson Papers, MG26 N1, vol. 58, File 8, Speeches: San Francisco: 1945.
19 Memorandum for the President, 2 June 1945, in Robarts Library, Records of the Department of State, Microfilm Publication M1244, MHF, Roll 9, H. Freeman Matthews Correspondence and Memorandums.
20 Memorandum Prepared by the United States Representative on the Preparatory Commission, 23 August 1945, in *FRUS, 1945*, vol. 1, 1439. Lester Pearson was one of five secondary candidates on Stettinius's list.
21 Anne O'Hare McCormick, "A Middle Power Keeps to a Middle Course," *New York Times*, 13 June 1945, 22.
22 Cockram to Stephenson, 16 June 1945, in NAUK, DO 35/1884.
23 UK Delegation to FO, 23 June 1945, in NAUK, CAB 21/2307.
24 Drew Pearson, "Washington Merry-Go-Round," *Washington Post*, 30 June 1945, cited in LAC, DEA Papers, RG25, Series B-3, vol. 2157, Postwar World Organization 1945. See also Machtig to Eden, 27 June 1945, in NAUK, DO 35/1883; Divine, *Second Chance*, 294; Stephen C. Schlesinger, *Act of Creation: The Founding of the United Nations* (Boulder, CO: Westview Press, 2003), 195; and Virginia C. Gildersleeve, *Many a Good Crusade: Memoirs of Virginia Cocheron Gildersleeve* (New York: Macmillan, 1954), 322.
25 Hickerson to Atherton, 4 August 1945, in Robarts Library, Records of the Department of State, Microfilm Publication M1244, MHF, Roll 4, John D. Hickerson Correspondence A-G 1934-47.
26 "Canada: The General Election: Canada at San Francisco," *The Round Table* 140 (September 1945): 362, 365.
27 MacDonald to Addison [SSDA], 6 November 1945, in DUL, Malcolm MacDonald Papers, 12/7.
28 Australian Public Opinion Poll (hereafter APOP), June-July 1945, in *POQ* 9, 3 (Fall 1945): 393; APOP, August 1945, in ibid. In contrast, when Canadians were asked about the conference in August, 82 percent said that they knew about it; see CIPO, 11 August 1945, in ibid., 391.
29 Hickerson to Atherton, 4 August 1945, in Robarts Library, Records of the Department of State, Microfilm Publication M1244, MHF, Roll 4, John D. Hickerson Correspondence A-G 1934-47.
30 English, *Shadow of Heaven*, 287.
31 Brennan, *Reporting the Nation's Business*, xi.
32 English, *Shadow of Heaven*, 280; see also 256.
33 A.D. Dunton, "San Francisco Conference: Canadian Delegation: Information," 25 June 1945, in LAC, DEA Papers, RG25, Series A-4, vol. 3456, File 6-1-1945/8.
34 Francis Flaherty, "Canadian Delegation Is Following Policy of Watching and Waiting," *Saturday Night*, 5 May 1945, 8.
35 Clark, Memorandum of Conversation with Norman Robertson, 13 July 1945, in NARA, RG84, Records of the Foreign Service Posts of the Department of State, Entry 2195a, 350/51/09/03, Canada, Ottawa Embassy, Security, Segregated General Records 1939-49, Box 116, 1945, 020-701.1, 020-500.
36 For more, see Escott Reid, *On Duty*, which covers the entire preparatory meetings. See also Published Documents, *DCER*, vol. 11, 799-863; Holmes, *The Shaping of Peace*, 262-63; and Hilliker, *Canada's Department of External Affairs*, 309-13.
37 King, diary entries, 3 and 4 October 1945, in Robarts Library, King Diary. See also Eayrs, *In Defence of Canada*, vol. 3, 139-40.
38 St. Laurent, 16 October 1945, in Canada, House of Commons, *Debates*, 1st Session, 20th Parliament, vol. 246, 6 September to 17 October 1945, 1185-1202. St. Laurent brought forth the motion because Mackenzie King was in meetings in London about, among other things, the Gouzenko affair.
39 Graydon, in Canada, ibid., 1203-8.
40 Coldwell, 18 October 1945, in Canada, ibid., vol. 247, 18 October to 23 November 1945, 1249-51.

41 Beaudoin, in Canada, ibid., 1275.
42 Fleming, in Canada, ibid., 1280.
43 One exception to this observation was John Diefenbaker. Diefenbaker had managed to attend the conference without being part of the official Canadian delegation (one of M.J. Coldwell's assistants took ill, and Diefenbaker received permission from Coldwell to attend in his place). His comments on San Francisco were profoundly idealistic; see Diefenbaker, 19 October 1845, in Canada, ibid., 1305-6. Soward's account of the debate is less nuanced and too focused on the Cold War; see *Canada in World Affairs*, 145-47.

Epilogue: Cherishing Illusions

1 Lionel Gelber, "Canada's New Stature," *Foreign Affairs* 24, 2 (January 1946): 277-80.
2 A.R.M. Lower, "Canada, the Second Great War, and the Future," *International Journal* 1, 2 (April 1946): 99.
3 King, *Industry and Humanity*, 12.
4 English, *Shadow of Heaven*, 268.
5 Granatstein, *Ottawa Men*, 79.
6 See for example, Arthur Andrew, *The Rise and Fall of a Middle Power: Canadian Diplomacy from King to Mulroney* (Toronto: J. Lorimer, 1993); and Andrew Cohen, *While Canada Slept: How We Lost Our Place in the World* (Toronto: McClelland and Stewart, 2003).
7 See for example, Denis Stairs, "Realists at Work," in *Canada and the Early Cold War*, ed. Greg Donaghy, 91-116 (Ottawa: Canadian Government Publishing, Department of Foreign Affairs and International Trade, 1998); and Stairs, "Trends in Canadian Foreign Policy: Past, Present, and Future," *Behind the Headlines* 59, 3 (Spring 2002): 1-7.
8 It is worth noting that while Reid wrote a series of memoirs and while Pearson's memoirs run to three volumes, the records of Hume Wrong and Norman Robertson, particularly for the period 1940-45, are exceptionally thin.
9 Peyton V. Lyon and Brian W. Tomlin, *Canada as an International Actor* (Toronto: Macmillan, 1979), 77.

Bibliography

Primary Sources

Public Archives

Canada

Archives of Ontario (Toronto, Ontario)
Timothy Eaton Papers

Bank of Canada Archives (Ottawa, Ontario)
Louis Rasminsky Papers

Glenbow Museum Archives (Calgary, Alberta)
John Horn Blackmore Papers

Library and Archives Canada (Ottawa, Ontario)
Academy of Motion Picture Arts and Sciences Fonds
Department of External Affairs Papers
Department of Finance Papers
National Film Board of Canada Fonds
Privy Council Office Papers
Wartime Information Board and Canadian Information Service Papers

Canadian Citizenship Council Papers
Canadian Institute of International Affairs Papers
League of Nations Society in Canada Papers

Brooke Claxton Papers
Jean Désy Papers
Blair Fraser Papers
John King Gordon Papers
Gordon Graydon Papers
Howard Charles Green Papers
Arnold Danford Patrick Heeney Papers
C.D. Howe Papers
Robert Boyer Inch Papers
W. Arthur Irwin Papers
W.L.M. King Papers
George W. McCracken Papers
Theodore F.M. Newton Papers
L.B. Pearson Papers
Maurice Pope Papers
John Erskine Read Papers

Escott Reid Papers
Albert Edgar Ritchie Papers
Norman A. Robertson Papers
Louis St. Laurent Papers
L. Dana Wilgress Papers
Hume Wrong Papers

McGill University Library, Rare Books and Special Collections Division (Montreal, Quebec)
Co-operative Commonwealth Federation/New Democratic Party Papers

Queen's University Archives (Kingston, Ontario)
T.A. Crerar Papers
Grant Dexter Papers

Robarts Library (Toronto, Ontario)
The Mackenzie King Diaries, 1893-1950
Records of the Department of State, Microfilm Publication M1244, Records of the Office of
   European Affairs (Matthews-Hickerson File), 1934-47

University of Calgary Library, Special Collections (Calgary, Alberta)
Bruce Hutchison Fonds

University of Toronto Archives (Toronto, Ontario)
Robert Selkirk Bothwell Papers
Alexander Brady Papers
G.P. de T. Glazebrook Papers
Vincent Massey Papers

University of Toronto, Trinity College Archives (Toronto, Ontario)
John Holmes Papers
George Ignatieff Papers

United Kingdom

Bodleian Library (Oxford)
Clement Attlee Papers
William Clark Papers
Lionel Curtis Papers
Archibald Clark Kerr [Inverchapel] Papers

Churchill Archives Centre (Cambridge)
Lawrence Burgis Papers
Sir Alexander George Montagu Cadogan Papers
Winston Churchill Papers
Lord Gladwyn [Jebb] Papers
Phillip Noel-Baker Papers
Edward Frederick Lindley Wood, Earl of Halifax, Papers

Durham University Library, Archives and Special Collections (Durham)
Malcolm MacDonald Papers

National Archives of England, Wales, and the United Kingdom (Kew)
Cabinet Office Papers
   A. Clement Attlee Papers
Dominions Office Papers
Foreign Office Papers
   Anthony Eden Papers
   Private Secretaries Papers
Prime Minister's Office Papers
Treasury Office Papers
   Frederick William Leith-Ross Papers

University of Birmingham Library, Special Collections (Birmingham)
Lord Avon [Anthony Eden] Papers

United States

Dag Hammarskjöld Library (United Nations, New York)
Oral History Collection

Franklin Delano Roosevelt Library (Hyde Park, NY)
Adolf Berle Papers
Oscar Cox Papers
Harry Hopkins Papers
Franklin Delano Roosevelt Papers
  Official Files
  Personal Files
  President's Secretary's Files
    Confidential Files
    Departmental Files
    Diplomatic Correspondence
    Safe Files
    Subject Files
Sumner Welles Papers
John G. Winant Papers

Library of Congress, Manuscript Division (Washington, DC)
Charles E. Bohlen Papers
Benjamin Gerig Papers
Cordell Hull Papers
Archibald MacLeish Papers
Leo Pasvolsky Papers

National Archives and Records Administration at College Park, Maryland
Records of the Department of State
  Alger Hiss Files
  Records of Harley Notter, 1939-1945
  Records of the Office of Assistant Secretary and Under-Secretary of State,
    Dean Ackson
  Records of the Office of United Nations Affairs
  Leo Pasvolsky File
  State Department Decimal Files, 1940-44 and 1945-49
Records of the Foreign Service Posts of the Department of State

Seeley G. Mudd Manuscript Library, Princeton University (Princeton, New Jersey)
Hamilton Fish Armstrong Papers
Council on Foreign Relations Papers
John Foster Dulles Papers
Arthur Krock Papers

Truman Presidential Museum and Library (Independence, MS), accessed on-line
Official Files
President's Secretary's Files

Personal Collections
Judith Robertson Papers
William Young Papers
  English Interviews
  Storey Interviews
  Young Interviews

Published Documents

Australia
Commonwealth of Australia. *United Nations Conference on International Organization: Report by the Australian Delegates*. Australia: Commonwealth Government Printer, 1945.

Canada
Canada. Department of External Affairs. *Charter of the United Nations Including the Statute of the International Court of Justice Together with the Interim Arrangements Establishing the Preparatory Commission of the United Nations Signed at San Francisco, June 26, 1945*. Treaty Series 1945. No. 7. Ottawa: King's Printer, 1945.
–. *Final Act of the International Civil Aviation Conference Held at Chicago from November 1 to December 7, 1944*. Treaty Series 1944. No. 36. Ottawa: King's Printer, 1945.
–. *First Report to the Governments of the United Nations by the Interim Commission on Food and Agriculture*. Conference Series 1945. No. 1. Ottawa: King's Printer, 1945.
–. *Report on the United Nations Conference on International Organization Held at San Francisco, 25th April-26th June 1945*. 1 September 1945.
Canada. Dominion Bureau of Statistics. Department of Trade and Commerce. *The Canada Year Book 1945*. Ottawa: Edmond Cloutier, 1945.
Canada. House of Commons. *Debates*. 1941-45.
Canada. Senate. *Debates*. 1943-45.
Canada. Wartime Information Board. *Canada at War*. 45 vols. 1941-45.
Canadian Foreign Policy, 1945-1954: Selected Speeches and Documents. Ed. R.A. MacKay. Toronto and Montreal: McClelland and Stewart, 1971.
Documents on Canadian External Relations. Vol. 7, *1939-1941*. Part 1. Ed. David R. Murray. Ottawa: Department of External Affairs, 1974.
Documents on Canadian External Relations. Vol. 9, *1942-1943*. Ed. John F. Hilliker. Ottawa: Minister of Supply and Services Canada, 1980.
Documents on Canadian External Relations. Vol. 10, *1944-1945*. Part 1. Ed. John F. Hilliker. Ottawa: Minister of Supply and Services Canada, 1987.
Documents on Canadian External Relations. Vol. 11, *1944-1945*. Part 2. Ed. John F. Hilliker. Ottawa: Minister of Supply and Services Canada, 1990.

Soviet Union
Ministry of Foreign Affairs of the U.S.S.R. *Correspondence between the Chairman of the Council of Ministers of the U.S.S.R. and the Presidents of the U.S.A. and the Prime Ministers of Great Britain during the Great Patriotic War of 1941-1945*. 2 vols. Moscow: Foreign Languages Publishing House, 1957.

United Kingdom
Confidential Dispatches: Analyses of America by the British Ambassador, 1939-1945. Ed. Thomas Hachey. Evanston, IL: New University Press, 1974.
Documents and Speeches on British Commonwealth Affairs, 1931-1952. Vol. 1. Ed. Nicholas Mansergh. London: Oxford University Press, 1953.

United Nations
Documents of the United Nations Conference on International Organization, San Francisco, 1945. Vol. 1, *General*. London and New York: United Nations Information Organization, 1945.
–. Vol. 3, *Dumbarton Oaks Proposals: Comments and Proposed Amendments, English Text*. London and New York: United Nations Information Organization, 1945.
–. Vol. 6, *Commission I, General Provisions*. London and New York: United Nations Information Organization, 1945.
–. Vol. 7, *Commission I, General Provisions*. London and New York: United Nations Information Organization, 1945.
–. Vol. 8, *Commission II, General Assembly*. London and New York: United Nations Information Organization, 1945.

–. Vol. 10, *Commission II, General Assembly*. London and New York: United Nations Information Organization, 1945.

–. Vol. 11, *Commission III, Security Council*. London and New York: United Nations Information Organization, 1945.

–. Vol. 12, *Commission III, Security Council*. London and New York: United Nations Information Organization, 1945.

–. Vol. 13, *Commission IV, Judicial Organization*. London and New York: United Nations Information Organization, 1945.

—. Vol. 14, *United Nations Committee of Jurists*. London and New York: United Nations Information Organization, 1945.

–. Vol. 15, *Coordination Committee, the Charter Lists*. London and New York: United Nations Information Organization, 1945

–. Vol. 17, *Documents of the Coordination Committee, Including Documents of the Advisory Committee of Jurists*. New York: United Nations, 1954.

United Nations Information Office. *Helping the People to Help Themselves: The Story of the United Nations Relief and Rehabilitation Administration*. New York: United Nations Information Office, 1944.

–. *Towards Freedom in the Air: The Story of the International Civil Aviation Conference*. New York: United Nations Information Office, 1945.

United States

The Dynamics of World Power: A Documentary History of United States Foreign Policy, 1945-1973. Vol. 5, *The United Nations*. Ed. Richard Hottelet. New York: Chelsea House Publishers, 1973.

Foreign Relations of the United States, 1941. Vol. 1, *General, the Soviet Union*. Washington, DC: Government Printing Office, 1958.

Foreign Relations of the United States, 1942. Vol. 1, *General, the British Commonwealth, the Far East*. Washington, DC: Government Printing Office, 1960.

Foreign Relations of the United States, 1943. Vol. 1, *General*. Washington, DC: Government Printing Office, 1963.

Foreign Relations of the United States, 1943. Vol. 3, *The British Commonwealth, Eastern Europe, the Far East*. Washington, DC: Government Printing Office, 1963.

Foreign Relations of the United States, 1944. Vol. 1, *General*. Washington, DC: Government Printing Office, 1966.

Foreign Relations of the United States, 1944. Vol. 2, *General, Economic and Social Matters*. Washington, DC: Government Printing Office, 1967.

Foreign Relations of the United States, 1944. Vol. 3, *The British Commonwealth and Europe*. Washington, DC: Government Printing Office, 1965.

Foreign Relations of the United States, 1945. Vol. 1, *General, the United Nations*. Washington, DC: Government Printing Office, 1967.

Foreign Relations of the United States, 1945. Vol. 2, *General, Political and Economic Matters*. Washington, DC: Government Printing Office, 1967.

Foreign Relations of the United States: The Conference at Quebec, 1944. Washington, DC: Government Printing Office, 1972.

Foreign Relations of the United States: The Conference of Berlin (The Potsdam Conference), 1945. Vol. 1. Washington, DC: Government Printing Office, 1960.

Foreign Relations of the United States: The Conferences at Cairo and Teheran, 1943. Washington, DC: Government Printing Office, 1961.

Foreign Relations of the United States: The Conferences at Malta and Yalta. Washington, DC: Government Printing Office, 1955.

Foreign Relations of the United States: The Conferences at Washington, 1941-1942, and Casablanca, 1943. Washington, DC: Government Printing Office, 1968.

Foreign Relations of the United States: The Conferences at Washington and Quebec, 1943. Washington, DC: Government Printing Office, 1970.

Public Papers of the Presidents of the United States: Harry S. Truman, 1945. Washington, DC: United States Government Printing Office, 1961.

United States. Department of State. *Bulletin.* 1942-45. Washington, DC: Government Printing Office, 1943-46.

–. *Making the Peace Treaties, 1941-1947.* Washington, DC: Government Printing Office, 1947.

–. *Report of the Delegation of the United States of America to the Inter-American Conference on Problems of War and Peace, Mexico City, Mexico, February 21-March 8, 1945.* Washington, DC: United States Government Printing Office, 1946.

–. *Report to the President on the Results of the San Francisco Conference by the Chairman of the United States Delegation, The Secretary of State, June 26, 1945.* Washington, DC: Department of State, 1945.

United States. Senate. *A Decade of American Foreign Policy: Basic Documents, 1941-49.* Washington, DC: United States Government Printing Office, 1950.

War and Peace Aims of the United Nations. Vol. 2, *From Casablanca to Tokio Bay, January 1, 1943-September 1, 1945.* Ed. Louise W. Holborn. Boston: World Peace Foundation, 1948.

Memoirs and Diaries

Acheson, Dean. *Present at the Creation: My Years in the State Department.* New York: W.W. Norton and Company, 1969.

Andrew, Arthur. *The Rise and Fall of a Middle Power: Canadian Diplomacy from King to Mulroney.* Toronto: J. Lorimer, 1993.

Byrnes, James F. *Speaking Frankly.* New York and London: Harper and Brothers, 1947.

Casey, Lord. *Personal Experience, 1939-1946.* London: Constable and Company, 1962.

Churchill, Winston S. *The Second World War.* Vol. 4, *The Hinge of Fate.* Boston: Houghton Mifflin, 1950.

–. *The Second World War.* Vol. 5, *Closing the Ring.* Boston: Houghton Mifflin, 1951.

–. *The Second World War.* Vol. 6, *Triumph and Tragedy.* Boston: Houghton Mifflin, 1953.

Coldwell, M.J. *Left Turn, Canada.* New York and Toronto: Duell, Sloan and Pearce, 1945.

Colville, John. *The Fringes of Power: Downing Street Diaries, 1939-1955.* London: Hodder and Stoughton, 1985.

Corbett, E.A. *We Have with Us Tonight.* Toronto: Ryerson Press, 1957.

Daniels, Jonathan. *White House Witness: 1942-1945.* New York: Doubleday, 1975.

de Gaulle, Charles. *The Complete War Memoirs of Charles de Gaulle.* Trans. Jonathan Griffin. New York: Simon and Schuster, 1964.

de Roussy de Sales, Raoul. *The Making of Yesterday: The Diaries of Raoul de Roussy de Sales.* New York: Reynal and Hitchcock, 1947.

The Diaries of Edward R. Stettinius Jr. Ed. Thomas M. Campbell and George C. Herring. New York: New Viewpoints, 1975.

The Diaries of Sir Alexander Cadogan, O.M., 1938-1945. Ed. David Dilks. New York: G.P. Putnam's Sons, 1972.

Djilas, Milovan. *Conversations with Stalin.* Trans. Michael B. Petrovich. 1962. Reprint, Orlando, FL: Harcourt and Brace, 1990.

Eden, Anthony. *The Eden Memoirs: The Reckoning.* London: Cassell and Company, 1965.

Eichelberger, Clark M. *Organizing for Peace: A Personal History of the Founding of the United Nations.* New York: Harper and Row, 1977.

Ferns, H.S. *Reading from Left to Right: One Man's Political History.* Toronto: University of Toronto Press, 1983.

Gildersleeve, Virginia C. *Many a Good Crusade: Memoirs of Virginia Crocheron Gildersleeve.* New York: Macmillan, 1954.

Gordon, Walter. *A Political Memoir.* Toronto: McClelland and Stewart, 1977.

Gray, James H. *Troublemaker! A Personal History.* Toronto: Macmillan of Canada, 1978.

Grew, Joseph. *Turbulent Era: A Diplomatic Record of Forty Years, 1904-1945.* Vol. 2. Ed. Walter Johnson. Cambridge, MA: The Riverside Press, 1952.

Gromyko, Andrei. *Memories.* Trans. Harold Shukman. London: Hutchinson, 1989.

Halifax, Lord (Edward Frederick Lindley Wood). *Fullness of Days.* New York: Dodd, Mead and Company, 1957.

Hasluck, Paul. *Diplomatic Witness: Australian Foreign Affairs, 1941-1947.* Melbourne: Melbourne University Press, 1980.

Hiss, Alger. *Recollections of a Life*. New York: Seaver Books, 1988.

The Historian as Diplomat: Charles Kingsley Webster and the United Nations, 1939-1946. Ed. P.A. Reynolds and R.J. Hughes. London: Martin Robertson, 1976.

Hull, Cordell. *The Memoirs of Cordell Hull*. Vol. 2. New York: Macmillan, 1948.

Hutchison, Bruce. *The Far Side of the Street*. Toronto: Macmillan, 1976.

Jebb, Gladwyn. *The Memoirs of Lord Gladwyn*. London: Weidenfeld and Nicolson, 1972.

Keenleyside, Hugh L. *Memoirs of Hugh L. Keenleyside: On the Bridge of Time*. Vol. 2. Toronto: McClelland and Stewart, 1982.

Lapalme, Georges-Émile. *Mémoires: Le Bruit des Choses Réveillées*. Vol. 1. Ottawa: Les Éditions Leméac, 1969.

Laurendeau, André. *La Crise de la Conscription 1942*. Montreal: Les Editions du Jour, 1962.

Leahy, William D. *I Was There: The Personal Story of the Chief of Staff to Presidents Roosevelt and Truman Based on His Notes and Diaries Made at the Time*. New York: Wittlesey House, 1950.

Long, Breckinridge. *The War Diary of Breckinridge Long: Selections from the Years 1939-1944*. Ed. Fred L. Israel. Lincoln: University of Nebraska Press, 1966.

Martin, Paul. *A Very Public Life*. Vol. 1, *Far From Home*. Ottawa: Deneau, 1983.

Massey, Vincent. *What's Past Is Prologue: The Memoirs of the Right Honourable Vincent Massey, C.H.* Toronto: Macmillan, 1963.

Pearson, Lester B. *Mike: The Memoirs of the Rt. Honourable Lester B. Pearson*. Vol. 1, *1897-1948*. Toronto: University of Toronto Press, 1972.

Pickersgill, J.W. *The Mackenzie King Record*. Vol. 1, *1939-1944*. Toronto: University of Toronto Press, 1960.

–. *My Years with Louis St. Laurent: A Political Memoir*. Toronto: University of Toronto Press, 1975.

–, and D.F. Forster. *The Mackenzie King Record*. Vol. 2, *1944-1945*. Toronto: University of Toronto Press, 1968.

–, and D.F. Forster. *The Mackenzie King Record*. Vol. 3, *1945-1946*. Toronto: University of Toronto Press, 1970.

–, and D.F. Forster. *The Mackenzie King Record*. Vol. 4, *1947-1948*. Toronto: University of Toronto Press, 1970.

Pope, Maurice A. *Soldiers and Politicians: The Memoirs of Lt.-Gen. Maurice A. Pope*. Toronto: University of Toronto Press, 1962.

Power, Charles G. *A Party Politician: The Memoirs of Chubby Power*. Toronto: Macmillan, 1966.

The Price of Vision: The Diary of Henry Wallace, 1942-1946. Ed. John Morton Blum. Boston: Houghton Mifflin, 1973.

The Private Papers of Senator Vandenberg. Ed. Arthur H. Vandenberg, Jr. Boston: Riverside Press, 1952.

Reid, Escott. *On Duty: A Canadian at the Making of the United Nations, 1945-1946*. Toronto: McClelland and Stewart, 1983.

–. *Radical Mandarin: The Memoirs of Escott Reid*. Toronto: University of Toronto Press, 1989.

Reston, James. *Deadline: A Memoir*. New York: Random House, 1991.

Ritchie, Charles. *The Siren Years: A Canadian Diplomat Abroad, 1937-1945*. Toronto: Macmillan, 1974.

Robertson, Gordon. *Memoirs of a Very Civil Servant, Mackenzie King to Pierre Trudeau*. Toronto: University of Toronto Press, 2000.

Sharp, Mitchell. *Which Reminds Me ... A Memoir*. Toronto: University of Toronto Press, 1994.

Soward, F.H. "Inside a Canadian Triangle: The University, the CIIA, and the Department of External Affairs, a Personal Record." *International Journal* 33, 1 (Winter 1977-78): 66-87.

Stettinius, Edward R., Jr. *Roosevelt and the Russians: The Yalta Conference*. Garden City, NY: Doubleday, 1949.

Stimson, Henry L., and McGeorge Bundy. *On Active Service in Peace and War*. New York: Harper and Brothers, 1947.

The Wartime Diaries of Lionel Robbins and James Meade, 1943-45. Ed. Susan Howson and Donald Moggridge. London: Macmillan, 1990.

Watt, Alan. *Australian Diplomat: Memoirs of Sir Alan Watt*. Sydney: Angus and Robertson Publishers, 1972.

The White House Papers of Harry L. Hopkins. Vol. 1. Ed. Robert E. Sherwood. London: Eyre and Spottiswoode, 1948.
–. Vol. 2. Ed. Robert E. Sherwood. London: Eyre and Spottiswoode, 1949.

Newspapers, Magazines, and Periodicals
American Journal of International Law
American Political Science Review
Behind the Headlines
Canadian Affairs
Canadian Bar Review
Canadian Forum
Canadian Historical Review
Canadian Journal of Economics and Political Science
Canadian Journal of Political Science
Dalhousie Review
Le Devoir
Dialogue
External Affairs
Financial Post
Foreign Affairs
Globe and Mail
International Affairs
International Journal
International Organization
Maclean's
Montreal Gazette
New York Times
Ottawa Journal
La Presse
Public Opinion Quarterly
Revue Études Internationales
The Round Table
Queen's Quarterly
Saturday Night
University of Toronto Law Journal
University of Toronto Quarterly
Winnipeg Free Press

Contemporary Scholarship
"Air Transport: A Canadian View." *The Round Table* 137 (December 1944): 38-45.
Anderson, Violet, ed. *This Is the Peace: Addresses Given at the Canadian Institute on Public Affairs, August 18 to 25, 1945.* Toronto: Ryerson Press, 1945.
Angus, H.F. "Canada and a Foreign Policy." *Dalhousie Review* (October 1934): 265-75.
Bidwell, Percy, ed. *The United States and the United Nations: Views on Postwar Relations.* New York: Council on Foreign Relations, 1943.
Bonnet, Henri. *The United Nations on the Way.* Chicago: World Citizens' Association, 1942.
Burpee, Lawrence J. "Good Faith among Nations." *Queen's Quarterly* 51 (Spring 1944): 78-87.
Campbell, John C. *The United States in World Affairs, 1945-1947.* New York and London: Harper and Brothers, 1947.
"Canada: Discussion of Commonwealth Relations." *The Round Table* 135 (June 1944): 270-76.
"Canada: The Future of the British Commonwealth." *The Round Table* 134 (March 1944): 186-92.
"Canada: The General Election: Canada at San Francisco." *The Round Table* 140 (September 1945): 359-65.

"Canada: What Is Her Future to Be?" *The Round Table* 131 (June 1943): 273-80.

Canadian Institute of International Affairs. *Canada and the United Nations: Report of the Proceedings of the Ninth Annual Conference of the Canadian Institute of International Affairs.* Toronto: 23-24 May 1942.

Claxton, Brooke. "The Place of Canada in Post-War Organization." *Canadian Journal of Economics and Political Science* 10, 4 (November 1944): 409-21.

Clokie, H. McD. "Moscow Conference." *Behind the Headlines* 3, 10 (1943).

"The Close of an Era: Twenty-Five Years of Mackenzie King." *Canadian Forum* 24, 284 (September 1944): 125-26.

"The Commonwealth and the Settlement." *The Round Table* 132 (September 1943): 306-12.

"The Commonwealth Conference." *Canadian Forum* 24, 281 (June 1944): 51-52.

"The Conference." *The Round Table* 135 (June 1944): 195-98.

"The Conference of 1944: Achievement and Opportunities." *The Round Table* 136 (September 1944): 311-17.

Council on Foreign Relations. *The War and Peace Studies of the Council on Foreign Relations, 1939-1945.* New York: Harold Pratt House, 1946.

Dafoe, J.W. "Canada and the Peace Conference of 1919." *Canadian Historical Review* 24, 3 (September 1943): 233-48.

Dean, Vera Michaels. *The Struggle for World Order.* New York: Foreign Policy Association, 1941.

Dexter, Grant. *Canada and the Building of Peace.* Toronto: Canadian Institute of International Affairs, 1944.

Dulles, John Foster. "The General Assembly." *Foreign Affairs* 24, 1 (October 1945): 1-11.

–. *War or Peace.* New York: Macmillan, 1950.

Duncan, Lewis. "Blueprint of World Order." *Canadian Bar Review* 22, 5 (May 1944): 405-11.

Eagleton, Clyde. "The Share of Canada in the Making of the United Nations." *University of Toronto Law Journal* 7, 2 (Lent Term 1948): 329-56.

–. "The United Nations: Peace and Security." *American Political Science Review* 39, 5 (October 1945): 934-92.

Empire Parliamentary Association. *Report of the Proceedings of the Parliamentary Conference Held in the Houses of Parliament.* Ottawa: Empire Parliamentary Association, Dominion of Canada Branch, 1943.

Evatt, Herbert Vere. *The United Nations.* Cambridge, MA: Harvard University Press, 1948.

Field, Harry H., and Louise M. Van Patten. "If the American People Made the Peace." *Public Opinion Quarterly* 8, 4 (Winter 1944-45): 500-12.

Fraser, Blair. "Our Diplomats at Work." *Behind the Headlines* 5, 3 (1945).

Fraser, C.F. "Canada's Foreign Relations." *Dalhousie Review* 22, 1 (1942-43): 48-54.

Fraser, John, and Graham Fraser, eds. *Blair Fraser Reports: Selections, 1944-1968.* Toronto: Macmillan, 1969.

Gallup, George. "Reporting Public Opinion in Five Nations." *Public Opinion Quarterly* 6, 3 (Fall 1942): 429-36.

Gallup, George, and Saul Forbes Rae. *The Pulse of Democracy: The Public Opinion Poll and How It Works.* New York: Simon and Schuster, 1940.

Gelber, Lionel. "Canada's New Stature." *Foreign Affairs* 24, 2 (January 1946): 277-89.

–. "English-Speaking Unity." *Saturday Night,* 12 October 1940, 13.

–. "A Greater Canada among Nations." *Behind the Headlines* 4, 2 (1944).

Glazebrook, G. de T. *Canada at the Paris Peace Conference.* London: Oxford University Press, 1942.

–. "The Middle Powers in the United Nations System." *International Organization* 1, 2 (June 1947): 307-15.

Godbout, Adélard. "Canada: Unity in Diversity." *Foreign Affairs* 21, 3 (April 1943): 452-61.

Goodrich, Leland M., and Edvard Hambro. *Charter of the United Nations: Commentary and Documents.* Boston: World Peace Foundation, 1946.

Graydon, Gordon. "Canada Deepens Her Roots in the Soil of World Affairs." *International Journal* 2, 4 (1946-47): 316-24.

Hall, H. Duncan. "The British Commonwealth as a Great Power." *Foreign Affairs* 23, 4 (July 1945): 594-608.

"Have We a Foreign Policy?" *Canadian Forum* 23, 275 (December 1943): 197-98.

Hodgetts, J.E. "The San Francisco Conference: Old Worlds for New?" *University of Toronto Quarterly* 14, 4 (July 1945): 431-40.

Humphrey, John P. "Dumbarton Oaks at San Francisco." *Canadian Forum* 25, 291 (April 1945): 6-10.

"The International Law of the Future." *Canadian Bar Review* 22, 4 (April 1944): 277-376.

Keenleyside, H.L. "Canada's Department of External Affairs." *International Journal* 1, 3 (July 1945): 189-214.

King, William Lyon Mackenzie. *Industry and Humanity.* 1918. Reprint, Toronto: University of Toronto Press, 1973.

–. "What Do the Liberals Stand For?" Introduction by Blair Fraser. *Maclean's* 58, 3 (1 February 1945): 10-11, 38-40.

King-Hall, Stephen. *Chatham House: A Brief Account of the Origins, Purposes, and Methods of The Royal Institute of International Affairs.* London: Oxford University Press, 1937.

Koo, Wellington, Jr. *Voting Procedures in International Political Organizations.* New York: Columbia University Press, 1947.

Lippmann, Walter. *The Good Society.* 1933. Reprint, New York: Grosset and Dunlap, 1943.

–. *U.S. Foreign Policy: Shield of the Republic.* Boston: Little, Brown and Company, 1943.

Lower, A.R.M. "Canada, the Second Great War, and the Future." *International Journal* 1, 2 (April 1946): 97-111.

MacDonald, Malcolm. "Canada, a New Moral Force in the World." *International Journal* 1, 2 (April 1946): 159-63.

MacFarlane, R.O. "Beginning at the End: Canada and the Post-War World, Part 3." *Behind the Headlines* 2, 5 (15 February 1942).

–. "Blueprints for a New World: Canada and the Post-War World, Part 2." *Behind the Headlines* 2, 4 (1 February 1942).

–. "Canada Tomorrow: Canada and the Post-War World." *Behind the Headlines* 2, 3 (January 1942).

McInnis, Edgar. *The War: Fifth Year.* London: Oxford University Press, 1945.

–. *The War: Fourth Year.* London: Oxford University Press, 1944.

–. *The War: Sixth Year.* London: Oxford University Press, 1946.

MacKay, R.A. "Mackenzie King: Architect of Canadian Sovereignty." *The Round Table* 40, 106 (September 1950): 304-7.

Mallory, J.R. "What Kind of Post-War Security?" *University of Toronto Quarterly* 14, 1 (1944-45): 90-100.

Mitrany, David. "The Functional Approach to World Organization." *International Affairs* 24, 1 (January 1948): 350-63.

Morton, W.L. "Behind Dumbarton Oaks." *Behind the Headlines* 5, 2 (1945).

–. *Canada and the World Tomorrow: Opportunity and Responsibility: Report of the Proceedings of the Ninth Annual Study Conference of the Canadian Institute of International Affairs, Hamilton, Ontario, 22-23 May 1943.* Toronto: CIIA, 1943.

National Industrial Conference Board. *British Postwar Planning.* New York: National Industrial Conference Board, 1943.

"The Next League of Nations." *Canadian Forum* 24, 282 (July 1944): 75-76.

Pearson, L.B. "Canada and the Post-War World." *Canadian Affairs* 1, 6 (1 April 1944).

–. "H. Hume Wrong." *External Affairs* 6, 3 (March 1954): 74-78.

"Planning Postwar Canada." *Canadian Forum* 23, 267 (April 1943): 11-16.

Prince, A.E. "The Commonwealth Prime Ministers' Conference." *Queen's Quarterly* 51 (Summer 1944): 194-203.

Rasminsky, Louis. "International Credit and Currency Plans." *Foreign Affairs* 22, 4 (July 1944): 589-603.

Riddell, Walter Alexander. *World Security by Conference.* Toronto: Ryerson Press, 1947.

Robinson, Howard, et al. *Toward International Organization.* New York and London: Harper and Brothers, 1942.

Robinson, Judith. "Canada's Split Personality." *Foreign Affairs* 22, 1 (October 1943): 70-77.

"San Francisco." *Canadian Forum* 25, 291 (April 1945): 3-4.

"San Francisco." *Canadian Forum* 25, 294 (July 1945): 81-82.

Sanders, Wilfrid. "Canada Looks toward Postwar." *Public Opinion Quarterly* 8, 4 (Winter 1944-45): 523-29.

Scott, F.R. "The End of Dominion Status." *American Journal of International Law* 38 (1944): 34-49.

Shotwell, James T. *The Great Decision.* New York: Macmillan, 1944.

Skilling, H. Gordon. *Canadian Representation Abroad: From Agency to Embassy.* Toronto: Ryerson Press, 1945.

–. "A Chance for World Security." *Canadian Affairs* 2, 8 (1 May 1945).

Smith, I. Norman. "San Francisco: The First Step." *Behind the Headlines* 5, 6 (September 1945).

Spitzer, Tadeuscz B. "Dumbarton Oaks Project of World Democracy." *Dalhousie Review* 25, 1 (April 1945): 1-13.

Stevenson, J.A. "Canada, Free and Dependent." *Foreign Affairs* 29, 3 (April 1951): 456-67.

–. "A New Era in Canada." *Foreign Affairs* 26, 3 (April 1948): 515-27.

–. "Topics of the Day: Germany in Defeat: The Canadian Election: Charter of the United Nations: Adjustments of 'Right' and 'Left.'" *Dalhousie Review* 25, 2 (1945): 234-43.

–. "Topics of the Day: Our Party Politics: Lord Halifax at Toronto: Mr. Churchill's Political Future: Our Problems of Immigration." *Dalhousie Review* 24, 1 (April 1944): 88-100.

–. "Topics of the Day: Outlook for 1944: Field Marshall Smuts and His Plans: An Amended 'League': Educating Opinion." *Dalhousie Review* 23, 4 (January 1944): 456-64.

Streit, Clarence K. *Union Now: A Proposal for a Federal Union of the Democracies of the North Atlantic.* London: Jonathan Cape, 1939.

Trotter, R.G. "Canada and the World Organization." *Canadian Historical Review* 26, 2 (June 1945): 128-47.

–. "Commonwealth: Pattern for Peace?" *Behind the Headlines* 4, 5 (1944).

–. "Future Canadian-American Relations." *Queen's Quarterly* 52 (Summer 1945): 215-29.

–. "National Interests within the British Commonwealth." *Queen's Quarterly* 51 (Winter 1944): 439-52.

"United Nations, Ltd." *Canadian Forum* 24, 286 (November 1944): 173-74.

Webster, Charles K. "The Making of the United Nations." *History* 32 (March-September 1947): 16-38.

Welles, Sumner. *Where Are We Heading?* New York and London: Harper and Brothers, 1946.

"What Canadians Think about Post-War Reconstruction." *Foreign Policy Reports* (1 March 1943).

Willkie, Wendell L. *One World.* New York: Simon and Schuster, 1943.

Wilson, Kenneth R. "The World Is Our Oyster." *Behind the Headlines* 4, 7 (1944).

World Citizens Association. *The World's Destiny and the United States: A Conference of Experts in International Relations.* Chicago: R.R. Donnelly and Sons, 1941.

Public Speeches

Atherton, Ray. "Looking Forward to the Post-War World." *The Empire Club of Canada: Addresses Delivered to the Members during the Year 1944-45*, 256-65. Toronto: T.H. Best Printing Company, 1945.

Churchill, Winston. *Onwards to Victory: War Speeches by the Right Hon. Winston S. Churchill.* Ed. Charles Eade. Boston: Little, Brown and Company, 1944.

Fotitch, Constantin. "The Small Nations in World Affairs." *The Empire Club of Canada: Addresses Delivered to the Members during the Year 1943-44*, 269-83. Toronto: T.H. Best Printing Company, 1944.

King, William Lyon Mackenzie. *Canada and the Fight for Freedom.* Toronto: Macmillan of Canada Limited, 1944.

–. *Canada and the War: Victory, Reconstruction and Peace.* Ottawa: 1945.

Riddell, R.G. "The Role of the Middle Powers in the United Nations." *Statements and Speeches* 48, 40 (Mount Holyoke College Institute on the United Nations, 22 June 1948).

Welles, Sumner. *Co-operation between Canada and the United States in the Search for World Peace.* Winnipeg: J.W. Dafoe Foundation, 1946.
–. *The World of the Four Freedoms.* New York: Columbia University Press, 1943.

Secondary Sources

Monographs

Aster, Sidney, ed. *The Second World War as a National Experience.* Ottawa: Canadian Committee for the History of the Second World War, 1981.

Bercuson, David Jay. *True Patriot: The Life of Brooke Claxton, 1898-1960.* Toronto: University of Toronto Press, 1993.

Berger, Carl. *The Sense of Power: Studies in the Ideas of Canadian Imperialism, 1867-1914.* Toronto and Buffalo: University of Toronto Press, 1970.

Bissell, Claude. *The Imperial Canadian: Vincent Massey in Office.* Toronto: University of Toronto Press, 1986.

Black, Conrad. *Franklin Delano Roosevelt: Champion of Freedom.* New York: Perseus Book Group, 2003.

Blum, John Morton. *V Was for Victory: Politics and American Culture during World War II.* New York and London: Harcourt Brace Jovanovich, 1976.

Bothwell, Robert, Ian Drummond, and John English. *Canada since 1945.* 1981. Rev. ed., Toronto: University of Toronto Press, 1989.

–, and William Kilbourn. *C.D. Howe: A Biography.* Toronto: McClelland and Stewart, 1979.

Brennan, Patrick H. *Reporting the Nation's Business: Press-Government Relations during the Liberal Years, 1935-1957.* Toronto: University of Toronto Press, 1994.

Brinkley, Douglas, and David R. Facey-Crowther, eds. *The Atlantic Charter.* New York: St. Martin's Press, 1994.

Buhite, Russell D. *Decisions at Yalta: An Appraisal of Summit Diplomacy.* Wilmington, DC: Scholarly Resources, 1986.

Campbell, Thomas M. *Masquerade Peace: America's UN Policy, 1944-1945.* Tallahassee: Florida State University Press, 1973.

Claude, Inis L., Jr. *Swords into Ploughshares: The Problems and Progress of International Organization.* 1956. 4th ed., New York: Random House, 1984.

Clemens, Diane Shaver. *Yalta.* New York: Oxford University Press, 1970.

Cohen, Andrew. *While Canada Slept: How We Lost Our Place in the World.* Toronto: McClelland and Stewart, 2003.

Cole, Taylor. *The Canadian Bureaucracy: A Study of Canadian Civil Servants and Other Public Employees, 1939-1947.* Durham, NC: Durham University Press, 1949.

Cole, Wayne S. *Roosevelt and the Isolationists, 1932-1945.* Lincoln and London: University of Nebraska Press, 1983.

Colley, Linda. *Britons: Forging the Nation, 1707-1837.* New Haven and London: Yale University Press, 1992.

Cook, Ramsay. *The Politics of John W. Dafoe and the Free Press.* Toronto: University of Toronto Press, 1963.

Corbett, P.E. *Law and Society in the Relations of States.* New York: Harcourt, Brace and Company, 1951.

Creighton, Donald. *The Forked Road: Canada, 1939-1957.* Toronto: McClelland and Stewart, 1976.

Crowley, Terry. *Marriage of Minds: Isabel and Oscar Skelton Reinventing Canada.* Toronto: University of Toronto Press, 2003.

Dallek, Robert. *Franklin D. Roosevelt and American Foreign Policy, 1932-1945.* 1979. Rev. ed. New York and Oxford: Oxford University Press, 1995.

Dallin, Alexander. *The Soviet Union and the United Nations.* New York: Frederick A. Praeger, 1962.

Divine, Robert A. *Second Chance: The Triumph of Internationalism in America during World War II.* New York: Atheneum, 1967.

Dobell, Peter C. *Canada's Search for New Roles: Foreign Policy in the Trudeau Era.* London: Royal Institute of International Affairs, 1972.

Donaghy, Greg. *Parallel Paths: Canadian-Australian Relations since the 1890s*. Ottawa: Department of Foreign Affairs and International Trade, 1995.

–. *Uncertain Horizons: Canadians and Their World in 1945*. Canada: Canadian Committee for the History of the Second World War, 1996.

–, ed. *Canada and the Early Cold War*. Ottawa: Canadian Government Publishing, Department of Foreign Affairs and International Trade, 1998.

–, and Stéphane Rousell, eds. *Escott Reid: Diplomat and Scholar*. Montreal and Kingston: McGill-Queen's University Press, 2004.

Donnison, F.S.V. *Civil Affairs and Military Government Central Organization and Planning*. London: Her Majesty's Stationary Office, 1966.

Downs, Norton, ed. *Essays in Honor of Conyers Read*. Hartford: University of Chicago Press, 1953.

Eayrs, James. *The Art of the Possible: Government and Foreign Policy in Canada*. Toronto: University of Toronto Press, 1961.

–. *In Defence of Canada*. Vol. 3, *Peacemaking and Deterrence*. Toronto: University of Toronto Press, 1972.

Edel, Wilbur. *The State Department, the Public, and the United Nations*. New York: Vantage Press, 1979.

Egerton, George, ed. *Political Memoir: Essays on the Politics of Memory*. London: Frank Cass and Company, 1994.

English, John. *Shadow of Heaven: The Life of Lester Pearson*. Vol. 1, *1897-1948*. Toronto: Lester and Orpen Dennys, 1989.

–, and J.O. Stubbs, eds. *Mackenzie King: Widening the Debate*. Toronto: Macmillan, 1978.

Errington, Jane. *The Lion, the Eagle, and Upper Canada: A Developing Colonial Ideology*. Montreal and Kingston: McGill-Queen's University Press, 1987.

Faris, Ron. *The Passionate Educators: Voluntary Associations and the Struggle for Control of Adult Educational Broadcasting in Canada, 1919-52*. Toronto: Peter Martin Associates, 1975.

Finlay, Karen A. *The Force of Culture: Vincent Massey and Canadian Sovereignty*. Toronto: University of Toronto Press, 2004.

Franck, Thomas M., and Edward Weisband, eds. *Secrecy and Foreign Policy*. New York: Oxford University Press, 1974.

Fraser, Blair. *The Search for Identity: Canada, 1945-1967*. Toronto: Doubleday Canada, 1967.

Friesen, Gerald. *Citizens and Nation: An Essay on History, Communication, and Canada*. Toronto: University of Toronto Press, 2000.

Fry, Michael, ed. *Freedom and Change: Essays in Honour of Lester B. Pearson*. Toronto: McClelland and Stewart, 1975.

Gaddis, John Lewis. *The United States and the Origins of the Cold War, 1941-1947*. New York and London: Columbia University Press, 1972.

Gaffield, Chad, and Karen L. Gould, eds. *Canadian Distinctiveness into the 21st Century*. Ottawa: University of Ottawa Press, 2003.

Goodwin, Geoffrey L. *Britain and the United Nations*. New York: Manhattan Publishing Company, 1957.

Granatstein, J.L. *Canada's War: The Politics of the Mackenzie King Government, 1939-1945*. 1975. Reprint, Toronto: University of Toronto Press, 1990.

–. *A Man of Influence: Norman A. Robertson and Canadian Statecraft, 1929-68*. Toronto: Deneau Publishers, 1981.

–. *The Ottawa Men: The Civil Service Mandarins, 1935-1957*. 1982. Reprint, Toronto: University of Toronto Press, 1998.

–. *The Politics of Survival: The Conservative Party of Canada, 1939-1945*. Toronto: University of Toronto Press, 1967.

Gustafson, Milton O., ed. *The National Archives and Foreign Relations Research*. Athens, OH: Ohio University Press, 1974.

Harper, John Lamberton. *American Visions of Europe: Franklin D. Roosevelt, George F. Kennan, and Dean G. Acheson*. Cambridge: Cambridge University Press, 1994.

Hearden, Patrick J. *Architects of Globalism: Building a New World Order during World War II*. Fayetteville: University of Kansas Press, 2002.

Heinrichs, Waldo. *Threshold of War: Franklin D. Roosevelt and American Entry into World War II*. New York and Oxford: Oxford University Press, 1988.

Henderson, George F. *W.L. Mackenzie King: A Bibliography and Research Guide*. Toronto: University of Toronto Press, 1998.

Hertzman, Lewis, John W. Warnock, and Thomas A. Hockin. *Alliances and Illusions: Canada and the NATO-NORAD Question*. Edmonton: M.G. Hurtig Publishers, 1969.

Hildebrand, Robert C. *Dumbarton Oaks: The Origins of the United Nations and the Search for Postwar Security*. Chapel Hill and London: University of North Carolina Press, 1990.

Hilliker, John. *Canada's Department of External Affairs*. Vol. 1, *The Early Years*. Montreal and Kingston: McGill-Queen's University Press, 1990.

Hillmer, Norman, and J.L. Granatstein. *Empire to Umpire: Canada and the World to the 1990s*. Toronto: Copp Clark Longman, 1994.

–, Robert Bothwell, Roger Sarty, and Claude Beauregard, eds. *A Country of Limitations: Canada and the World in 1939*. Ottawa: Canadian Committee for the History of the Second World War, 1996.

Hockin, Thomas A., ed. *Apex of Power: The Prime Minister and Political Leadership in Canada*. 1971. 2nd ed., Scarborough: Prentice Hall, 1977.

Holmes, John W. *The Better Part of Valour: Essays on Canadian Diplomacy*. Toronto and Montreal: McClelland and Stewart, 1970.

–. *Canada: A Middle-Aged Power*. Toronto: McClelland and Stewart, 1976.

–. *Life with Uncle: The Canadian-American Relationship*. Toronto: University of Toronto Press, 1981.

–. *The Shaping of Peace: Canada and the Search for World Order, 1943-1957*. Vol. 1. Toronto: University of Toronto Press, 1979.

–. *The Shaping of Peace: Canada and the Search for World Order, 1943-1957*. Vol. 2. Toronto: University of Toronto Press, 1982.

Hoopes, Townsend, and Douglas Brinkley. *FDR and the Creation of the U.N.* New Haven and London: Yale University Press, 1997.

Hudson, W.J. *Australia and the New World Order: Evatt at San Francisco, 1945*. Canberra: Australian National University, 1993.

Iklé, Fred Charles. *Every War Must End*. Rev. ed. New York: Columbia University Press, 1991.

Iriye, Akira. *Global Community: The Role of International Organizations in the Making of the Contemporary World*. Berkeley: University of California Press, 2002.

Isaacson, Walter, and Evan Thomas. *The Wise Men: Six Friends and the World They Made*. New York: Simon and Schuster, 1986.

Keating, Tom. *Canada and World Order: The Multilateralist Tradition in Canadian Foreign Policy*. Toronto: McClelland and Stewart, 1993.

Kilbourn, William, ed. *Canada: A Guide to the Peaceable Kingdom*. Toronto: Macmillan of Canada, 1970.

Kimball, Warren F. *The Juggler: Franklin Roosevelt as Wartime Statesman*. Princeton: Princeton University Press, 1991.

–, ed. *Churchill and Roosevelt: The Complete Correspondence*. Vol. 1, *Alliance Emerging: October 1933-November 1942*. Princeton: Princeton University Press, 1984.

–, ed. *Churchill and Roosevelt: The Complete Correspondence*. Vol. 2, *Alliance Forged: November 1942-February 1944*. Princeton: Princeton University Press, 1984.

–, ed. *Churchill and Roosevelt: The Complete Correspondence*. Vol. 3, *Alliance Declining: February 1944-April 1945*. Princeton: Princeton University Press, 1984.

Lewis, William Roger. *Imperialism at Bay, 1941-1945: The United States and the Decolonization of the British Empire*. Oxford: Clarendon Press, 1977.

Lingard, C. Cecil, and Reginald G. Trotter. *Canada in World Affairs: September 1941 to May 1944*. Toronto: Oxford University Press, 1950.

Luard, Evan. *A History of the United Nations*. Vol. 1, *The Years of Western Domination, 1945-1955*. London and Basingstoke: Macmillan, 1982.

Luck, Edward C. *Mixed Messages: American Politics and International Organization, 1919-1999*. Washington, DC: Brookings Institution Press, 1999.

Lyon, Peyton V., and Brian W. Tomlin. *Canada as an International Actor.* Toronto: Macmillan, 1979.

Mackenzie, David. *Canada and International Civil Aviation, 1932-1948.* Toronto: University of Toronto Press, 1989.

McKenzie, Francine. *Redefining the Bonds of Commonwealth, 1939-1948: The Politics of Preference.* New York: Palgrave Macmillan, 2002.

McKercher, B.J.C., and Lawrence Aronsen, eds. *The North Atlantic Triangle in a Changing World: Anglo-American-Canadian Relations, 1902-1956.* Toronto: University of Toronto Press, 1996.

McKillop, A.B. *Matters of Mind: The University in Ontario, 1791-1951.* Toronto: University of Toronto Press, 1994.

MacMillan, Margaret, and Francine McKenzie, eds. *Parties Long Estranged: Canada and Australia in the Twentieth Century.* Vancouver and Toronto: University of British Columbia Press, 2003.

McNeil, William Hardy. *America, Britain and Russia: Their Co-operation and Conflict, 1941-1946.* London: Oxford University Press, 1953.

Madison, G.B., Paul Fairfield, and Ingrid Harris. *Is There a Canadian Philosophy? Reflections on the Canadian Identity.* Ottawa: University of Ottawa Press, 2000.

Mansergh, Nicholas. *Survey of British Commonwealth Affairs: Problems of Wartime Co-operation and Post-War Change, 1939-1952.* London: Oxford University Press, 1958.

Massey, Vincent. *On Being Canadian.* Toronto: J.M. Dent and Sons, 1948.

Mastny, Vojtech. *Russia's Road to the Cold War: Diplomacy, Warfare, and the Politics of Communism, 1941-1945.* New York: Columbia University Press, 1979.

May, Ernest R. *"Lessons" of the Past: The Use and Misuse of History in American Foreign Policy.* New York: Oxford University Press, 1973.

Melakopides, Costas. *Pragmatic Idealism: Canadian Foreign Policy, 1945-1995.* Montreal and Kingston: McGill-Queen's University Press, 1998.

Mitrany, David. *The Functional Theory of Politics.* London: Martin Robertson, 1975.

–. *A Working Peace System.* Chicago: Quadrangle Books, 1966.

Montefiore, Simon Sebag. *Stalin: The Court of the Red Tsar.* London: Weidenfeld and Nicolson, 2003.

Morgan, Ted. *FDR: A Biography.* New York: Simon and Shuster, 1985.

Morton, W.L. *The Canadian Identity.* 1961. 2nd ed., Toronto and Buffalo: University of Toronto Press, 1972.

Muirhead, Bruce. *Against the Odds: The Public Life and Times of Louis Rasminsky.* Toronto: University of Toronto Press, 1999.

–. *The Development of Postwar Canadian Trade Policy: The Failure of the Anglo-European Option.* Montreal and Kingston: McGill-Queen's University Press, 1992.

Neilson, Keith, and Roy A. Prete, eds. *Coalition Warfare: An Uneasy Accord.* Waterloo: Wilfrid Laurier University Press, 1983.

Nossal, Kim Richard. *The Politics of Canadian Foreign Policy.* 1985. 3rd ed., Scarborough: Prentice Hall, 1997.

Notter, Harley. *Postwar Foreign Policy Preparation, 1939-1945.* Washington, DC: Department of State, 1949.

Orders, P.G.A. *Britain, Australia, New Zealand and the Challenge of the United States, 1939-46.* Great Britain: Palgrave Macmillan, 2003.

Ostrower, Gary B. *The United Nations and the United States.* New York: Twayne Publishers, 1998.

Owram, Douglas. *The Government Generation: Canadian Intellectuals and the State, 1900-1945.* Toronto: University of Toronto Press, 1986.

Pearson, Lester B., et al. *A Critical Evaluation of the United Nations.* Vancouver: University of British Columbia Press, 1961.

Reynolds, David. *The Creation of the Anglo-American Alliance, 1937-1941: A Study in Diplomatic Competitive Co-operation.* Chapel Hill: University of North Carolina Press, 1982.

–, et al., eds. *Allies at War: The Soviet, American and British Experience, 1939-1945.* New York: St. Martin's Press, 1994.

Robins, Dorothy B. *Experiment in Democracy: The Story of U.S. Citizen Organizations in Forging the Charter of the United Nations.* New York: Parkside Press, 1971.

Rothstein, Robert L. *Planning, Prediction, and Policymaking in Foreign Affairs: Theory and Practice.* Boston: Little, Brown and Company, 1972.

Russell, Ruth B. *A History of the United Nations Charter: The Role of the United States, 1940-1945.* Washington, DC: The Brookings Institution, 1958.

Sainsbury, Keith. *Churchill and Roosevelt at War: The War They Fought and the Peace They Hoped to Make.* Houndmills, Basingstoke, Hampshire, GB: Macmillan, 1994.

Sanger, Clyde. *Malcolm MacDonald: Bringing an End to Empire.* Montreal and Kingston: McGill-Queen's University Press, 1995.

–, ed. *Canadians and the United Nations.* Ottawa: Minister of Supply and Services, 1988.

Schlesinger, Stephen C. *Act of Creation: The Founding of the United Nations.* Boulder, CO: Westview Press, 2003.

Schulzinger, Robert D. *The Wise Men of Foreign Affairs: The History of the Council on Foreign Relations.* New York: Columbia University Press, 1984.

Smith, Gaddis. *American Diplomacy during the Second World War, 1941-1945.* 1965. 2nd ed., New York: Alfred A. Knopf, 1985.

Snell, John L., ed. *The Meaning of Yalta: Big Three Diplomacy and the New Balance of Power.* Baton Rouge: Louisiana State University Press, 1956.

Soward, F.H. *Canada in World Affairs: From Normandy to Paris, 1944-1946.* London: Oxford University Press, 1950.

–, and Edgar McInnis. *Canada and the United Nations.* New York: Manhattan Publishing Company, 1956.

Stacey, C.P. *Arms, Men and Governments: The War Policies of Canada, 1939-1945.* Ottawa: Queen's Printer, 1970.

–. *Canada and the Age of Conflict.* Vol. 2, *The Mackenzie King Era.* Toronto: University of Toronto Press, 1981.

–. *Mackenzie King and the Atlantic Triangle.* Toronto: Macmillan, 1976.

Steel, Ronald. *Walter Lippmann and the American Century.* Boston and Toronto: Little, Brown and Company, 1980.

Stewart, Walter. *The Life and Times of M.J. Coldwell.* Toronto: Stoddart, 2000.

Stoler, Mark A. *Allies and Adversaries: The Joint Chiefs of Staff, the Grand Alliance, and U.S. Strategy in World War II.* Chapel Hill and London: University of North Carolina Press, 2000.

Strauss, William, and Neil Howe. *Generations: The History of America's Future, 1584-2069.* New York: William Morrow and Company, 1991.

Stromberg, Roland N. *Collective Security and American Foreign Policy: From the League of Nations to NATO.* New York: Frederick A. Praeger, 1963.

Swettenham, John. *McNaughton.* Vol. 2, *1939-1943.* Toronto: Ryerson Press, 1969.

–. *McNaughton.* Vol. 3, *1944-1946.* Toronto: Ryerson Press, 1969.

Thorne, Christopher. *Allies of a Kind: The United States, Britain and the War Against Japan, 1941-1945.* London: Hamish Hamilton, 1978.

Thorpe, D.R. *Eden: The Life and Times of Anthony Eden, First Earl of Avon, 1897-1977.* London: Chatto and Windus, 2003.

Tucker, Michael. *Canadian Foreign Policy: Contemporary Issues and Themes.* Toronto: McGraw-Hill Ryerson, 1980.

Underhill, Frank H. *The Image of Confederation.* Toronto: CBC Publications, 1964.

Whitaker, Reginald. *The Government Party: Organizing and Financing the Liberal Party of Canada, 1930-58.* Toronto and Buffalo: University of Toronto Press, 1977.

Wilson, Theodore A. *The First Summit: Roosevelt and Churchill at Placentia Bay, 1941.* 1969. Rev. ed., Lawrence, KS: University of Kansas Press, 1991.

Woodbridge, George. *UNRRA: The History of the United Nations Relief and Rehabilitation Administration.* Vol. 1. New York: Columbia University Press, 1950.

Woodward, Sir Llewellyn. *British Foreign Policy in the Second World War.* Vol. 5. London: Her Majesty's Stationary Office, 1976.

Woolner, David B., ed. *The Second Quebec Conference Revisited.* 1st ed. New York: St. Martin's Press, 1998.

Articles

Bloomfield, Lincoln P. "Policy Planning Redefined: What the Planners Really Think." *International Journal* 32, 4 (Autumn 1977): 813-28.

Bothwell, Robert, and J.L. Granatstein. "Canada and the Wartime Negotiations over Civil Aviation: The Functional Principle in Operation." *International History Review* 2, 4 (October 1980): 585-601.

Brecher, Irving. "In Defence of Preventive War." *International Journal* 58, 3 (Summer 2003): 253-80.

Chapnick, Adam. "The Canadian Middle Power Myth." *International Journal* 55, 2 (Spring 2000): 188-206.

–. "The Middle Power." *Canadian Foreign Policy* 7, 2 (Winter 1999): 73-82.

–. "Principle for Profit: The Functional Principle and the Development of Canadian Foreign Policy, 1943-1947." *Journal of Canadian Studies* 37, 2 (Summer 2002): 68-85.

Cull, Nicholas J. "Reluctant Persuaders: Canadian Propaganda in the United States, 1939-1945." *British Journal of Canadian Studies* 14, 2 (1999): 207-22.

Donaghy, Greg. "Solidarity Forever: The Cooperative Commonwealth Federation and Its Search for an International Role, 1939-1949." *International Journal of Canadian Studies* 5 (Spring 1992): 89-111.

Goodrich, Leland M. "From League of Nations to United Nations." *International Organization* 1, 1 (February 1947): 3-21.

Gow, J.I. "Les Québécois, la Guerre et la Paix, 1945-1960." *Canadian Journal of Political Science* 3, 1 (1970): 88-122.

Hilliker, John. "No Bread at the Peace Table: Canada and the European Settlement, 1943-47." *Canadian Historical Review* 61, 1 (March 1980): 69-86.

Hillmer, Norman. "O.D. Skelton: Called and Chosen." *Dialogue* 14, 2 (April 1990): 37-39.

Holsti, K.J. "National Role Conceptions in the Study of Foreign Policy." *International Studies Quarterly* 14, 3 (September 1970): 233-309.

Hughes, E.J. "Winston Churchill and the Formation of the United Nations Organization." *Journal of Contemporary History* 9, 4 (October 1974): 177-94.

Little, Douglas. "Crackpot Realists and Other Heroes: The Rise and Fall of the Postwar American Diplomatic Elite." *Diplomatic History* 13, 1 (Winter 1989): 99-111.

Madar, Daniel, and Denis Stairs. "Alone on Killers' Row: The Policy Analysis Group and the Department of External Affairs." *International Journal* 32, 4 (Autumn 1977): 727-55.

Miller, A.J. "Canada at San Francisco: A Reappraisal of the Influence of the 'Functional Concept.'" Unpublished paper accessed with permission through the Library of the Canadian Institute of International Affairs.

–. "From Function to Functionalism: The Evolution of a Principle in Canadian External Relations." Unpublished paper presented to Annual Meeting, Canadian Political Science Association, University of Saskatchewan, May 1979. Accessed with permission through the Library of the Canadian Institute of International Affairs.

–. "The Functional Principle in Canada's External Relations." *International Journal* 35, 2 (Spring 1980): 309-28.

Molot, Maureen Appel. "Where Do We, Should We, or Can We Sit? A Review of Canadian Foreign Policy Literature." *International Journal of Canadian Studies* 1-2 (Spring-Fall 1990): 77-96.

Munton, Don, and Donald Page. "Planning in the East Block: The Post-Hostilities Problems Committees in Canada, 1943-45." *International Journal* 32, 4 (Autumn 1977): 677-726.

Page, Donald. "The Institute's 'Popular Arm': The League of Nations Society in Canada." *International Journal* 33, 1 (Winter 1977-78): 28-65.

Porter, John. "Higher Public Servants and the Bureaucratic Elite in Canada." *Journal of Economics and Political Science* 24, 4 (November 1958): 483-501.

Schlesinger, Arthur, Jr. "Origins of the Cold War." *Foreign Affairs* 46, 1 (October 1967): 22-52.

Schlesinger, Stephen C. "FDR's Five Policemen: Creating the United Nations." *World Policy Journal* 11, 3 (Fall 1994): 88-93.

Stairs, Denis. "The Political Culture of Canadian Foreign Policy." *Canadian Journal of Political Science* 15, 4 (December 1982): 667-90.
–. "Public Opinion and External Affairs: Reflections on the Domestication of Canadian Foreign Policy." *International Journal* 33, 1 (Winter 1977-78): 128-49.
–. "Trends in Canadian Foreign Policy: Past, Present, and Future." *Behind the Headlines* 59, 3 (Spring 2002): 1-7.
Tardy, Thierry. "L'héritage de la SDN, l'espoir de l'ONU: Le rôle de l'ONU dans la gestion de la sécurité internationale." *Revue Études Internationales* 31, 4 (Décembre 2000): 691-708.
Watt, D.C. "Every War Must End: War-Time Planning for Post-War Security, in Britain and America in the Wars of 1914-18 and 1939-45: The Roles of Historical Example and of Professional Historians." *Transactions of the Royal Historical Society* 5th series, 28 (London: Offices of the Royal Historical Society, 1978): 159-73.
Widenor, William C. "American Planning for the United Nations: Have We Been Asking the Right Questions?" *Diplomatic History* 6, 3 (Summer 1982): 245-65.

Unpublished Theses
Anderson, John C. "Mackenzie King and Collective Security: The League of Nations and the United Nations." MA thesis, University of Alberta, 1977.
Anglin, Douglas G. "Canadian Policy towards International Institutions, 1939-1950." PhD dissertation, Oxford University, 1956.
Armstrong-Reid, Susan. "Canada's Role in the United Nations Relief and Rehabilitation Administration, 1942-1947." PhD dissertation, University of Toronto, 1981.
Gow, James Iain. "The Opinions of French Canadians in Quebec on the Problems of War and Peace, 1945-1960." PhD dissertation, Université de Laval, 1969.
May, Alexander. "The Round Table, 1910-66." PhD dissertation, Oxford University, 1995.
Merrick, John Robert. "Canada and the Origins of the United Nations, 1941-1945." MA thesis, Queen's University, 1974.
Metcalfe, Heather. "Canadian Public Opinion towards the Growth of the Canadian American Relationship during the Second World War, as Reflected in the Print Media." MA thesis, University of Calgary, 2002.
Miller, John. "Functionalism and Canadian Foreign Policy: An Analysis of Canadian Voting Behaviour in the General Assembly of the United Nations, 1946-1966." PhD dissertation, McGill University, 1970.
Ossman, Albert John, Jr. "The Development of Canadian Foreign Policy." PhD dissertation, Syracuse University, 1963.
Plant, John David Edward. "The Origins and Development of Australia's Policy and Posture at the United Nations Conference on International Organization, San Francisco, 1945." PhD dissertation, Australian National University, 1967.
Rasmussen, Kathleen Britt. "Canada and the Reconstruction of the International Economy, 1941-1947." PhD dissertation, University of Toronto, 2001.
Sauer, Angelika. "The Respectable Course: Canada's Department of External Affairs, the Great Powers, and the German Problem 1943-1947." PhD dissertation, University of Waterloo, 1994.
Schwark, Stephen John. "The State Department Plans for Peace, 1941-1945." PhD dissertation, Harvard University, 1985.
Stipernitz, Boris. "Kanada und die Gründung der Vereinten Nationen, 1939-1945." PhD dissertation, Universität zu Köln, 2001.
Young, William Robert. "Making the Truth Graphic: The Canadian Government's Home Front Information Structure and Programmes during World War II." PhD dissertation, University of British Columbia, 1978.

Interviews
Judith Robertson. 19 July 2002. Toronto.
June Rogers. 24 September 2002. Toronto.
James A. Gibson. 25 September 2002. Toronto.

Index